HARDEN'S

London Food Shops 2002/03

Where to buy Harden's guides
Harden's guides are on sale in most major bookshops. In case of difficulty, call Harden's on (020) 7839 4763 or visit www.hardens.com.

mail@hardens.com
We welcome any comments you may have on this guide, by e-mail at the above address, or by post.

Research Manager: Antonia Russell
Production Manager: Elizabeth Warman
Additional research by Sarah Ashpole & Frances Gill

© Harden's Limited, 2002

ISBN 1-873721-48-X

British Library Cataloguing-in-Publication data:
a catalogue record for this book is available from the British Library.

Printed and bound in Finland by
WS Bookwell Ltd

Harden's Limited
14 Buckingham Street
London WC2N 6DF

The contents of this book are believed correct at the time of printing. Nevertheless, the publishers can accept no responsibility for errors, changes in or omissions from the details given.

No part of this publication may be reproduced or transmitted in any form or by any means, electronically or mechanically, including photocopying, recording or any information storage or retrieval system, without prior permission in writing from the publishers.

Contents

	Page
Introduction	7
How this book was researched	8
Survey results	9
1 The 'Big Ten'	11
2 Bread	17
3 Cheese	29
4 Chocolates & sweets	35
5 Coffee & tea	41
6 Cookware	45
7 Ethnic shops	51
8 Fish & seafood	58
9 Fruit & vegetables	66
10 Grocers & delicatessens	72
11 Health & organic foods	91
12 Herbs & spices	98
13 Markets	102
14 Meat, game & poultry	107
15 Pâtisserie	119
16 Wine	125
Maps	138
Area overviews	158
Alphabetical index	166

Introduction

Is it Puritanism? Meanness? Ignorance? Is it because Victorian workers lost all links with nature when they went to work in the satanic mills? Are we "just too busy nowadays"? The explanations for the renowned British indifference to the quality of food are many and varied. One reality is clear, however – our food-shopping is now dominated by the 'easy' option, the supermarkets. Recent figures suggest the independent food shops' decline continues unabated.*

So is this guide just a elegy for specialist suppliers? Far from it. For good or ill, the capital has always been something of 'another country', and the last five years have seen the beginnings of what may turn out to be counter-revolution in Londoners' attitude to food. There is a growing understanding that food need not be an industrial product, and that it can have character worth paying for.

The capital's shopping scene is reflecting this emerging interest in food. Future social historians may cite the emergence of Borough Market – which began on a very small scale in late-1997 – as the sign of a sea change in attitude: who, in the mid-1990s would have thought that Londoners could regard trekking across town to seek out fresh and sometimes exotic fare as the basis of a regular Saturday morning excursion? But thousands of shoppers every week now demonstrate that it can.

Hence this book – the first ever guide to the capital's food shops based on what real London food-shoppers think are the capital's key food resources. Like all our guides, it is primarily to be *used*, not read. Please take it with you when you're out and about on a food-shopping mission. Let it help you find shops you might not otherwise know about (or might know about, but not think of patronising). Let it encourage you – as it has us – to try new suppliers of familiar foodstuffs, and to make provisioning expeditions to new corners of the capital. There is much to find.

We are quite sure that many worthy places will have eluded us, and, with your help, we can make the next edition of this guide even better. **To take part in our next food shops survey, and perhaps also our annual survey of restaurants in London and across the UK, please send us your name and address – ideally to mail@hardens.com, or alternatively to the address shown on page 4.**

Richard Harden   **Peter Harden**

---

*A report published by Retail Knowledge Bank, a research company, shortly before this guide went to press suggested that since 1990 – a period which has seen moderate increases in consumption of both fish and meat – butchers' sales nationally were down by nearly a quarter, and fishmongers' by over half.

How this book was researched

In the survey on which this guide is based, reporters (who numbered some 900) were asked to nominate their favourite shops, and to give numerical ratings to: i) the quality of the food; ii) the service; and iii) the ambience – how pleasant a place to shop is it? These responses are the basis of the selection of stores in the guide, and also determine the level of enthusiasm which may be apparent in the respective write-ups. Comments from reporters are in "quotation marks" in the individual write-ups.

All the shops in this book are 'recommended' to a greater or lesser extent, and we have therefore kept the rating system as simple as possible. It is as follows:

★ An establishment attracting much commentary and notably high average survey ratings

☆ An establishment attracting similarly high average survey ratings, but a lower volume of support.

Stars are awarded strictly for **produce quality** (not for service or ambience). They are also awarded on a **category-by-category** basis – Sainsbury's, for example, is 'starred' for its bread, but not for its cheese & dairy produce. Stars are awarded solely on the basis of the results of the survey: thus, recently-opened shops, or those attracting little comment, cannot qualify.

Prices

The general price level of any individual establishment will usually be obvious from its description and location. Only where reporters stress how expensive (or cheap) a place is have we mentioned price or value in the write-ups.

Symbols

- ☕ – Café or other eat-in facilities
- 🚚 – Local deliveries within London
- 📬 – Mail order service
- S – Open Sundays
- 🌞 – Open early (8am or earlier)
- ☽ – Open late (7pm or later)

These symbols are only general indications, and may not apply to all days of the week, or all the branches of a chain.

Small print
Map reference – shown immediately after the telephone number.
(For supermarkets and larger chains, only selected branches are shown.)
Opening hours – Note that most shops are closed on bank holidays; many are open longer hours before Christmas
Credit & debit cards – unless otherwise stated, Mastercard, Visa, Switch and American Express are accepted.

Survey results

Survey – most mentioned

These are the food, wine and cookware sources which were most frequently mentioned by reporters (though not necessarily the ones which scored the highest ratings).

1. Selfridges
2. Waitrose
3. Harrods
4. Borough Market
5. Sainsbury's
6. Neal's Yard Dairy
7. Pâtisserie Valerie
8. Maison Blanc
9. Fortnum & Mason
10. Divertimenti

11. Oddbins
12. Marks & Spencer
13. John Lewis/Peter Jones
14. Harvey Nichols
15. C Lidgate
16. Planet Organic
17. Fresh & Wild
18. Tesco
19. Portobello Road Market
20. Bluebird

21. &Clarke's
22. Carluccio's
23. Baker & Spice
24. Whittard of Chelsea
25. Villandry
26. Paxton & Whitfield
27. Jeroboams
28. Paul
29. Rococo Chocolates
30. Majestic Wine

31. Spitalfields Organic Market
32. The Spice Shop
33. Luigi's Delicatessen
34. Nicolas
35. Northcote Road Market
36. La Fromagerie
37. Berry Bros. & Rudd
38. Berwick Street Market
39. I Camisa & Son
40. Godiva

1. The 'Big Ten'

These are the ten general supplies which – at least so far as the Londoners who took part in our survey are concerned – stand head and shoulders above the rest. Other general suppliers – from Safeway, which attracted only a quarter of the volume of commentary achieved by Bluebird, downwards – are listed in **Chapter 7 Grocers & delicatessens**. In descending order of number of references, the Big Ten were:

1 Selfridges
2 Waitrose
3 Harrods
4 Borough Market
5 Sainsbury's
6 Fortnum & Mason
7 Marks & Spencer
8 Harvey Nichols
9 Tesco
10 Bluebird

Apart from the introductions below, each member of the Big Ten also has write-ups in the individual categories in which it generated a high level of feedback; these are listed below, in descending order of the number of survey mentions.

Bluebird SW3
350 King's Rd   5–3C
☎ (020) 7559 1000   www.conran.co.uk
As you would expect, Sir Terence Conran brought a high level of style to the food shopping experience when he opened this Chelsea emporium in 1997. High prices are a recurrent cause of comment but – unlike most Conran restaurants – reporters do feel that, especially in the following areas (in descending order of number of reports), there is some justification for them:

1   Grocers & delicatessens ★
2   Bread ★
3= Fruit & vegetables ★
3= Cheese & dairy ★
5   Fish & seafood ★

For an on-the-premises snack, the ground floor café – with its King's Road people-watching possibilities – is much to be preferred to the overpriced restaurant above. / HOURS Mon-Wed 9am-8pm, Thu-Sat 9am-9pm, Sun 11am-5pm TUBE Sloane Square/South Kensington

The Big Ten

Borough Market SE1
Borough High St   9–4C
🖳 www.boroughmarket.org.uk
There has been a food market at Borough for almost a millennium (and the long-standing early-morning wholesale fruit and veg market continues to this day). For consumers, though, it's the retail market – which first came into being after Henrietta Green organised a 'one-off' event in 1997 – which has become a phenomenon, attracting thousands weekly. The types of food reporters seek out are as follows:

1   Fruit & vegetables ★
2   Meat, game & poultry ★
3   Fish & seafood ★
4   Herbs & spices ★
5   Cheese & dairy ★
6   Bread ★

Regular stalls that came in for particular survey praise include Northfield Farm and Ginger Pig (both naturally-reared meat), Sillfield Farm (meat and cheese), Flour Power (bread), Turnips (fruit and vegetables), Brindisa (Spanish goods), Furness Fish (fish and potted shrimps), Shell Seekers (scallops) and Booths (mushrooms).
Overcrowding is one of the market's main problems, and its trustees have ambitious plans for expansion and upgrading – see the website for details and a progress report. The market has no café as such, but it offers a number of on-the-hoof snacking possibilities, from venison burgers to chocolate brownies (as well as numerous 'tasting' possibilities). / HOURS Fri noon-5pm, Sat 9am-4pm (wholesale fruit & veg Mon-Fri 3am-10am) CREDIT CARDS no credit cards TUBE London Bridge

Fortnum & Mason W1
181 Piccadilly   3–3D
☎ (020) 7734 8040   🖳 www.fortnumandmason.co.uk
Worldwide fame has its drawbacks. Even among our reporters (by definition, 'locals'), it's for the small, portable and not-too-perishable specialities – so convenient for tourists to take home – that the famous food hall of St James's glittering Georgian store is best known. Although five produce categories were singled out as being of special interest by reporters, the first two together accounted for well over half of total nominations:

1   Coffee & tea ★
2   Chocolate & sweets ★
3   Grocers & delicatessens ★
4   Pâtisserie ★
5   Wine

Fortnum's offers a number of dining possibilties. Most characterful is the Fountain Restaurant, adjacent to the food hall, which is especially popular for afternoon tea. / HOURS Mon-Sat 10am-6.30pm TUBE Piccadilly Circus/Green Park

The Big Ten

Harrods SW1
87 Brompton Rd 5–1D
☎ (020) 7730 1234 www.harrods.com
"What you can't find here is not worth looking for" – sheer variety of "top-notch" produce makes these famous Knightsbridge food halls, with their "magnificent" (listed) décor a hugely popular destination. (If you visit mainly to gawp, under no circumstances omit the "wonderful", daily-changing fish sculpture.) The store is seen principally as a collection of specialists – "unusually, the staff know their products" – and the high level of service is a particular plus for many reporters (outweighing, it would seem, the need for multiple queuing and paying). Almost all the departments are thought worthy of individual note. In descending order of number of references, they were:

1 Fish & seafood ★
2 Chocolates & sweets ★
3 Grocers & delicatessens ★
4= Meat, game & poultry ★
4= Coffee & tea ★
6 Cheese & dairy ★
7= Fruit & vegetables ★
7= Cookware (2nd floor) ★
9 Bread ★
10 Pâtisserie ★
11 Wine

The Waterstone's bookshop (2nd floor) has one of the capital's widest ranges of cookery titles. Harrods claims some two dozen food and drink outlets in total: of particular note, in the Food Halls themselves, are the bars where you can sample sushi, seafood and cheese. / HOURS Mon, Tue & Sat 10am-6pm, Wed-Fri 10am-7pm

Harvey Nichols SW1
109-125 Knightsbridge 5–1D
☎ (020) 7235 5000 www.harveynichols.com
"Varied and sometimes exciting" produce leads some to make the trek up to the space-age fifth-floor 'foodmarket' of this famous Knightsbridge store. It's as a general supplier that it finds most support, however, and – probably reflecting its smaller scale – most of its specialist offerings are eclipsed by those of Harrods and Selfridges. Reporters commended Harvey Nicks in the following categories:

1 Grocers & delicatessens
2 Fish & seafood ★
3= Meat, game & poultry
3= Bread ☆
5 Wine

The Big Ten

Harvey Nichols cont'd
A café, sushi bar, restaurant and cocktail bar are all close to hand; the first, in particular, suffers from excessive popularity at busy times. / HOURS Mon, Tue & Sat 10am-7pm, Wed-Fri 10am-8pm, Sun noon-6pm TUBE *Knightsbridge*

Marks & Spencer   S ☽
☎ (0845) 609 0200 www.marksandspencer.com
BRANCHES AT:
   Locations throughout London

Sad to say, the pioneer of quality food on the high street is "not as far ahead as it once was, and quality has declined over the years". It's striking how little true enthusiasm reporters express for most of its range – indeed, the store rates special mention in only four categories, with the first accounting for almost half the total number of references (and none rated highly enough to qualify for a 'star'):

1   Fruit & vegetables
2   Bread
3   Cheese & dairy
4   Meat, game & poultry

/ HOURS *Most stores open Mon-Sat 9am-8pm (central branches open later), Sun noon-6pm*

Sainsbury's   S ☀ ☽ 🚚
☎ (0845) 301 2020 www.sainsburys.com
BRANCHES AT:
   Locations throughout London

In all qualitative respects, the capital's biggest supermarket chain emerges as a pretty clear – if somewhat distant – runner-up to Waitrose. "Reliability" and "value for money" are themes which often emerge, with "plenty of parking" and "long hours" among supporting attractions often cited. Two departments are particularly praised (the one attracting the greatest volume of commentary perhaps something of a surprise):

1   Herbs & spices
2   Fruit & vegetables
3   Fish & seafood ★
4   Cheese & dairy
5   Bread ★
6   Health & organic foods
7   Wine
8   Meat, game & poultry

The chain has recently been involved in a frantic upgrading and expansion initiative in the capital, introducing many 'Local' supermarkets (essentially large convenience stores) and 'Centrals': the latter, apart from being, well, central, tend to carry extensive premium ranges (with extensive ready meal and organic selections, for example). / HOURS *Some larger stores 24 hours*

The Big Ten

Selfridges W1
400 Oxford St   3–1A
☎ (020) 7629 1234   www.selfridges.co.uk
Judged in terms of sheer volume of survey commentary, Oxford Street's "luxury food hall" would appear to be the capital's leading food resource. It's very tempting to compare it with Harrods – which attracts almost as much commentary – but reporters' commentary on the two giants is in fact sharply divergent. Almost half of those who comment on Selfridges note its attractions as a general supplier (a sort of super-Sainsbury's), whereas almost three-quarters of Harrods reporters stress the individual attractions of its various specialities. "A fantastic selection of world produce" was the theme of many of Selfridges 'generalist' fans, with the range of ethnic, kosher and Middle Eastern items attracting particular attention. Notwithstanding strength as a general supplier, no fewer than ten of the shop's departments earned recognition for their individual merits:

1. Fish & seafood ★
2. Cookware (in basement) ★
3. Grocers & delicatessens ★
4. Chocolates & sweets ★
5. Cheese & dairy ★
6. Meat, game & poultry ★
7. Bread ★
8. Fruit & vegetables ★
9. Herbs & spices ★
10. Wine ☆

Note also that the book department (basement) has one of the largest ranges of food and cookery titles in London. The store offers many eating and drinking possibilities – in the Food Hall itself, the Oyster Bar and pâtisserie counter are of most interest. / HOURS *Mon-Fri 10am-8pm, Sat 9.30am-8pm, Sun noon-6pm* TUBE *Bond Street*

Tesco
 www.tesco.com
BRANCHES AT:
   Locations throughout London
It may be the leader at the national level, but so far as reporters are concerned – in terms of both quantity and the quality of survey feedback – Tesco emerged as a very clear third in the supermarket stakes, well behind Waitrose and Sainsbury's. Despite the considerable volume of commentary, only three departments emerged as worthy of particular note:

1= Bread
1= Fruit & vegetables
3 Wine

The Big Ten

Tesco cont'd
Rather like Sainsbury's, Tesco shops range all the way from local 'Metro' and 'Express' branches (the latter attached to garages) to 'Extra' hypermarkets. / HOURS *Some larger stores 24 hours*

Waitrose
☎ (01344) 424680 Customer service
🌐 www.waitrose.com
BRANCHES AT:
  Locations throughout London

Nationally speaking, Waitrose is considered a minnow of the supermarket world. Its "bourgeois" charms, however, make it the survey's undisputed Number One Supermarket. Unsurprisingly, it is "sourcing quality food from good producers" that seems to be at the root of the high approval rating, but "decent service" and the "human" scale of operations are all important parts of a formula that "makes supermarket shopping bearable" for many reporters. Waitrose boasts eight departments worthy of note in their own right. These are:

1 Wine
2 Fruit & vegetables
3 Fish & seafood
4 Herbs & spices
5= Cheese & dairy ★
5= Meat, game & poultry ★
7 Bread ★
8= Health & organic foods

/ HOURS *Hours vary: generally Mon-Sat 8.30am-9pm, Sun 11am-5pm*

2. Bread

Where did we buy our bread ten years ago? Almost all the places that grab reporters' attention have come into existence over the past decade, and there's no sign at all that the huge improvements in the range of bakers is coming to an end. Until recently, it was the locals (such as Baker & Spice and &Clarke's) who made the running, but the last couple of years have seen the arrival on these shores of two outstanding names from across the Channel – Paul (France's largest bakery chain) and Poilâne (the most celebrated). The small Belgravia offshoot of Poilâne only opened in 2000, but its (admittedly tiny) range of products is already rated more highly than those of any other food shop in town.

North London emerges as a great place for bread-lovers, the place of baking in Jewish life presumably explaining the existence of a concentration of bakers of note around Hampstead and Golders Green.

Many of the top producers of quality bread listed here also distribute their products at (more upmarket) food markets and delicatessens throughout the capital.

The suppliers which attracted the most attention from reporters were:

1. Baker & Spice ★
2. &Clarke's ★
3. Poilâne ★
4. Maison Blanc ★
5. Paul ★
6. De Gustibus ★
7. Euphorium ★
8. Bluebird ★
9. St John ★
10. Northcote Road Market ★

Note that many of the following shops also carry a basic pâtisserie range. Specialists are listed in **Chapter 15 Pâtisserie**.

L'Amandine Patisserie
BRANCHES AT:
  229 Earls Court Rd, SW5 5–2A
  ☎ (020) 7244 0400
  122 Wandsworth Bridge Rd, SW6 10–1B
  ☎ (020) 7371 8871
  48 Turnham Green Ter, W4 7–2A
  ☎ (020) 8995 1995

Bread

L'Amandine Patisserie cont'd
40 Haven Grn, W5   1–2A
☎ (020) 8991 1010
7 Bellevue Rd, SW17   10–2C
☎ (020) 8672 7252

"Fresh bread seven days a week" makes these competent west London café/boulangerie/pâtisseries useful stand-bys. / HOURS Open Mon-Sun, all branches open by 8am CREDIT CARDS no Amex.

Bagatelle Boutique SW7   Ⓢ ☀ ☾ 🚚 ★
44 Harrington Rd   5–2B
☎ (020) 7581 1551   🖰 www.bagatelle.co.uk

"Real French bread" (of the baguette variety), is available every day of the week at this supplier in the heart of South Kensington; it's better known as a pâtisserie. / HOURS Mon-Sat 8am-8pm, Sun 8am-6pm TUBE South Kensington SEE ALSO Patisserie.

Baker & Spice   Ⓢ ☀ ☾ ★
BRANCHES AT:
46 Walton St, SW3   5–1D
☎ (020) 7589 4734
75 Salusbury Rd, NW6   1–2B
☎ (020) 7604 3636

With its *"wonderful"* and *"tempting" selection"* of breads (and pastries too), this small baker's main branch behind Harrods is the top destination in town; some do find the products from the century-old ovens *"expensive"* for what they are, though, and *"snooty"* service is a recurrent complaint. / HOURS Mon-Sat 7am-7pm (NW6 Mon-Fri 7am-8pm), Sun 8.30am-2pm CREDIT CARDS no Amex SEE ALSO Patisserie.

Belmont Bakery   Ⓢ ☀
BRANCHES AT:
11 Stanley Rd, Teddington, TW11   1–4A
☎ (020) 8977 2773
92 Queens Rd, Twickenham, TW1   1–4A
☎ (020) 8892 5078
52 Heath Rd, Twickenham, TW1   1–4A
☎ (020) 8892 3796

"Good fresh bread and a choice of home-baked products" helps make this Twickenham trio a classic small *"family bakery"* chain; *"poor service"*, however, can let the side down. / HOURS Mon-Sat 7am-5pm (Queens Rd 5.30pm).

Bloomsbury Cheeses WC1   🖃 ☾ ☆
61 Judd St   8–4C
☎ (020) 7387 7645   🖰 www.cthc.demon.co.uk

A handy supplier, if you live or work in these parts, of *"very good and unusual bread from the &Clarkes bakery"*. / HOURS Mon-Fri 10am-7pm, Sat 10am-5.30pm CREDIT CARDS no Amex TUBE Russell Square/Kings Cross SEE ALSO Cheese & dairy.

19 *Bread*

Bluebird SW3
350 King's Rd   5–3C
☎ (020) 7559 1000   www.conran.co.uk
The "very good range and quality" of baked goods on offer at this striking Chelsea emporium is one of the areas in which reporters find its premium pricing generally justified. / HOURS *Mon-Wed 9am-8pm, Thu-Sat 9am-9pm, Sun 11am-5pm* TUBE *Sloane Square/South Kensington* SEE ALSO *Big Ten; Cheese & dairy; Fish & seafood; Fruit & vegetables; Grocers & delicatessens.*

Bonne Bouche
BRANCHES AT:
  6 Strutton Ground, SW1   2–4C
  ☎ (020) 7222 5464
  38 Tachbrook St, SW1   2–4C
  ☎ (020) 7630 1626
  2 Thayer St, W1   3–1A
  ☎ (020) 7486 9584
  22 Bute St, SW7   5–2B
  ☎ (020) 7584 9839
  129 Praed St, W2   6–1D
  ☎ (020) 7724 5784

Somewhere in style between your typical high street baker and a more specialist operator, this small chain boasts a "good range" and fills a useful gap in the market; the bread is, in our view, rather better than the cakes. / HOURS *Hours vary: generally Mon-Sat 8.30am-6pm; W1 open Sun 9am-6pm.*

Borough Market SE1
Borough High St   9–4C
 www.boroughmarket.org.uk
London's leading market offers "a variety of excellent bread stalls". / HOURS *Fri noon-5pm, Sat 9am-4pm (wholesale fruit & veg Mon-Fri 3am-10am)* CREDIT CARDS *no credit cards* TUBE *London Bridge* SEE ALSO *Big Ten; Cheese & dairy; Fish & seafood; Fruit & vegetables; Herbs & spices; Markets; Meat, game & poultry.*

Bread Shop
BRANCHES AT:
  17 Brewer St, W1   3–2D
  ☎ (020) 7434 3408
  65 St John's Wood High St, NW8   8–3A
  ☎ (020) 7586 5311

A "wonderful" (if "pricey") selection of continental breads "both traditional and 'new'" ensures strong support for this self-explanatory business; the strikingly modern St John's Wood original now has a Soho offshoot; German baking a speciality. / HOURS *W1 Mon-Fri 8am-7.30pm, Sat 8am-8pm, Sun noon-6pm; NW8 Mon-Fri 7am-6.30pm, Sat 7am-6pm, Sun 8am-4.30pm* CREDIT CARDS *no credit cards.*

Bread

The Breadstall W11 ⓢ 🌅 ☆
172 Portobello Rd   6–1B
☎ (020) 7221 3122
This rather confusingly-named shop also has two stalls on the adjoining Portobello Road street market where the business originated (Fri & Sat only); it's "eye-opening selection" of baked goods wins quite a local following. / HOURS Mon-Sun 8am-6pm CREDIT CARDS no credit cards TUBE Ladbroke Grove/Notting Hill Gate.

Brick Lane Beigel Bake E1 ⓢ 🌅 ☽ ★
159 Brick Ln   1–2D
☎ (020) 7729 0616
"Open 24 hours a day for fabulous bagels", this "East End institution" fared as well in the survey for this guide as it always has for our restaurant survey; prices really are very low – a dozen plain bagels, £1.44, for example – making this one of the best-quality budget destinations in town. / HOURS 24 hrs daily CREDIT CARDS no credit cards or cheques TUBE Liverpool Street/Bethnal Green.

Carluccios WC2 ☽ ★
28 Neal St   4–2C
☎ (020) 7240 1487
"Great breads of all kinds, but all very pricey" – the focaccia, ciabatta, and so on of this famous Covent Garden Italian deli are particularly approved. / HOURS Mon-Thu 11am-7pm, Fri 10am-7pm, Sat 10am-6pm SEE ALSO Grocers & delicatessens.

Carmelli Bakeries NW11 ⓢ 🌅 ☽ ★
128 Golders Green Rd   1–1B
☎ (020) 8455 3063
Thanks to "the best bagels in London" – plus "all styles of kosher bread and cakes", as well as cheesecake – the main problem with this Golders Green institution is that it can be just too popular; "avoid during the Saturday night rush". / HOURS Mon-Wed 7am-1am, Thu all night, Fri 7am-2pm, Sat all night through to Mon 1am CREDIT CARDS no credit cards TUBE Golders Green.

&Clarke's W8 🌅 ☽ ★
122 Kensington Church St   6–2B
☎ (020) 7229 2190   www.sallyclarke.com
Sally Clarke was one of the pioneers of quality bread in the capital, and the shop she opened in 1988, adjacent to her Kensington restaurant, is still London's second-biggest name in quality baking; indeed, such are the attractions of her "delicious and varied" range that this narrow shop can get "too crowded", and service can suffer; some of the 35 types of bread baked daily are also available from Waitrose and other third-party suppliers. / HOURS Mon-Fri 8am-8pm, Sat 9am-4pm TUBE Notting Hill Gate SEE ALSO Cheese & dairy; Chocolates & sweets; Patisserie.

Bread

Comptoir Gascon EC1
63 Charterhouse St   9–1A
☎ (020) 7608 0851
A "fine range of high-quality breads" – from familiar baguettes and croissants to sturdy 8-seed loaves and hazelnut bread – is on offer at this upmarket new Farringdon delicatessen. / HOURS Mon-Fri 8am-8pm, Sat 9am-6pm TUBE Farringdon
SEE ALSO Grocers & delicatessens.

Cullens
BRANCHES AT:
Locations throughout London
"Regular supplies of hot French bread all day" are a popular feature of these convenience stores (which otherwise were little commented on by reporters). / HOURS 11 branches, generally open Mon-Sun 8am-11pm.

Daniel's Bagel Bakery NW11
12-13 Hallswelle Pde   1–1B
☎ (020) 8455 5826
"The best bagels and cholla in London" – and an extensive range of other baked products – win nothing but praise for this kosher establishment, which also offers a small selection of delicatessen items. / HOURS Sun-Wed 7am-9pm, Thu 7am-10pm, Fri 7am-90mins before Shabbat CREDIT CARDS no credit cards TUBE Golders Green.

De Gustibus
🖱 www.degustibus.co.uk
BRANCHES AT:
53 Blandford St, W1   2–1A
☎ (020) 7486 6608
6 Southwark St, SE1   9–4C
☎ (020) 7407 3625
53-55 Carter Ln, EC4   9–2A
☎ (020) 7236 0056
"Wonderful" sourdough and an "enormous selection" of other breads win pretty much unanimous support for this "artisan baker", which now has shops in Borough Market and the City as well as the Marylebone original; all baking takes place on the premises. / HOURS W1 Mon-Fri 7am-4.30pm, Sat 8.30am-2pm; EC4 Mon-Fri 8am-5pm; SE1 Mon-Fri 6am-5pm, Sat 7am-4pm.

Dunn's N8
6 The Broadway   1–1C
☎ (020) 8340 1614
"There are as many helpful staff as there are varieties of bread and cake", at this universally popular fifth-generation family bakery in Crouch End; "excellent" doughnuts win particular praise, and there is an extensive range of classic English baked fare. / HOURS Mon-Sat 7am-6pm CREDIT CARDS no Amex TUBE Finsbury Park.

Bread

Euphorium Bakery N1
202 Upper St   8–2D
☎ (020) 7704 6905
"A much better bakery than it ever was a restaurant" – indeed, the latter is now closed – this Islington spot is north London's top bakery; its range may be *"limited"*, but fans say that the likes of *"awesome focaccia"* and *"the best croissants in town"* make it *"worth the inevitable wait for service"*. / HOURS Mon-Fri 7am-7pm, Sat 8am-6pm, Sun 9am-3.30pm CREDIT CARDS no Amex TUBE Highbury & Islington SEE ALSO Patisserie.

Exeter Street Bakery
BRANCHES AT:
  15 Exeter St, WC2   4–3D
  ☎ (020) 7379 1881
  1b Argyll Rd, W8   5–1A
  ☎ (020) 7937 8484
Richard Polo is the name behind two of the longer-running success-stories on the London restaurant scene, Orso and Joe Allen; both establishments are also represented in New York, so it's perhaps no surprise that his new Italian bakeries – in Covent Garden and Kensington – have a rather American feel. / HOURS WC2 Mon-Sat 8am-6.30pm, Sun 9am-6pm; W8 Mon-Sat 8am-6.30pm, Sun 9am-6pm CREDIT CARDS no Amex.

Fresh & Wild
🌐 www.freshandwild.com
BRANCHES AT:
  69-75 Brewer St, W1   3–2D
  ☎ (020) 7434 3179
  210 Westbourne Grove, W11   6–1B
  ☎ (020) 7229 1063
  32-40 Stoke Newington Church St, N16   1–1C
  ☎ (020) 7254 2332
  49 Parkway, NW1   8–3B
  ☎ (020) 7428 7575
  305 Lavender Hill, SW11   10–2C
  ☎ (020) 7585 1488
  194 Old St, EC1   9–1C
  ☎ (020) 7250 1708
"A good range of breads from different high-quality bakers" is a feature of these organic supermarkets. / HOURS W1 Mon-Fri 7.30am-9pm, Sat 9am-9pm, Sun 11.30am-8.30pm; other shops generally slightly shorter hours SEE ALSO Health & organic foods.

Grodzinski NW11
223 Golders Green Rd   1–1B
☎ (020) 8458 3654
"Excellent rye bread" and *"brilliant bagels"* win broad support for this kosher institution in Golders Green. / HOURS Mon, Wed & Sun 6am-11pm, Tue 6am-9pm, Thu 6am-1am, Fri 6am-dusk CREDIT CARDS no credit cards TUBE Golders Green.

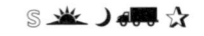

Bread

Harrods SW1
87 Brompton Rd   5–1D
☎ (020) 7730 1234   www.harrods.com
"A wide range of fresh breads to suit all moods and tastes" – the bakery selection at the Knightsbridge food hall is indeed impressive; if you can't find what you're looking for here... / HOURS Mon, Tue & Sat 10am-6pm, Wed-Fri 10am-7pm SEE ALSO Big Ten; Cheese & dairy; Chocolates & sweets; Coffee & tea; Cookware; Fish & seafood; Fruit & vegetables; Grocers & delicatessens; Meat, game & poultry; Patisserie; Wine.

Harvey Nichols SW1
109-125 Knightsbridge   5–1D
☎ (020) 7235 5000   www.harveynichols.com
A *"great, wide"* selection of breads and other baked items is one of the bigger attractions of this fifth-floor Knightsbridge food hall. / HOURS Mon, Tue & Sat 10am-7pm, Wed-Fri 10am-8pm, Sun noon-6pm TUBE Knightsbridge SEE ALSO Big Ten; Fish & seafood; Grocers & delicatessens; Meat, game & poultry; Wine.

Jones Dairy E2
23 Ezra St   1–2D
☎ (020) 7739 5372
There's a *"fabulous selection of breads"* at this charming spot near the Columbia Road Flower Market, which is more noted by reporters for its baked products than its cheeses – there's plenty of *"olde worlde charm"* too. / HOURS Fri & Sat 8am-1pm, Sun 8am-3pm CREDIT CARDS no credit cards TUBE Liverpool Street/Bethnal Green SEE ALSO Cheese & dairy.

Konditor & Cook
BRANCHES AT:
  66 The Cut, SE1   9–4A
  ☎ (020) 7261 0465
  22 Cornwall Rd, SE1   9–4A
  ☎ (020) 7261 0456
  10 Stoney St, SE1   9–4C
  ☎ (020) 7407 5100
Though it's much better known for its pâtisserie, this stylish small chain has quite a name for its *"imaginative"* and *"delicious"* range of breads. / HOURS Mon-Fri 7.30am-6.30pm, Sat 8.30am-2.30pm; The Cut Mon-Fri 8.30am-11pm, Sat 10.30am-11pm SEE ALSO Patisserie.

Lighthouse Bakery SW11
64 Northcote Rd   10–2C
☎ (020) 7228 4537   www.lighthousebakery.co.uk
Established in 2000, this 'artisanal' Battersea bakery is not yet as well known as the neighbouring market's bread stall; fans, however, say it offers *"better quality"* (if *"less choice"*) – it specialises in English breads (so, naturally, one of the co-owners is an American!) / HOURS Tue-Sat 8.30am-5pm TUBE BR Clapham Junction.

Bread

Maison Blanc S ★
www.maisonblanc.co.uk
BRANCHES AT:
  62 Hampstead High St, NW3 8–2A
  ☎ (020) 7431 8338
  37 St John's Wood High St, NW8 8–3A
  ☎ (020) 7586 1982
  303 Fulham Rd, SW10 5–3B
  ☎ (020) 7795 2663
  11 Elystan St, SW3 5–2C
  ☎ (020) 7584 6913
  102 Holland Park Ave, W11 6–2A
  ☎ (020) 7221 2494
  7 Thayer St, W1 2–1A
  ☎ (020) 7224 0228
  26 Turnham Green Terr, W4 7–2A
  ☎ (020) 8995 7220
  7a Kensington Church St, W8 5–1A
  ☎ (020) 7937 4767

Those in search of authentic boulangerie are almost unanimous in their support for this popular chain; "slow" service is something of a bugbear (though it's "friendly" at least), but Sunday opening (with "fresh deliveries") is a particular plus. / HOURS *usual hours Mon-Sat 8am-7pm (SW3 5.30pm), Sun 9am-6pm (SW3 3.30pm)* CREDIT CARDS *no Amex* SEE ALSO *Chocolates & sweets; Patisserie.*

AF Manuel SW15 ☕ ☀ ★
64 Lower Richmond Rd 1–4A
☎ (020) 8788 6363

"Outstanding simple English breads" (including "the best granary loaf in the world") and "classic" Chelsea buns make this long-established family baker in Putney a unanimously popular recommendation. / HOURS *Mon-Sat 7am-4pm* CREDIT CARDS *no credit cards* TUBE *Putney Bridge.*

Marks & Spencer S ☾
☎ (0845) 609 0200 www.marksandspencer.com
BRANCHES AT:
  Locations throughout London

An "excellent range" and "good quality" – with "brilliant batch loaves" a highlight – win consistent support for the baked offerings of this high street chain. / HOURS *Most stores open Mon-Sat 9am-8pm (central branches open later), Sun noon-6pm* SEE ALSO *Big Ten; Cheese & dairy; Fruit & vegetables; Meat, game & poultry.*

Mr Christian's W11 S ☀ ☾ ☆
11 Elgin Cr 6–1A
☎ (020) 7229 0501

Especially on Saturdays – when the bread stall in front of this long-established Notting Hill delicatessen is something of a Portobello Market institution – reporters vote this a "fantastic" destination, thanks to its "excellent variety". / HOURS *Mon-Fri 6am-7pm, Sat 5.30am-6.30pm, Sun 7am-4pm* TUBE *Notting Hill Gate/Ladbroke Grove* SEE ALSO *Grocers & delicatessens.*

Bread

Neal's Yard Bakery WC2 ☕ ★
6 Neal's Yd 4–2C
☎ (020) 7836 5199
"Never boring", say fans of the bakery in the courtyard behind the more famous Covent Garden cheese shop – though the range, primarily wholemeal, "doesn't change", neither does the quality; also cakes. / HOURS Mon-Sat 9am-5pm CREDIT CARDS no credit cards TUBE Covent Garden.

Northcote Road Market SW11 ★
Northcote Rd 10–2C
"Very good bread and cakes" – plus bagels from Brick Lane – make the baking stall at this Battersea market one of the latter's leading attractions; it's "always packed", and some find the pressure tells on the attitude of the staff. / HOURS Mon-Sat 9am-5pm, Wed 9am-1pm TUBE BR Clapham Junction SEE ALSO Fruit & vegetables; Markets.

Old Post Office Bakery SW9) 🚚 ☆
76 Landor Rd 10–1D
☎ (020) 7326 4408
The "best organic wholewheat bread in south London" makes this recently-established Clapham venture a place of pilgrimage for some reporters; some find the limited opening hours "frustrating", though; the range is also available from Fresh & Wild. / HOURS Mon, Wed &Thu 11am-7pm, Tue 11am-5pm, Fri 11am-6pm CREDIT CARDS no credit cards TUBE Clapham North.

Paul Ⓢ ☀) ★
BRANCHES AT:
  115 Marylebone High St, W1 2–1A
  29 Bedford St, WC2 4–3C
  ☎ (020) 7836 3304
There's a reason this Covent Garden establishment (soon with a Marylebone stablemate) strikes reporters as "a real French bread shop" – it's a branch of France's largest boulangerie/pâtisserie chain; the whole operation attracts little but praise (though true Brits may bemoan "the absence of anything organic and little that's wholemeal"). / HOURS WC2 Mon-Fri 7.30am-9pm, Sat & Sun 9am-9pm; W1 still to open as we go to press SEE ALSO Patisserie.

Pierre Pechon Ⓢ ☀)
BRANCHES AT:
  127 Queensway, W2 6–2C
  ☎ (020) 7229 0746
  4 Chepstow Rd, W2 6–1B
  ☎ (020) 7229 5289
  27 Kensington Church St, W8 5–1A
  ☎ (020) 7937 9574
A "good choice" of "very fresh" Gallic baking is available from this small group of long-established west London café/pâtisseries. / HOURS W2 Sun-Wed 7am-7pm, Thu-Sat 7am-8pm; W8 shorter hours SEE ALSO Patisserie.

Bread 26

Poilâne SW1
46 Elizabeth St 2–4A
☎ (020) 7808 4910 🖥 www.poilane.fr
Lionel Poilâne is "rightly celebrated as the king of bakers", and his family's Paris bakery (established on the rue du Cherche-Midi in 1932) has become a place of pilgrimage – in many quarters the Poilâne name has become synonymous with old-style (sourdough) French bread; though only established in June 2000, this completely authentic Belgravia outpost – where the tiny range also includes apple tarts, croissants and "the best brioches in the world" – already attracts nothing short of adulation. / HOURS Mon-Fri 7.30am-7.30pm, Sat 7.30am-6pm TUBE Sloane Square.

Roni's Bagel Bakery NW6
250 West End Ln 1–1B
☎ (020) 7794 6663
"Open early till late, including bank holidays" – this West Hampstead bakery drew a smaller response from reporters than some of its competitors, but all positive. / HOURS Mon-Sun 7am-midnight CREDIT CARDS no credit cards TUBE West Hampstead.

Rumbolds NW3
45 South End Rd 8–1A
☎ (020) 7794 2344
"Lovely fresh bread" is one of the attractions of this old-style bakery in Hampstead – one of the more accessible north London spots for those in search of quality classic English goodies. / HOURS Mon-Sat 8am-5pm TUBE Belsize Park/Hampstead.

Sainsbury's
☎ (0845) 301 2020 🖥 www.sainsburys.com
BRANCHES AT:
　Locations throughout London
Even some not otherwise enamoured of the Sainsbury experience speak of the "always lovely" bakery products which are one of its greatest strengths, with highlights including "good organic bread" and "great fresh loaves that actually last a couple of days". / HOURS Some larger stores 24 hours SEE ALSO Big Ten; Cheese & dairy; Fish & seafood; Fruit & vegetables; Health & organic foods; Herbs & spices; Meat, game & poultry; Wine.

Selfridges W1
400 Oxford St 3–1A
☎ (020) 7629 1234 🖥 www.selfridges.co.uk
There's a "great selection" of "fresh" baking at 'London's most talked-about food hall', and sometimes "big queues" too. / HOURS Mon-Fri 10am-8pm, Sat 9.30am-8pm, Sun noon-6pm TUBE Bond Street SEE ALSO Big Ten; Cheese & dairy; Chocolates & sweets; Cookware; Ethnic shops; Fish & seafood; Fruit & vegetables; Grocers & delicatessens; Herbs & spices; Meat, game & poultry; Wine.

Bread

St John EC1 ☕ ☾ ★
26 St John St 9–1B
☎ (020) 7251 0848 www.stjohnrestaurant.co.uk
"Great bread and cakes" make the shop adjoining the famously carnivorous Smithfield restaurant a destination in its own right; "solid, home-made chunky breads" – many from "interesting" English recipes – are the house speciality, plus such exotica as "divine Eccles cakes". / HOURS Mon-Sat 9am-11pm TUBE Farringdon.

Stagnells Bakeries N19 ☀
59 Junction Rd 8–1C
☎ (020) 7272 1724
You get "nothing fancy, just excellent white and wholemeal", from this Archway bakery; "there are queues in the early morning". / HOURS Mon-Thu 7.45am-5.30pm, Fri 7.45am-6pm, Sat 7.45am-5pm CREDIT CARDS no credit cards TUBE Archway.

Tachbrook Street Market SW1
Tachbrook St 2–4B
☎ (020) 7641 1090
This "friendly" market stall has quite a local reputation for its "fresh and tasty" loaves (and its small pâtisserie range). / HOURS Mon-Sat 9.30am-4.30pm TUBE Pimlico/Victoria SEE ALSO Fruit & vegetables; Markets.

Tesco Ⓢ ☀ ☾ 🚚
 www.tesco.com
BRANCHES AT:
  Locations throughout London
"Plenty of variety at the larger stores" – the bakery was the product area of our largest supermarket chain most often mentioned by reporters. / HOURS Some larger stores 24 hours SEE ALSO Big Ten; Fruit & vegetables; Wine.

Villandry W1 ☕ Ⓢ ☀ ☾ ★
170 Gt Portland St 2–1B
☎ (020) 7631 3131
A "good but pricey" range – including pain Poilâne and "delicious focaccia" – makes this wide-ranging Marylebone food hall a particularly useful source on the bakery front. / HOURS Mon-Sat 8am-10pm, Sun 9.30am-4pm TUBE Great Portland Street SEE ALSO Grocers & delicatessens.

Waitrose Ⓢ ☾ 🚚 ★
☎ (01344) 424680 Customer service
 www.waitrose.com
BRANCHES AT:
  Locations throughout London
The survey's highest-rated supermarket supplier – hardly surprising when, apart from their own (competent and quite extensive) range, they also sell the likes of Poilâne and &Clarke's! / HOURS Hours vary: generally Mon-Sat 8.30am-9pm, Sun 11am-5pm SEE ALSO Big Ten; Cheese & dairy; Fish & seafood; Fruit & vegetables; Health & organic foods; Herbs & spices; Meat, game & poultry; Wine.

Bread

Yasir Halim Patisserie N13 Ⓢ ☾ ★
493 Green Lanes   1–1C
☎ (020) 8340 8090
"The best bread in the world" – well, so say fans – is among the features which makes this Palmers Green spot reporters' leading Turkish food emporium. / HOURS Mon-Sun 9am-10pm CREDIT CARDS no Amex SEE ALSO Ethnic shops.

3. Cheese & dairy

London offers a 'strong field' of specialist cheese suppliers, the top five all being independents. The leader – by a very long way – is Neal's Yard Dairy, which has become a destination of mystical significance for lovers of our native cheeses. The original Covent Garden shop and its Borough Market offshoot attracted over a quarter of the total number of nominations as the best place to buy cheese – a level of domination of customer perception unequalled in any of the other sectors covered by this book.

The top ten most commented-upon suppliers were:

1 Neal's Yard Dairy ★
2 Paxton & Whitfield ★
3 Jeroboams ★
4 La Fromagerie ★
5 Hamish Johnston ★
6= Harrods ★
6= Rippon Cheese Stores ★
8 Selfridges ★
9 Sainsbury's
10 International Cheese Centre ☆

Bloomsbury Cheeses WC1
61 Judd St 8–4C
☎ (020) 7387 7645 ✆ www.cthc.demon.co.uk
A "good selection of cheeses" makes this tiny shop well worth knowing about, especially in a part of town without many specialist food suppliers of note. / HOURS Mon-Fri 10am-7pm, Sat 10am-5.30pm CREDIT CARDS no Amex TUBE Russell Square/Kings Cross SEE ALSO Bread.

Bluebird SW3
350 King's Rd 5–3C
☎ (020) 7559 1000 ✆ www.conran.co.uk
Cheese is one of the highlights of Conran's Chelsea food emporium – "very good range and quality, but expensive". / HOURS Mon-Wed 9am-8pm, Thu-Sat 9am-9pm, Sun 11am-5pm TUBE Sloane Square/South Kensington SEE ALSO Big Ten; Bread; Fish & seafood; Fruit & vegetables; Grocers & delicatessens.

Cheese & dairy

Borough Market SE1 ★
Borough High St 9–4C
🖥 www.boroughmarket.org.uk
The cheese offerings at London's foodiest market tend to be eclipsed by the presence of the larger of the two Neal's Yard branches; the market itself, however, is home to a number of specialist cheese stalls offering "good quality and choice". / HOURS Fri noon-5pm, Sat 9am-4pm (wholesale fruit & veg Mon-Fri 3am-10am) CREDIT CARDS no credit cards TUBE London Bridge SEE ALSO Big Ten; Bread; Fish & seafood; Fruit & vegetables; Herbs & spices; Markets; Meat, game & poultry.

The Cheese Block SE22 ★
69 Lordship Ln 1–4D
☎ (020) 8299 3636
"A good variety of cheeses" ("plus bread, and other deli fare") makes this very well stocked shop a "great local resource for the good people of East Dulwich" – "lengthy queues" can sometimes result. / HOURS Mon-Fri 9.30am-6.30pm, Sat 9am-6pm CREDIT CARDS no Amex TUBE BR East Dulwich.

The Cheese Board SE10 🚚 ☆
26 Royal Hill 1–3D
☎ (020) 8305 0401 🖥 www.cheese-board.co.uk
"Wonderful 'new' cheeses plus a few old favourites" help make this well-stocked Greenwich shop a popular destination. / HOURS Mon-Wed & Sat 9am-5pm, Thu 9am-1pm, Fri 9am-5.30pm TUBE BR Greenwich.

Cheeses N10 🚚 ☆
13 Fortis Green Rd 1–1C
☎ (020) 8444 9141
A "great, tiny local shop" – this Muswell Hill establishment packs quite a range (some 150 varieties, largely English and French) into its small compass. / HOURS Tue-Thu 10am-5.45pm, Fri 10am-6pm, Sat 9.30am-6pm CREDIT CARDS no Amex TUBE Bounds Green/East Finchley.

&Clarke's W8 ☼) ★
122 Kensington Church St 6–2B
☎ (020) 7229 2190 🖥 www.sallyclarke.com
It stocks British and Irish cheeses only, but Sally Clarke's famous bakery is worth knowing about as one of the surprisingly few purveyors of quality cheeses in leafy Kensington; quality is unanimously hailed as tiptop. / HOURS Mon-Fri 8am-8pm, Sat 9am-4pm TUBE Notting Hill Gate SEE ALSO Bread; Chocolates & sweets; Patisserie.

Cheese & dairy

La Fromagerie N5 ⓢ ☽ 🚚 ★
30 Highbury Pk   8–2D
☎ (020) 7359 7440   www.lafromagerie.co.uk
"Unbeatable" cheese – uniquely in London the shop practices 'affinage' (bringing 'raw' cheeses to perfection, à la française) – makes Patricia Michelson's tiny Highbury shop unequalled for popularity in north London (and it supplies to some of the capital's foremost restaurants); the range is "incredible" and the "knowledgeable" service is usually "friendly" too (though the odd "brusque" encounter is not unknown). / HOURS Mon 10.30am-7.30pm, Tue-Fri 9.30am-7.30pm, Sat 9.30am-7pm, Sun 10am-5pm TUBE Highbury Park.

Hamish Johnston SW11 ★
48 Northcote Rd   10–2C
☎ (020) 7738 0741
"The best cheese south of the river"; "a great selection, British and French" is available at this Battersea shop, where staff are "knowledgeable, and keen to help". / HOURS Mon-Sat 9am-6pm TUBE BR Clapham Junction.

Harrods SW1 ☕ ☽ 🚚 ★
87 Brompton Rd   5–1D
☎ (020) 7730 1234   www.harrods.com
It's not just the "great variety" that makes cheese one of this Knightsbridge food hall's most impressive departments – they are "always in good condition" too, which is no mean achievement with more than 350 lines from 15 countries in stock; those desperate for an immediate fix can snack at the adjoining Bar Fromage. / HOURS Mon, Tue & Sat 10am-6pm, Wed-Fri 10am-7pm SEE ALSO Big Ten; Bread; Chocolates & sweets; Coffee & tea; Cookware; Fish & seafood; Fruit & vegetables; Grocers & delicatessens; Meat, game & poultry; Patisserie; Wine.

International Cheese Centre ☀ ☽ ☆
BRANCHES AT:
  The Parade, Victoria Station, SW1   2–4B
  ☎ (020) 7828 2886
  Unit 5 Marylebone Station, Melcombe Pl, NW1   8–4A
  ☎ (020) 7724 1432
  Liverpool Street Station, EC2   9–2D
  ☎ (020) 7628 6637
"Always a great range from Britain and Europe" – the capital's only specialist cheese mini-chain attracts consistently favourable commentary. / HOURS Mon-Wed 8am-8pm, Thu & Fri 8am-8.30pm, Sat 11am-7.30pm CREDIT CARDS no Amex.

Cheese & dairy

Jeroboams

🏠 Ⓢ ☾ ★

🖰 www.jeroboams.co.uk
BRANCHES AT:
  51 Elizabeth St, SW1   2–4A
  ☎ (020) 7823 5623
  96 Holland Park Ave, W11   6–2A
  ☎ (020) 7727 9359

Though they offer a general range of "hams, jams and other home-made produce", it's the cheese – "an unusual selection, of excellent quality" – which is the undoubted highlight at this upmarket small deli chain. / HOURS Mon-Fri 9am-7.30pm, Sat 8.30am-7pm, Sun 10am-4pm SEE ALSO Grocers & delicatessens.

Jones Dairy E2

☕ Ⓢ 🌅 ☆

23 Ezra St   1–2D
☎ (020) 7739 5372

British and Dutch farmhouse cheeses are the speciality of this atmospheric East End destination. / HOURS Fri & Sat 8am-1pm, Sun 8am-3pm CREDIT CARDS no credit cards TUBE Liverpool Street/Bethnal Green SEE ALSO Bread.

C Lidgate W11

🌅 🚚 ★

110 Holland Park Ave   6–2A
☎ (020) 7727 8243

This hugely-celebrated Holland Park butcher also offers a small range of cheeses, all "in perfect condition". / HOURS Mon-Sat 7.30am-6pm (Sat 5pm) CREDIT CARDS no Amex TUBE Holland Park SEE ALSO Meat, game & poultry.

Marks & Spencer

Ⓢ ☾

☎ (0845) 609 0200   🖰 www.marksandspencer.com
BRANCHES AT:
  Locations throughout London

"Great range, poor availability" – four words say it all about the cheese on offer, intermittently, at the high street store. / HOURS Most stores open Mon-Sat 9am-8pm (central branches open later), Sun noon-6pm SEE ALSO Big Ten; Bread; Fruit & vegetables; Meat, game & poultry.

Neal's Yard Dairy

☾ ★

BRANCHES AT:
  17 Shorts Gdns, WC2   4–2C
  ☎ (020) 7240 5700
  6-8 Park St, SE1   9–4C
  ☎ (020) 7645 3554

"A great selection of British and Irish cheeses" (plus the odd Gallic interloper nowadays) and "informed and enthusiastic service" make this atmospheric Covent Garden shop London's cheese-lovers' favourite by far; success has brought a second branch at the company's south London warehouse – some say "Borough is better", the original shop being just "too small" and "crowded" for some tastes. / HOURS WC2 Mon-Sat 9am-7pm; SE1 Mon-Fri 9am-6pm, Sat 10am-4pm.

Cheese & dairy

North End Road Market SW6
North End Rd   5–3A
☎ (020) 8748 3020 ext 4936
The market includes a cheese stall of some note. / HOURS Mon-Sat 7am-5pm, Thu 7am-1pm TUBE Fulham Broadway SEE ALSO Fruit & vegetables; Markets.

Paxton & Whitfield SW1
93 Jermyn St   3–3D
☎ (020) 7930 0259   www.cheesemongers.co.uk
"Old-fashioned in the nicest sense", this "timeless" St James's institution (est 1797) still offers a "very wide range of excellent quality" which, for many reporters, maintains a justified claim to being "the best cheese shop in London"; the staff are notably "knowledgeable" and "friendly" (particularly for somewhere that's "stranded in touristville"). / HOURS Mon-Sat 9.30am-6pm TUBE Piccadilly Circus.

Real Cheese Shop SW13
62 Barnes High St   10–1A
☎ (020) 8878 6676
This Barnes shop may be "very compact", but its "unassuming" approach and the "wide variety" it offers makes it a very popular local destination. / HOURS Tue-Sat 9am-5pm CREDIT CARDS no Amex TUBE Hammersmith.

Rippon Cheese Stores SW1
26 Upper Tachbrook St   2–4B
☎ (020) 7931 0628
"Great service" – usually presided over by Mr Rippon – and "fantastic variety" are carving out a big reputation for this ordinary-looking Pimlico shop; the retail operation is, in fact, the 'tip of the iceberg' of an operation that supplies many top restaurants. / HOURS Mon-Sat 8am-5.15pm CREDIT CARDS no Amex TUBE Pimlico/Victoria.

Sainsbury's
☎ (0845) 301 2020   www.sainsburys.com
BRANCHES AT:
   Locations throughout London
"A surprisingly good choice" (especially in shops with a 'Special Selection') made Sainsbury's the survey's most-often nominated supermarket cheese supplier – quality was, however, not felt to be quite up to that of Waitrose. / HOURS Some larger stores 24 hours SEE ALSO Big Ten; Bread; Fish & seafood; Fruit & vegetables; Health & organic foods; Herbs & spices; Meat, game & poultry; Wine.

Selfridges W1
400 Oxford St   3–1A
☎ (020) 7629 1234   www.selfridges.co.uk
"Good variety and quality" and "knowledgeable staff" win a good following for the cheesy offerings of the survey's most-mentioned food hall. / HOURS Mon-Fri 10am-8pm, Sat 9.30am-8pm, Sun noon-6pm TUBE Bond Street SEE ALSO Big Ten; Chocolates & sweets; Cookware; Ethnic shops; Fish & seafood; Fruit & vegetables; Grocers & delicatessens; Herbs & spices; Meat, game & poultry; Wine.

Cheese & dairy

Waitrose Ⓢʃ🚚★
☎ (01344) 424680 Customer service
🖱 www.waitrose.com
BRANCHES AT:
  Locations throughout London
"Very good quality cheese at the counter" (plus *"a good Gallic pre-packed selection"*) *puts Waitrose some way ahead of the other supermarkets in the quality stakes.* / HOURS *Hours vary: generally Mon-Sat 8.30am-9pm, Sun 11am-5pm* SEE ALSO *Big Ten; Bread; Fish & seafood; Fruit & vegetables; Health & organic foods; Herbs & spices; Meat, game & poultry; Wine.*

MAIL ORDER

Huge Cheese Direct SW8
A37-42 New Covent Garden Mkt 10–1D
☎ (020) 7819 6099 🖱 www.hugecheesedirect.co.uk
Perhaps not the most elegant website we've ever seen, but – viewed most easily through the 'Quick Entry' page – it does offer a good range of cheeses for next day delivery, plus other goodies such as biscuits, jams, mustards and vinegars; also pain Poilâne.

4. Chocolates & sweets

Cheese and chocolate are often thought of as rather similar addictive delights, and the pattern of London's quality shops reflects this. As with the top ten cheese stores, nine of the top ten chocolate shops are 'specialists' of one sort or another, and all are good enough to merit a star. Only one multiple – the UK's only major high street chocolate chain – is represented.

Most commented-upon suppliers:

1. Rococo Chocolates ★
2. Godiva ★
3. Thorntons
4. The Chocolate Society ★
5. Harrods ★
6= Fortnum & Mason ★
6= Charbonnel et Walker ★
8. Selfridges ★
9. Leonidas ★
10. Prestat ★

A La Reine Astrid W1
27 Burlington Arcade   3–3C
☎ (020) 7499 8558
Part of the Parisian invasion of the London food scene, this chic recent Mayfair arrival from the 8ème is already winning praise for its "delicious" pralines. / HOURS Mon-Sat 10am-6pm CREDIT CARDS no Amex TUBE Green Park/Piccadilly Circus.

Ackermans NW6
9 Goldhurst Ter   8–3A
☎ (020) 7624 2742 www.thehouseofchocolates.com
Perhaps rather under-celebrated by those outside its immediate area, this "tiny" south Hampstead shop attracts ecstatic support for its "wonderful traditional chocolates"; truffles, 'thins' and animal figures are among the products attracting particular praise. / HOURS Mon-Fri 10am-6pm, Sat 10am-5.30pm (open Sun at peak times) TUBE Finchley Road.

Ambala NW1
112 Drummond St   8–3C
☎ (020) 7387 7886
The capital's leading subcontinental sweetmeat supplier stocks all kinds of Indian and Pakistani confectionery (plus savouries, such as pakoras). / HOURS Mon-Sun 9am-8.30pm CREDIT CARDS no credit cards TUBE Euston/Euston Square SEE ALSO Ethnic shops.

Chocolates & sweets

L'Artisan du Chocolat SW1
89 Lower Sloane St   5–2D
☎ (020) 7824 8365
Handmade in Kent by choc-obsessives, the products at this expensively understated new Pimlico shop come in a bewildering variety of flavours; some press commentators already regard it as among the very top places in town. / HOURS Mon-Sat 10am-7pm CREDIT CARDS no Amex TUBE Sloane Square.

Casemir
⌁ www.casemirchocolates.co.uk
BRANCHES AT:
  13 Piccadilly Arcade, SW1   3–3D
  ☎ (020) 7629 8825
  5 Tetherdown, N10   1–1C
  ☎ (020) 8365 2132
Established in Antwerp in 1928, and in London since 1986, this north London outfit has recently opened a rather more central retail operation in St James's; products are made by hand, from Belgian chocolate; (the nifty website provides a useful source of further information). / HOURS W1 Mon-Fri 9.30am-6.30pm, Sat 9.30am-6pm; N10 Fri & Sat only 10am-5.30pm.

Charbonnel et Walker W1
1 The Royal Arcade, 28 Old Bond St   3–3C
☎ (020) 7491 0939
"Delicious chocolates packed in fabulous boxes" makes this multiple royal warrant-holding Mayfair shop (est 1875, and Queen Victoria's preferred supplier) one of the very best operators in its field; "incomparable drinking chocolate" was praised by a large number of reporters. / HOURS Mon-Fri 10am-6pm, Sat 10am-6pm TUBE Green Park.

Choccywoccydoodah W1
47 Harrowby St   6–1D
☎ (020) 7724 5465 ⌁ www.choccywoccydoodah.com
Based in Brighton (where production takes place), these craftsmen in chocolate bring a rather rococo style to bespoke productions; weddings cakes are a speciality, but anything can be commissioned – see the impressive website for further details. / HOURS Tue-Sat 11am-6pm (closed 2pm-3pm) CREDIT CARDS no credit cards TUBE Edgware Road.

The Chocolate Society SW1
36 Elizabeth St   2–4A
☎ (020) 7259 9222, (01423) 322230
⌁ www.chocolate.co.uk
"Superb quality chocolates" of "wicked richness" make this Belgravia shop – and enthusiasts' club – a destination worth seeking out; the total experience of a visit, however, can fall short of the quality of the basic products, and a minority of reporters find service "less caring" or "less organised" than they would hope. / HOURS Mon-Fri 9.30am-5.30pm, Sat 9.30am-4pm CREDIT CARDS no Amex TUBE Victoria.

Chocolates & sweets

&Clarke's W8
122 Kensington Church St   6–2B
☎ (020) 7229 2190   www.sallyclarke.com
It's best known for baked goods, but Sally Clarke's celebrated Kensington shop also has something of a cult following for "the best truffles anywhere". / HOURS Mon-Fri 8am-8pm, Sat 9am-4pm TUBE Notting Hill Gate SEE ALSO Bread; Cheese & dairy; Patisserie.

Dugans Chocolates N1
149 Upper St   8–3D
☎ (020) 7354 4666
This "tiny, tiny" Islington shop strikes some as "a bit claustrophobic", but its Belgian and 'nostalgia' chocolates offer "orgasmic" compensation. / HOURS Mon-Sat 10.30am-6.30pm, Sun 11am-5pm TUBE Angel/Highbury & Islington.

Fortnum & Mason W1
181 Piccadilly   3–3D
☎ (020) 7734 8040   www.fortnumandmason.co.uk
"It's hard to find anyone to rival Fortnums' quality, presentation, packaging and service", says one reporter, and the general consensus endorses this view; "lovely truffles" are a highlight, but even "just breathing in the fumes here is divine". / HOURS Mon-Sat 10am-6.30pm TUBE Piccadilly Circus/Green Park SEE ALSO Big Ten; Coffee & tea; Grocers & delicatessens; Patisserie; Wine.

Godiva
www.godiva.com
BRANCHES AT:
  247 Regent St, W1   3–1C
  ☎ (020) 7495 2845
  17 The Piazza, Covent Garden, WC2   4–3D
  ☎ 020 7836 5706
  150 Fenchurch St, EC3   9–3C
  ☎ (020) 7623 2287
"The best of London's Belgian choccy shops" – established in Brussels in 1926, and named, rather curiously, after a Coventry lass – has a huge number of supporters for the "sumptuous" quality of its pralines; with over a thousand outlets internationally, it's perhaps no great surprise that some of its shops can seem a touch "sterile". / HOURS WC2 Mon-Sat 10am-8pm, Sun noon-6pm; W1 Mon-Sat 9.30am-7pm, Sun noon-6pm; EC3 Mon-Fri 9am-6pm.

Harrods SW1
87 Brompton Rd   5–1D
☎ (020) 7730 1234   www.harrods.com
"The best selection of chocolate under one roof" – including most of the 'big names' – ensures a winning reputation for what's probably the capital's largest space devoted to confectionery, set in these incomparable Knightsbridge food halls. / HOURS Mon, Tue & Sat 10am-6pm, Wed-Fri 10am-7pm SEE ALSO Big Ten; Bread; Cheese & dairy; Coffee & tea; Cookware; Fish & seafood; Fruit & vegetables; Grocers & delicatessens; Meat, game & poultry; Patisserie; Wine.

Chocolates & sweets

The House of Chocolates TW9
13 The Grn, Richmond   1–4A
☎ (020) 8332 1503
Two hundred and twenty square feet is not a great deal of space, but it is when packed wall-to-wall with chocolates from a variety of names such as Godiva, Neuhaus and Kimberlys (an English outfit specialising in fruit centres); this "decadent" Richmond shop also offers an unusually wide range of bespoke wrappings that are "great for gifts". / HOURS Mon-Sat 10am-6.30pm (also Sun near Christmas & Easter) TUBE Richmond.

Indulgence SW19
79 Ridgway   10–2B
☎ (020) 8944 8955
Down Wimbledon way, it's useful to note that this 'fine food shop' includes Godiva and Charbonnel et Walker amongst its range. / HOURS Tue-Sun 9am-5.30pm CREDIT CARDS no Amex TUBE Wimbledon.

Leonidas EC4
110 Fleet St   9–2A
☎ (020) 7353 3590   www.leonidas.com
Not as well known as Godiva, but the 'other' Belgian supplier is in fact older (est 1913), has rather more outlets worldwide and is rated almost as highly by reporters for its "rich and delicious" range of pralines and 'creams'; some of the shops, though, really are rather depressing. / HOURS Mon-Fri 7am-6pm CREDIT CARDS no Amex TUBE St Pauls/Blackfriars.

Maison Blanc
www.maisonblanc.co.uk
BRANCHES AT:
  62 Hampstead High St, NW3   8–2A
  ☎ (020) 7431 8338
  37 St John's Wood High St, NW8   8–3A
  ☎ (020) 7586 1982
  303 Fulham Rd, SW10   5–3B
  ☎ (020) 7795 2663
  11 Elystan St, SW3   5–2C
  ☎ (020) 7584 6913
  102 Holland Park Ave, W11   6–2A
  ☎ (020) 7221 2494
  7 Thayer St, W1   2–1A
  ☎ (020) 7224 0228
  26 Turnham Green Terr, W4   7–2A
  ☎ (020) 8995 7220
  7a Kensington Church St, W8   5–1A
  ☎ (020) 7937 4767
"Pure chocolate is pure chocolate here" – the popular pâtisserie chain does more than bread and cakes. / HOURS usual hours Mon-Sat 8am-7pm (SW3 5.30pm), Sun 9am-6pm (SW3 3.30pm) CREDIT CARDS no Amex SEE ALSO Bread; Patisserie.

Chocolates & sweets

Marine Ices NW3
8 Haverstock Hill   8–2B
☎ (020) 7482 9003
Over 70 years in business, this Chalk Farm pizzeria and gelateria is one of the capital's few ice-cream 'destinations'; 15 varieties are available to take away. / HOURS Mon-Fri 10.30am-11pm, Sat 11am-11pm, Sun 11am-10pm TUBE Chalk Farm.

WM Martyn N10   ★
135 Muswell Hill Broadway   1–1C
☎ (020) 8883 5642
"Excellent plain dark chocolates and candied fruits" are among the particularly commended ranges at this eminent Muswell Hill grocer. / HOURS Mon-Wed, Fri 9.30am-5.30pm, Thu 9.30am-1pm, Sat 9am-5.30pm CREDIT CARDS no Amex TUBE Highgate SEE ALSO Coffee & tea; Herbs & spices.

Maxwell & Kennedy
BRANCHES AT:
Whiteleys, 151 Queensway, W2   6–2C
☎ (020) 7221 9627
Broadway Shopping Centre, W6   7–2C
☎ (020) 8563 2800
Cabot Place West, Canary Whf, E14   2–2D
☎ (020) 7512 9113
Aldgate Barrs, Whitechapel High St, E1   9–2D
☎ (020) 7481 2031
The Mall, Liverpool Street Station, EC2   9–2D
☎ (020) 7638 2847
"Every chocolate tastes like heaven", say supporters of this small chain of confectioners; it received surprisingly little commentary, but all very positive. / HOURS W2 Mon-Sat 10am-8pm, Sun 12-6pm; EC2 Mon-Fri 8am-8pm, Sat 10am-6pm; other branches slightly shorter hours.

Prestat SW1   ★
14 Princes Arcade   3–3D
☎ (020) 7629 4838   www.prestat.co.uk
"Delicious" truffles are the top tip from fans of this chocolatier in an arcade off Jermyn Street; established in 1902, "its standards have not changed over the years". / HOURS Mon-Fri 9.30am-6pm, Sat 9.30am-5pm TUBE Green Park/Piccadilly Circus.

Rococo Chocolates SW3   ★
321 King's Rd   5–3B
☎ (020) 7352 5857   www.rococochocolates.com
If you're looking for "a fantastic speciality shop", reporters are in little doubt that this "magnificent" (and aptly-named) Chelsea establishment is the place – "a genuine passion for chocolate" makes it the survey's clear No.1 in the category. / HOURS Mon-Sat 10am-6.30pm, Sun noon-5pm TUBE Sloane Square.

Chocolates & sweets 40

Sandrine SW14 ☆
239 Upper Richmond Rd West   10–2A
☎ (020) 8878 8168
"A specialist in hand-made Belgian chocolates" (and "elegantly wrapped" too) that's much approved by the folk of East Sheen. / HOURS *Mon-Sat 10am-5.30pm* TUBE *BR Mortlake.*

Selfridges W1   🍵 Ⓢ ☾ 🚚 ★
400 Oxford St   3–1A
☎ (020) 7629 1234   www.selfridges.co.uk
London's most talked-about food hall offers "beautiful displays" and "all the brands under one roof" – what more could a chocoholic want? / HOURS *Mon-Fri 10am-8pm, Sat 9.30am-8pm, Sun noon-6pm* TUBE *Bond Street* SEE ALSO *Big Ten; Bread; Cheese & dairy; Cookware; Ethnic shops; Fish & seafood; Fruit & vegetables; Grocers & delicatessens; Herbs & spices; Meat, game & poultry; Wine.*

Theobroma Cacao W4   📷 🍵 Ⓢ ★
43 Turnham Green Ter   7–2A
☎ (020) 8996 0431
Being in Chiswick, it doesn't attract nearly the same volume of support, but fans insist that this characterful, modernistic shop is "just as good as Rococo in Chelsea, maybe even better"; "the most wonderful hot chocolate drinks", consumed on the premises, attract particular support. / HOURS *Mon-Sat 9.30am-6pm, Sun 10.45am-5pm* TUBE *Turnham Green.*

Thorntons   📷
www.thorntons.co.uk
BRANCHES AT:
  Locations throughout London
Thanks to the consistent standards of its "good-value, everyday chocolates", the UK's largest high-street chocolatier chain was a respectable survey performer; however, when it comes to toffee – "lovely", "to die for", "the best in the world" – reporters approach something closer to ecstasy. / HOURS *18 branches: generally Mon-Sat 9am-5.30pm, some branches open Sun.*

MAIL ORDER

Sara Jayne SW12   📷
53 Cavendish Rd
☎ (020) 8673 6300
Self-professed 'chocolate evangelist' Sara Jayne Stanes has not only written a book on the subject, but even offers tutored tastings – her definitive hand-made truffles are available by mail order. / CREDIT CARDS *no credit cards.*

5. Coffee & tea

Perhaps because coffee sellers (as opposed to coffee shops) seem to be the area of retail which style forgot, specialist coffee merchants have a profile so low they are almost invisible. But if you know where to look, London has a number of excellent specialists. As ever, for quality, independents are very much to the fore. The ten most commented-upon suppliers were:

1. Whittard of Chelsea
2. Fortnum & Mason ★
3. Monmouth Coffee Company ★
4. Algerian Coffee Stores ★
5. Harrods ★
6. Starbucks
7. HR Higgins ★
8. Twining & Co ★
9. WM Martyn ★
10. Tea & Coffee Plant ★

Algerian Coffee Stores W1 ☾ ★
52 Old Compton St   4–3A
☎ (020) 7437 2480   www.algcoffee.co.uk
It may be "cramped", but this venerable Soho shop (est 1887) has it all – "a very good selection of coffees and teas", "very educated staff", "wonderful aromas" and "bags of ancient charm"; in fact it's one of those few places where almost everyone praises almost everything! / HOURS Mon-Sat 9am-7pm TUBE *Leicester Square.*

Angelucci W1
23b Frith St   4–2A
☎ (020) 7437 5889
In spite of its central, Soho location and its longevity (est 1929), this specialist coffee supplier was not much commented on in the survey; its "fantastic range" – 35 types, including "very good decaffeinated" – was, however, enthusiastically approved by aficionados. / HOURS Mon-Wed 9am-5pm, Thu 9am-1pm, Fri & Sat 9am-5pm CREDIT CARDS *no credit cards* TUBE *Tottenham Court Road/Leicester Square.*

Berry Bros. & Rudd SW1
3 St James's St   3–4D
☎ (020) 7396 9600   www.bbr.com
A little-known fact with which to amaze your friends – London's top wine shop started off life as a tea merchant and they still provide the raw materials for some "superb" brews. / HOURS Mon-Fri 9am-5.30pm, Sat 10am-4pm TUBE *Green Park* SEE ALSO *Wine.*

Coffee & tea

Drurys WC2
3 New Row   4–3C
☎ (020) 7836 1960   www.drury.uk.com
A "great selection" – over 60 teas and more than 25 coffees – is one of the strengths of this Covent Garden merchant, which also offers a web-based ordering service. / HOURS Mon-Fri 8.30am-6pm, Sat 11am-5pm CREDIT CARDS no Amex TUBE Covent Garden/Leicester Square.

Fortnum & Mason W1
181 Piccadilly   3–3D
☎ (020) 7734 8040   www.fortnumandmason.co.uk
"Great exotic teas" – "the best in London", say fans – and "fantastic own-brand coffees" are market-leading strengths of Piccadilly's world-famous food store. / HOURS Mon-Sat 10am-6.30pm TUBE Piccadilly Circus/Green Park SEE ALSO Big Ten; Chocolates & sweets; Grocers & delicatessens; Patisserie; Wine.

Harrods SW1
87 Brompton Rd   5–1D
☎ (020) 7730 1234   www.harrods.com
Mr Harrod was, after all, a grocer and the Knightsbridge food halls which bear his name are distinguished to this day by a range of "fresh and flavoursome" teas and "excellent" coffees the equal of any in town. / HOURS Mon, Tue & Sat 10am-6pm, Wed-Fri 10am-7pm SEE ALSO Big Ten; Bread; Cheese & dairy; Chocolates & sweets; Cookware; Fish & seafood; Fruit & vegetables; Grocers & delicatessens; Meat, game & poultry; Patisserie; Wine.

HR Higgins (Coffee-Man) W1
79 Duke St   3–2A
☎ (020) 7629 3913   www.hrhiggins.co.uk
"There are no rivals we know of", says one reporter who has gone to the trouble of placing a regular mail order with Her Majesty's coffee merchant; for others too, the "excellent range" and the "knowledgeable and helpful staff" make this shop near Selfridges – established 60 years ago – "simply the best"; excellent website. / HOURS Mon-Fri 9.30am-5.30pm, Sat 10am-5pm TUBE Bond Street.

Markus Coffee Co W2
13 Connaught St, Marble Arch   6–1D
☎ (020) 7723 4020
"A superb range of excellent coffee" distinguishes this shop near Marble Arch, which has been trading since 1957; they also sell sugars and honey. / HOURS Mon-Fri 8.30-5.30, Sat 8.30-1pm CREDIT CARDS no Amex TUBE Marble Arch.

Coffee & tea

WM Martyn N10 ★
135 Muswell Hill Broadway   1–1C
☎ (020) 8883 5642
"Stuck in the 1950s, and all the more fun for that", this fifth-generation Muswell Hill grocers has a big reputation for its "great dried goods", including those rich in caffeine; all coffee-roasting and tea-blending takes place on the premises. / HOURS Mon-Wed, Fri 9.30am-5.30pm, Thu 9.30am-1pm, Sat 9am-5.30pm CREDIT CARDS no Amex TUBE Highgate SEE ALSO Chocolates & sweets; Herbs & spices.

Monmouth Coffee Company ★
www.monmouthcoffee.co.uk
BRANCHES AT:
  27 Monmouth St, WC2   4–2B
  ☎ (020) 7645 3561
  2 Park St, SE1   9–4C
  ☎ (020) 7645 3585
"They really know their beans" at this "old favourite" Covent Garden shop (with a Borough Market offshoot), which offers "a very decent range of quality coffee at fair prices"; "it ain't broke", say fans – "so please don't modernise it!" / HOURS Mon-Sat 8am-5pm (WC2 6.30pm).

Starbucks
www.starbucks.com
BRANCHES AT:
  Locations throughout London
Given that our restaurant survey feedback on Uncle Sam's leading coffee shop chain is hardly encouraging, it's something of a surprise that a number of reporters speak of the "wonderful" quality of its take-away beans; as they are to be found in most parts of town, and open at most hours of the day and night, its shops are certainly worth bearing in mind for 'emergency' supplies. / HOURS Most branches open long hours.

Tea & Coffee Plant W11 ★
170 Portobello Rd   6–1B
☎ (020) 7221 8137   www.coffee.uk.com
"Top-notch" coffee is to be had at this unpretentious-looking Notting Hill shop; "irresistible", says one convert – "you can smell it throughout the market". / HOURS Tue-Sat 10.30am-6pm CREDIT CARDS no Amex TUBE Notting Hill Gate/Ladbroke Grove.

The Tea House WC2
15 Neal St   4–2C
☎ (020) 7240 7539
"A fabulous choice of teas, herbal and otherwise", plus every sort of tea-related accessory you might hope for. / HOURS Mon-Wed 10am-7pm, Thu 10am-7.30pm, Fri 10.30am-7pm, Sat 10am-7pm, Sun noon-6pm TUBE Covent Garden.

Coffee & tea

R Twining & Co WC2 ★
216 Strand   2–2D
☎ (020) 7353 3511, Twinings Direct (0870) 241 3667
🖰 www.twinings.com
For an "incomparable" tea selection, seek out the fascinating eighteenth-century shop of the famous tea-shippers in the Strand (whose shop has the dubious distinction of being Westminster's longest-established ratepayer); you can, of course, buy the branded boxes on offer at any corner shop, but the 'export' selections are also available here – some of which are also available from the website. / HOURS Mon-Fri 9.30am-4.45pm TUBE Temple.

Whittard of Chelsea
☎ (08000) 154394   🖰 www.whittard.com
BRANCHES AT:
   Locations throughout London
"A pretty good and reliable stockist"; London's only specialist tea and coffee multiple – now a quoted company with a presence on many high streets – strikes some reporters as rather "too commercial" nowadays, but most feel that it still offers "reasonable goods at reasonable prices". / HOURS Hours vary; some central branches open Sun

MAIL ORDER

Betty's & Taylors of Harrogate HG2
Pagoda Hs, Plumpton Pk, Harrogate
☎ (0845) 345 3636   🖰 www.bettysbypost.com
Yorkshire tea straight from Yorkshire is one of the caffeine-fix options available from the mail order service of the famous Harrogate tearooms.

Clipper Teas DT8
Beaminster, Dorset
☎ (01308) 863344   🖰 www.clipper-teas.com
'The world's most enlightened tea company', so it claims (on account of its ethical agro-policies), offers an "excellent and easy" mail order service; organic and Fairtrade products a speciality. / CREDIT CARDS no Amex.

6. Cookware

When it comes to cookware, it's a real fight at the top of our survey between the specialist suppliers and the department stores. It's appropriate, then, that the top two names – which, in terms of volume of commentary, stand well clear of the rest of the field – include one representative from each camp.

The top ten most commented-upon suppliers were:

1. Divertimenti ★
2. John Lewis/Peter Jones
3. David Mellor ★
4. Selfridges ★
5. Gill Wing Cookshop
6. La Cuisinière
7. Harrods ★
8. Lakeland (mail order) ★
9. Jerry's Home Store
10. Richard Dare ★

(Please note that reporters were asked only to comment on cookware; we hope to cover tableware fully in the next edition.)

Amy's Cook & Dine NW3
13 Harben Pde, Finchley Rd 8–2A
☎ (020) 7221 6703
There's some local support for this Swiss Cottage kitchen equipment shop – the flagship of a chain with various shops around London (some of which carry a fair degree of culinary stock, and some not). / HOURS Mon-Sat 9.30am-6.30pm, Sun 10am-6pm TUBE Swiss Cottage.

Anything Left-Handed W1
57 Brewer St 3–2D
☎ (020) 7437 3910 www.anythingleft-handed.co.uk
A Soho emporium of gadgets for the left-handed – a startlingly modern concept when it was launched in 1968 – whose range includes a good selection of kitchen tools, from can-openers to corkscrews. / HOURS Mon-Sat 10am-5.30pm CREDIT CARDS no Amex TUBE Piccadilly Circus.

Books for Cooks W11 ♨ ★
4 Blenheim Cr 6–1A
☎ (020) 7221 1992 www.booksforcooks.com
"The UK's best cookbook shop" – "if you can't find that elusive recipe book anywhere else" (including some out-of-print titles), *these Tardis-like Notting Hill premises are almost certainly your best bet.* / HOURS Tue-Sat 10am-6pm TUBE Ladbroke Grove/Notting Hill Gate.

Cookware   46

The Conran Shop
-ᑫ www.conran.com
BRANCHES AT:
  55 Marylebone High St, W1   2–1A
  ☎ (020) 7723 2223
  Michelin Hs, 81 Fulham Rd, SW3   5–2C
  ☎ (020) 7589 7401

If you're looking for an "eclectic" (but quite limited) selection ("lots of shiny utensils"), the cookware departments of these design-led shops at Brompton Cross and in Marylebone may be worth checking out. / HOURS *Mon-Sat 10am-6pm (or later); Sun noon-6pm*

La Cuisinière SW11
81-83 Northcote Rd   10–2C
☎ (020) 7223 4487 -ᑫ www.la-cuisiniere.co.uk
This popular Clapham establishment may be "very small" and "rather crowded", but fans say that thanks to the "good range of products" on offer, "you can always find what you need". / HOURS *Mon-Sat 9.30am-6pm* TUBE *BR Clapham Junction.*

David Mellor SW1
4 Sloane Sq   5–2D
☎ (020) 7730 4259 -ᑫ www.davidmellordesign.com
"Every pan and device imaginable" is available at this "beautifully laid out" Belgravia shop, which "concentrates totally on best quality items and no gimmicks"; the shop's particular reputation – outside the strict scope of this guide – is for "top-class cutlery". / HOURS *Mon-Sat 9.30am-6pm* CREDIT CARDS *no Amex* TUBE *Sloane Square.*

Dentons SW4
2-4 Clapham High St   10–1D
☎ (020) 7450 0493 -ᑫ www.dentonscatering.co.uk
"Mainly professional catering equipment" is the speciality of this Clapham establishment", but the range of "useful household items" is also praised. / HOURS *Mon-Fri 8.45am-3pm, Sat 8.45am-1pm* TUBE *Clapham North.*

Divertimenti
-ᑫ www.divertimenti.co.uk
BRANCHES AT:
  33-34 Marylebone High St, W1   2–1A
  ☎ (020) 7935 0689
  139-141 Fulham Rd, SW3   5–2C
  ☎ (020) 7581 8065

"A great range of products" – "everything the keen cook (amateur or professional) could want", from "fascinating gadgets" to "lovely bowls and plates" – wins huge support for these Chelsea and Marylebone emporia; indeed, the vast volume of commentary they attracted pushed them into reporters' top ten 'food' shops of any type. / HOURS *Mon-Sat 9.30am-6pm, Sun noon-5.30pm.*

Cookware

Estilo Kitchen Shop SW19
37 High St 10–2B
☎ (020) 8944 6868
A "varied selection" which includes "many unusual items" – from a potato-peeler to a £400 fish kettle, apparently – commends this small Wimbledon shop to local reporters. / HOURS Mon-Sat 10am-6pm, Sun noon-5pm TUBE Wimbledon.

Fairfax Kitchen Shop NW3
1 Regency Pde, Finchley Rd 8–3A
☎ (020) 7722 7646 www.fairfaxcookshop.com
"The espresso machine selection is the best in London", insists one supporter of this Swiss Cottage shop; it offers "an excellent range of quality cookware" generally, but "appliances are a speciality". / HOURS Mon-Sat 9.30am-5.30pm TUBE Swiss Cottage.

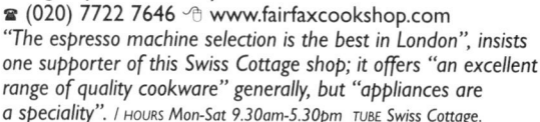

Gill Wing Cookshop N1
190 Upper St 8–2D
☎ (020) 7226 5392
"Not cheap, but a great place to browse and stock up" – this Islington shop may be a bit "crowded", but it offers "anything and everything you could possibly need, and all very stylish"; a branch was opening in Crouch End as we went to press (45 Park Rd, 020 8348 3451). / HOURS Mon-Sat 9.30am-6pm, Sun 10am-6pm CREDIT CARDS no Amex TUBE Highbury & Islington/Angel.

Habitat
www.habitat.net
BRANCHES AT:
  196 Tottenham Court Rd, W1 2–1C
  ☎ (020) 7631 3880
  206 King's Rd, SW3 5–3C
  ☎ (020) 7351 1211
  19-20 Kings Mall, King St, W6 7–2C
  ☎ (020) 8741 7111
  26-40 Kensington High St, W8 5–1A
  ☎ (020) 7795 6055
  191-197 Finchley Rd, NW3 8–2A
  ☎ (020) 7328 3444
Not a specialist supplier, of course, but these home interiors shops received a modest volume of praise for their range of "modern and simple" bits and pieces, which some find "great for gifts". / HOURS Hours vary: all branches open Mon-Sun.

Harrods SW1
87 Brompton Rd 5–1D
☎ (020) 7730 1234 www.harrods.com
"High-quality" products and an "authoritative" range – "everything you'll ever need" – win quite a big following for this large department, on the second floor of the Knightsbridge store. / HOURS Mon, Tue & Sat 10am-6pm, Wed-Fri 10am-7pm SEE ALSO Big Ten; Bread; Cheese & dairy; Chocolates & sweets; Coffee & tea; Fish & seafood; Fruit & vegetables; Grocers & delicatessens; Meat, game & poultry; Patisserie; Wine.

Cookware

Heal's
🌐 www.heals.co.uk
BRANCHES AT:
  196 Tottenham Court Rd, W1   2–1C
  ☎ (020) 7636 1666
  234 King's Rd, SW3   5–3C
  ☎ (020) 7349 8411

The famous furniture shop – now with a Chelsea branch in addition to its Bloomsbury base – also offers a "wide range" of general housewares, including "good-quality" kitchen equipment; service is "helpful" too. / HOURS Mon-Sat 10am-6pm or later; Sun W1 closed, SW3 noon-6pm.

Ikea NW10
2 Drury Way   1–1A
☎ (020) 8208 5600   🌐 www.ikea.co.uk

"Good, cheap wares" – the "great value and range" of the cookware make some reporters prepared to brave the famously confusing shopping experience of these vast Scandinavian emporia. / HOURS Mon-Fri 10am-10pm, Sat 9am-7pm, Sun 11am-5pm

Jerry's Home Store W1
80-81 Tottenham Court Rd   2–1C
☎ (020) 7436 7177   🌐 www.jerryshomestore.com

If it's "quirky" and "exclusive" products you're looking for – usually "with an American influence" ("from candy-floss makers to muffin mix") – it's worth checking out the limited but "fun" range at this fashionable home furnishings store; (the shop was sold as we went to press, and its former Chelsea branch closed – further changes may be afoot.) / HOURS Mon-Sat 10am-6.30pm (Thu 8pm), Sun noon-6pm TUBE Goodge Street.

John Lewis/Peter Jones
🌐 www.johnlewis.com
BRANCHES AT:
  Sloane Sq, SW1   5–2D
  ☎ (020) 7730 3434
  Oxford St, W1   3–1B
  ☎ (020) 7629 7711

Kitchen equipment is just the sort of area where you'd expect the "straightforward and unpretentious" charms of the never-knowingly-undersold department stores to come to the fore and, indeed, in reporters' view, if you're looking for "reasonable prices" but "lots of choice", you'd be hard put to do better; "I often end up there after looking at specialist shops", says one reporter, "and get a better deal here". / HOURS Mon-Wed, Fri 9.30am-6pm, Thu 10am-8pm, Sat 9am-6pm CREDIT CARDS no Amex.

Cookware

Kitchen Ideas 🗗 ★
BRANCHES AT:
   70 Westbourne Grove, W2   6–1B
   ☎ (020) 7229 3388
   23 New Broadway, W5   1–2A
   ☎ (020) 8566 5620
"Very unassuming" and "practical", "not chichi, but useful" – these Bayswater and Ealing shops are praised for "having everything, and cheaper than anywhere else", in particular a great range of stainless steel cookware; they are "happy to place special orders" too. / HOURS Mon-Sat 9.30am-6pm.

Leon Jaeggi W1 🗗
77 Shaftesbury Ave   4–3A
☎ (020) 7580 1974
Primarily a supplier to the trade – and carrying a very wide stock range – this Soho shop is a "professional operator that's helpful even to amateur cooks". / HOURS Mon-Sat 9am-5.30pm CREDIT CARDS no Amex TUBE Piccadilly Circus/Leicester Square.

Pages Catering Equipment WC2 ☆
121 Shaftesbury Ave   4–2B
☎ (020) 7565 5959
This large – by Soho standards – cookware shop stocks an excellent range of equipment; it caters mainly to the trade (VAT is not included in marked prices), and service can be "a bit grudging for mere mortals", but "the low prices more than make up for it". / HOURS Mon-Fri 9am-6pm, Sat 10am-5pm TUBE Leicester Square.

Richard Dare NW1 ★
93 Regents Park Rd   8–3B
☎ (020) 7722 9428
"The window displays lure you in" to this "small but wonderful" Primrose Hill shop – once you're inside, the reporters all speak of the "excellent range" to be found on "shelves loaded with tempting dishes, tins and pans". / HOURS Mon-Fri 9.30am-6pm, Sat 10am-6pm TUBE Chalk Farm.

Selfridges W1 ☕ Ⓢ) 🚚 ★
400 Oxford St   3–1A
☎ (020) 7629 1234 🖥 www.selfridges.co.uk
"Everything for aspiring cooks" – at least in the way of equipment – can be found in the "appliance heaven" to be found in the department store's basement; "looking for a choice of implements, when other suppliers just have one?" – this may well be the place for you. / HOURS Mon-Fri 10am-8pm, Sat 9.30am-8pm, Sun noon-6pm TUBE Bond Street SEE ALSO Big Ten; Bread; Cheese & dairy; Chocolates & sweets; Ethnic shops; Fish & seafood; Fruit & vegetables; Grocers & delicatessens; Herbs & spices; Meat, game & poultry; Wine.

Cookware

Summerill & Bishop W11
100 Portland Rd   6–2A
☎ (020) 7221 4566
This "expensive but imaginative" Holland Park shop is really more about tableware than cookware, but if you're looking for something beautiful and different it's certainly worth a look. / HOURS *Mon-Sat 10am-6pm* TUBE *Holland Park.*

MAIL ORDER

Cucina Direct SW15
PO Box 6611
☎ (020) 8246 4311   www.cucinadirect.co.uk
"It makes you want to cook!"; this "very well presented website/catalogue" offers an "excellent range", and is consistently well commented on by those who prefer to 'let their fingers do the walking'.

The Internet Cookshop RH12
24-26 East St, Horsham, West Sussex
☎ (0845) 601 2815   www.internetcook-shop.com
Fans say its "excellent all-round" and this easy-to-use website (the mail order branch of a West Sussex cookshop) certainly offers an impressive range; the wedding list service might be of interest to kitchen-mad couples-to-be. / CREDIT CARDS *no Amex.*

Kitchenware.co.uk BS16
25 Badminton Rd, Downend, Bristol
☎ (0117) 9070903   www.kitchenware.co.uk
This self-explanatory site is "easy to navigate" – if you're looking for a good range of kitchen equipment brought straight to your screen, it is worth a visit. / CREDIT CARDS *no Amex.*

Lakeland LA23   ★
Alexandra Buildings, Windermere, Cumbria
☎ (015394) 88300   www.lakeland.co.uk
This "efficient" mail and internet service wins many friends with its "good range" – much more extensive than you'd imagine, and including much kitchen hardware – and for its very helpful service" and "prompt delivery"; "great gadgetry for people who actually run homes rather than who play at doing so". / CREDIT CARDS *no Amex.*

7. Ethnic shops

Few shoppers nowadays would think of the produce associated with France, Italy and Spain as being in any sense 'ethnic'. Relevant shops are therefore included in **Chapter 10 Grocers & delicatessens** rather than listed in this chapter. Here, we have included only shops which specialise in ingredients appropriate to the cooking of somewhat more exotic climes: unsurprisingly, Asia predominates. The lack of establishments thought star-worthy by reporters may reflect the fact that produce which has travelled long distances can never be quite at the cutting edge of freshness and ripeness – one of the two more commented-on 'ethnic' shops particularly highly ranked by reporters is a seller of sweets in ethnic style, but of local manufacture!

The most commented-upon suppliers were:

1. Wing Yip
2. Talad Thai
3. Loon Fung
4. Yasir Halim Patisserie ★
5. Tawana
6. New Loon Moon
7. Green Valley
8. Oriental City
9. Ambala ★
10. See Woo Hong

Many markets (see **Chapter 13 Markets**) also carry significant amounts of ethnic produce.

Adamou W4 Ⓢ
126 Chiswick High Rd   7–2A
☎ (020) 8994 0752
"Very personal" service distinguishes this Greek "general store" of long standing in Chiswick; it's "knowledgeable" too – "who else knows or cares about pomegranate molasses!?" / HOURS Mon-Sat 8.30am-6.30pm, Sun 10am-2pm CREDIT CARDS no credit cards TUBE Turnham Green.

Ambala NW1 Ⓢ ☾ ★
112 Drummond St   8–3C
☎ (020) 7387 7886
"The best Indian sweets around, so fresh" win a wide following for this "sophisticated" shop in the Little India by Euston Station; "it's noted for its sweet stuff", confides one supporter, "but savouries are even better". / HOURS Mon-Sun 9am-8.30pm CREDIT CARDS no credit cards TUBE Euston/Euston Square SEE ALSO Chocolates & sweets.

Ethnic shops

Arigato W1
48-50 Brewer St   3–2D
☎ (020) 7287 1722
If you're looking for "wonderful and plentiful" supplies for Japanese cooking, this Soho oriental offers one of the better ranges on offer in central London, from chilled and frozen goods to fresh take-away sushi, sake and sauces. / HOURS *Mon-Sat 10am-9pm, Sun 11am-8pm* CREDIT CARDS *no Amex* TUBE *Leicester Square.*

Athenian Grocery W2
16 Moscow Rd   6–2C
☎ (020) 7229 6280
Just by the Greek Orthodox cathedral, it's perhaps no surprise that this half-centenarian family business is voted "best for all Greek supplies" by a number of reporters; fresh vegetables are imported on a daily basis. / HOURS *Mon-Sat 8.30am-7pm, Sun 9.30am-1pm* CREDIT CARDS *no credit cards* TUBE *Queensway/Bayswater.*

The Australia & NZ Shop WC2
26 Henrietta St   4–3C
☎ (020) 7836 2292   www.australiashop.co.uk
Aussies desperate for Pavlova Magic and Tim Tams, and Kiwis craving Pineapple Lumps need only head for Covent Garden, where the basement of this all-things-Antipodean shop is devoted to food; a smaller, related, outlet across the road stocks foodstuffs from South Africa and Canada. / HOURS *Mon-Sat 10.30am-6.30pm, Sun 11am-5pm* TUBE *Covent Garden.*

Country Market NW11
7 Russell Pde   1–1B
☎ (020) 8455 0134
"Every kosher item you could want" (some 10,000 lines) is to be had at this Golders Green institution, which claims to be the largest kosher shop in the whole of Europe. / HOURS *Mon-Fri & Sun 8am-10pm (Fri closes at sunset), closed Sat* TUBE *Brent Cross/Golders Green.*

Damas Gate W12
81-85 Uxbridge Rd   7–1C
☎ (020) 8743 5116
"Cheap, local and I like it" – Shepherd's Bush reporters are all very satisfied with this wide-ranging Middle Eastern supermarket, whose selection includes some "excellent falafel". / HOURS *Mon-Sun 9am-9pm* TUBE *Shepherds Bush.*

Deepak Cash & Carry SW17
953 Garratt Ln   10–2B
☎ (020) 8767 7819
A "mind-boggling range of Indian produce at rock bottom prices" (plus Asian and Caribbean specialities) can be had at this Tooting shop. / HOURS *Mon-Sat 9am-7.30pm, Sun 10am-5pm* CREDIT CARDS *no Amex* TUBE *Tooting Broadway.*

Ethnic shops

Golden Gate Grocers
BRANCHES AT:
16 Newport Pl, WC2   4–3B
☎ (020) 7437 0014
14 Lisle St, WC2   4–3A
☎ (020) 7437 0014
"Helpful to Anglos as well as Asians", these Chinatown supermarkets offer a good range of exotic fruit and vegetables alongside the usual suspects, and supporters say they are "the best source for Chinese ingredients" generally. / HOURS Mon-Sun 9am-8.30pm.

Graham's Butchers N2
134 East End Rd   1–1C
☎ (020) 8883 6187
A "very friendly" East Finchley butcher whose specialities include the likes of biltong and boerewors. / HOURS Tue-Fri 8.30am-5.30pm, Sat 8.30am-4pm, Sun 9am-1pm CREDIT CARDS no credit cards TUBE East Finchley SEE ALSO Meat, game & poultry.

Green Valley W1
36 Upper Berkeley St   2–2A
☎ (020) 7402 7385
Arabs far from home – or others wishing to have a go at their cuisines – will find "a very wide range of all types of products" at this recently refurbished and expanded Middle Eastern food hall, near Marble Arch; take-away dishes are prepared in the basement kitchens – "stunning salads" and "fantastic cakes" find particular approval. / HOURS Mon-Sun 8am-midnight CREDIT CARDS no Amex TUBE Marble Arch.

Greenfields Supermarket W1
25 Crawford St   2–1A
☎ (020) 7723 2510
"A very good, and very busy Lebanese supermarket", just off Baker Street; "friendly" service and "an excellent delivery service" are among the features which commend it. / HOURS Mon-Fri 8am-10pm, Sat & Sun 9am-10pm CREDIT CARDS no credit cards TUBE Marylebone SEE ALSO Herbs & spices.

Hoo Hing NW10
North Circular Road   1–2A
☎ (020) 8838 3388   www.hoohing.com
It's probably not the glamour of the location (just off the North Circular) which makes this "very useful Chinese supermarket" a popular recommendation, so it must have something to do with the prices and the range (which also includes Japanese and Korean specialities). / HOURS Mon-Fri 9.30am-7pm, Sat 11am-5pm, Sun 10am-7pm TUBE BR Hanger Lane.

Ethnic shops

Japan Centre W1
212 Piccadilly   3–3D
☎ (020) 7434 4218   www.japancentre.com
An impressive array of oriental goods – mainly packaged, although some fresh and others frozen – is available to those who truffle out the cramped basement of this Japanese store, just a few steps from Piccadilly Circus. / HOURS Mon-Sat 10am-7pm, Sun 11am-7pm CREDIT CARDS no Amex TUBE Piccadilly Circus.

Loon Fung Supermarket W1
42-43 Gerrard St   4–3A
☎ (020) 7437 7332
"Great for Chinese, Japanese and South East Asian" – "everything you need for Asian cooking, cheaper than at Sainsbury's" is to be had at this "authentic" and very popular "benchmark" Chinatown supermarket; it's "brighter" after its recent renovation too. / HOURS Mon-Sun 10am-8pm CREDIT CARDS no Amex TUBE Leicester Square.

Le Maroc W10
94 Golborne Rd   6–1A
☎ (020) 8968 9783
"A cool Moroccan shop" in North Kensington, with "an intriguing choice of products", that includes tea, tajines and olives. / HOURS Mon-Sat 9am-7pm, Sun 2pm-4pm CREDIT CARDS no credit cards TUBE Ladbroke Grove.

New Loon Moon W1
9 Gerrard St   4–3A
☎ (020) 7734 3887
Not nearly as well known as Loon Fung, on the other side of the street, the 'other' Chinatown supermarket is in fact somewhat more highly rated by reporters for its "interesting selection" and "good value". / HOURS Mon-Sun 10.30am-8pm TUBE Leicester Square.

Newport Supermarket WC2
32-33 Newport Ct   4–3B
☎ (020) 7437 2386
Perhaps the fact that it's off the main Chinatown drag reduces footfall at (and therefore commentary on) this large supermarket, which attracted relatively little survey commentary; fans, though, commend its "wide variety of Chinese food" and its "low prices". / HOURS Mon-Sun 10.30am-7.30pm CREDIT CARDS min order £20, no Amex TUBE Leicester Square.

Oriental City NW9
399 Edgware Rd   1–1A
☎ (020) 8200 0009   www.orientalcity.net
Anyone with an interest in oriental cuisine should make the trek to Colindale to visit the largest Japanese shopping mall in Europe (formerly called Yoahan Plaza); it offers "a simply astounding selection of oriental food"; "all things Japanese" are a highlight, as are the "great fish counter" and "the best selection of Thai fruit this side of Bangkok". / HOURS Mon-Sun 10am-7pm TUBE Colindale.

Ethnic shops

Panzer's NW8
13-19 Circus Rd   8–3A
☎ (020) 7722 8596   www.panzers.co.uk
Not strictly an ethnic shop, but this famous St John's Wood delicatessen boasts as wide a range of kosher fare as you could wish for. / HOURS Mon-Fri 8am-7pm, Sat 8am-6pm, Sun 9am-2pm CREDIT CARDS no Amex TUBE St John's Wood SEE ALSO Fruit & vegetables; Grocers & delicatessens.

Reza W8
345 Kensington High St   7–1D
☎ (020) 7603 0924
For "a very broad selection" of Iranian produce – "especially sweet things" (including "delicious saffron ice cream") – this "inspirational" Kensington store has a number of admirers. / HOURS Mon-Sun 9am-9pm TUBE High Street Kensington.

See Woo Hong WC2
18-20 Lisle St   4–3A
☎ (020) 7439 8325
For a true "pile it high, sell it cheap" experience, you won't do much better than this "very well stocked" Chinatown emporium; as you'd hope, fans reckon it offers "good value" too. / HOURS Mon-Sun 10am-8pm CREDIT CARDS Switch & Delta only TUBE Leicester Square.

Selfridges W1
400 Oxford St   3–1A
☎ (020) 7629 1234   www.selfridges.co.uk
Though it's not a specialist supplier, it's worth noting that our survey's most-mentioned food hall offers a wide range of 'ethnic' supplies, especially if you're looking for the flavour of the Middle East. / HOURS Mon-Fri 10am-8pm, Sat 9.30am-8pm, Sun noon-6pm TUBE Bond Street SEE ALSO Big Ten; Bread; Cheese & dairy; Chocolates & sweets; Cookware; Fish & seafood; Fruit & vegetables; Grocers & delicatessens; Herbs & spices; Meat, game & poultry; Wine.

Sri Thai W6
56 Shepherds Bush Rd   7–1C
☎ (020) 7602 0621
"A cornucopia of exotic produce"; "for everything Thai you need" – including "good fruit and veg" – this "modest" and "unstylish-looking" shop south of Shepherd's Bush has a surprisingly broad following. / HOURS Mon-Sun 9am-7pm CREDIT CARDS no credit cards TUBE Hammersmith.

Super Bahar W8
349a Kensington High St   7–1D
☎ (020) 7603 5083
Anyone wanting to cook Persian-style will want to check out this specialist general store, not far from Olympia; Iranian caviar a speciality. / HOURS Mon-Sun 10am-9pm CREDIT CARDS no credit cards TUBE High Street Kensington.

Ethnic shops

Taj Stores E1
112-114 Brick Ln   1–2D
☎ (020) 7377 0061   www.cuisinenet.co.uk/tajstores
An East End institution offering "everything for Indian cuisine", including "good, fresh vegetables and fruit and frozen Indian ingredients", as well as the herbs and spices which are the house speciality. / HOURS Mon-Sun 9am-9pm TUBE Aldgate East SEE ALSO Herbs & spices.

Talad Thai SW15
326 Upper Richmond Rd   10–2A
☎ (020) 8789 8084
"All the Asian ingredients, you need, very cheaply" – "more in this small shop than in most oriental supermarkets" – win a disproportionate following for this Thai grocer in Putney; "sauces, spices, herbs and fresh produce" are among the ranges attracting particular praise. / HOURS Mon-Sat 9am-8pm, Sun 10am-8pm CREDIT CARDS no credit cards TUBE East Putney SEE ALSO Herbs & spices.

Tawana
BRANCHES AT:
   18-20 Chepstow Rd, W2   6–1B
   ☎ (020) 7221 6316
   179 Wandsworth High St, SW18
   ☎ (020) 8874 7742
"Most eastern ingredients" can be tracked down at these Bayswater and Wandsworth emporia; ingredients "fresh from Thailand" – "best on Wednesday and Sunday, when the new stock comes in" – a speciality. / HOURS W2 Mon-Sun 9.30am-8pm; SW18 Mon-Sun 10.30am-7.30pm.

Tooting Market SW17
Upper Tooting Rd, between Mitcham Rd, Upper Tooting Rd & Totterdam St   10–2C
A good source of subcontinental fare. / HOURS Mon-Sat 9.30am-5pm, Wed 9.30am-1pm TUBE Tooting Broadway SEE ALSO Herbs & spices; Markets.

Turkish Food Centre E8
89 Ridley Rd   1–1D
☎ (020) 7254 6754
"Great value-for-money and delicious freshly-baked Turkish bread" are highlights at this self-explanatory Dalston shop; the great majority of the stock comes from Turkey, but other Middle Eastern countries are also represented. / HOURS Mon-Sun 8am-8.30pm CREDIT CARDS no Amex TUBE BR Dalston Lane.

Wing Yip NW2
395 Edgware Rd   1–1A
☎ (020) 8450 0422   www.wingyip.com
Service is "robotic" and the layout "baffling", but many reporters still find it an "amazing experience" to visit this Hendon oriental supermarket; a "huge range" – including "all manner of jars and fresh items", as well as "frozen produce" – is on offer, and value is "very good". / HOURS Mon-Sat 9.30am-7pm, Sun 11.30am-5.30pm CREDIT CARDS no Amex TUBE Dollis Hill.

Ethnic shops

Yasir Halim Patisserie N13 Ⓢ ☽ ★
493 Green Lanes   1–1C
☎ (020) 8340 8090
This well-known Turkish Cypriot shop in Edmonton is best known as a bakery, but it's "also a butcher and greengrocer – you name it"; in fact, if you're looking for Middle Eastern specialities of any sort, this is one of the top few places in town. / HOURS Mon-Sun 9am-10pm CREDIT CARDS no Amex SEE ALSO Bread.

Yildiz N19 ☀ ☽ ★
47 Junction Rd   8–1C
☎ (020) 7561 9050
"Treats galore, straight from Cyprus" ("with new deliveries nearly every day") – including "pickles, pulses, houmous and sweet treats" – make this reporters' top tip for Turkish fare; service that's unanimously celebrated as "always friendly, helpful and cheerful" makes no small contribution. / HOURS Mon-Sat 7am-9pm CREDIT CARDS no credit cards TUBE Archway.

Fish & seafood 58

8. Fish & seafood

Certainly nationally, and probably in London too, fishmongers have been in decline for many years. The picture is not nearly as bleak as it may seem however: as the profusion of stars below indicates, Londoners rate many of the survivors very highly, and the number of new arrivals in recent years may herald something of a revival.

The ten most commented-upon suppliers were:

1. Steve Hatt ★
2. Harrods ★
3. Chalmers & Gray ★
4. Selfridges ★
5. JF Blagden's ★
6. Fish! Shop
7. Waitrose
8. Copes Seafood Company
9. Sandy's ★
10. Golborne Fisheries ★

B&M Seafood NW5
258 Kentish Town Rd   8–2C
☎ (020) 7485 0346
This "good-quality, proper fishmonger" is unanimously appreciated by reporters from Kentish Town; they sell meat too, which is also recommended. / HOURS *Mon-Sat 8am-6pm (no fish on Mon)* CREDIT CARDS *no Amex* TUBE *Kentish Town.*

Bibendum SW3
Michelin Hs, 81 Fulham Rd   5–2C
☎ (020) 7589 0864   www.bibendum.co.uk
"Excellent but expensive" – the stall at the entrance to the Chelsea Conran Shop offers a high-glamour fish and seafood-buying experience. / HOURS *Mon-Fri 9am-8pm, Sat 9am-7pm* TUBE *South Kensington.*

Billingsgate E14
Trafalgar Way   11–1C
☎ (020) 7987 1118   fis.com/billingsgate/
"Get up early for the freshest fish in London" – there's nothing to stop you from buying where the professionals do, at the fishmarket which moved from its ancient City site to distant Docklands in 1982; on its 13-acre site, there are some 100 stands as well as 30 shops and two cafés – "oddly enough, they do great bacon and eggs". / HOURS *Tue-Sat 5am-8.30am* TUBE *DLR West India Quay* SEE ALSO *Markets.*

Fish & seafood

JF Blagden's W1 ★
65 Paddington St   2–1A
☎ (020) 7935 8321
"Outstanding quality" and "very friendly" and "knowledgeable" service" win many fans for this By Appointment Marylebone fishmonger, which some claim as "the best in the capital" – opening hours are "limited, but they do deliver"; also poultry and game in season. / HOURS Mon 7.30am-4pm, Tue-Fri 7.30am-5pm, Sat 7.30am-4pm CREDIT CARDS no credit cards TUBE Baker Street.

Bluebird SW3 ★
350 King's Rd   5–3C
☎ (020) 7559 1000   www.conran.co.uk
"Fresh and imaginatively presented" – the fish selection in Conran's Chelsea food hall is claimed as "the best in south west London" by some reporters. / HOURS Mon-Wed 9am-8pm, Thu-Sat 9am-9pm, Sun 11am-5pm TUBE Sloane Square/South Kensington SEE ALSO Big Ten; Bread; Cheese & dairy; Fruit & vegetables; Grocers & delicatessens.

Borough Market SE1 ★
Borough High St   9–4C
  www.boroughmarket.org.uk
"Get there early", but perhaps especially if you want to enjoy the "really fresh fish" on offer at London's most popular market. / HOURS Fri noon-5pm, Sat 9am-4pm (wholesale fruit & veg Mon-Fri 3am-10am) CREDIT CARDS no credit cards TUBE London Bridge SEE ALSO Big Ten; Bread; Cheese & dairy; Fruit & vegetables; Herbs & spices; Markets; Meat, game & poultry.

Brixton Market SW9
Brixton Station Rd, Popes Rd, Atlantic Rd, Electric Rd & Electric Avenue   10–2D
If you're looking for "unusual fish at reasonable prices", this mêlée of a market (which is great for all things Caribbean) was particularly recommended – "if you can face the crush". / HOURS Mon-Sat 8am-5.30pm, Wed 8am-1pm TUBE Brixton SEE ALSO Fruit & vegetables; Herbs & spices; Markets.

Brown's NW8 ★
37-39 Charlbert St   8–3A
☎ (020) 7722 8237
"St John's Wood's best", this long-established fishmonger is praised for its "top-class" fish and seafood, and for its "friendly" and "knowledgeable" service. / HOURS Tue-Sat 8am-5pm TUBE St John's Wood.

TH Carr W5 ☆
139 Pitshanger Ln   1–2A
☎ (020) 8997 5639
A local reporter praises the "exceptional" quality of this long-established Ealing fishmonger; salmon (wild in season) is something of a speciality. / HOURS Mon 9am-1pm, Tue & Thu-Fri 8am-5.30pm, Wed 8am-1pm, Sat 8am-4pm TUBE Ealing Broadway.

Fish & seafood

Caviar House W1
161 Piccadilly 3–3C
☎ (020) 7409 0445
This grand St James's shop, part of an international chain established in Copenhagen in 1950, attracted little attention from reporters; if money is no object, its range of "epicurean delights" – featuring caviar and smoked salmon (and also fine wine) – is worth considering. / HOURS Mon-Sat 9am-7.30pm TUBE Green Park.

Chalmers & Gray W11
67 Notting Hill Gate 6–2B
☎ (020) 7221 6177
A "great selection" of "very fresh" fish – "good enough to make sashimi with" – makes this "traditional" Notting Hill fishmonger one of the best in town. / HOURS Mon-Fri 8am-6pm, Sat 8am-5pm CREDIT CARDS no Amex TUBE Notting Hill Gate.

Chelsea Fishery SW3
10 Cale St 5–2C
☎ (020) 7589 9432
"A limited selection" (mainly English, rather than exotic) but "always of the highest quality" – local reporters sing the praises of this Chelsea Green shop. / HOURS Tue-Sat 9am-4.30pm (Sat till 2.30pm) CREDIT CARDS no credit cards TUBE Sloane Square/South Kensington.

Condon Fishmongers SW8
363 Wandsworth Rd 10–1D
☎ (020) 7622 2934
"A marvellous fishmonger, if you don't mind standing on the pavement", this north Clapham stall offers a "good range of fish" of "outstanding" quality; smoked fish – from their own smokery – is a highlight. / HOURS Tue-Fri 8.45am-5.30pm (Thu till 1pm) Sat 8.45am-4.30pm CREDIT CARDS no credit cards TUBE Stockwell.

Copes Seafood Company SW6
700 Fulham Rd 10–1B
☎ (020) 7371 7300
"Very good fresh fish" – "and they tell you how to cook it too" – makes this "tiny" but "friendly" shop Fulhamites' most popular destination for fish and seafood. / HOURS Mon-Fri 10am-8pm, Sat 9am-6pm CREDIT CARDS no Amex TUBE Parsons Green.

Covent Garden Fishmongers W4
37 Turnham Green Ter 7–2A
☎ (020) 8995 9273
Rather confusingly located in Chiswick, this "friendly" fishmonger offers "a good range" – it does a lot of restaurant business – and "good advice too". / HOURS Tue-Sat 8am-5.30pm (Thu & Sat 5pm) CREDIT CARDS no Amex.

Fish & seafood

The Fish Shop W8
201 Kensington Church St 6–2B
☎ (020) 7243 6626
"Lovely people, lovely fish" – the stylish shop adjacent to the fashionable restaurant Kensington Place is a "small but well stocked" establishment; its range includes some "wonderful ready meals". / HOURS Tue-Fri 9am-7pm, Sat 9am-5pm CREDIT CARDS no Amex TUBE Notting Hill Gate.

Fish! Shop SE1
Cathedral St 9–4C
☎ (020) 7407 3801 www.fishdiner.co.uk
"Good-quality" but "expensive" – the smart fish shop attached to the exclamatorily-named restaurant by Borough Market is praised for its "good quality" and its "knowledgeable" staff; fish-related cookware and gadgets also available. / HOURS Mon-Fri 10am-6pm, Sat 10am-4pm TUBE London Bridge.

France Fresh Fish N4
99 Stroud Green Rd 8–1D
☎ (020) 7263 9767
It "doesn't look like much", but if you're looking for Caribbean or tropical fish this Finsbury Park specialist is well worth checking out; it has "good prices and quality" and "very helpful staff". / HOURS Mon-Sat 9am-6.30pm TUBE Finsbury Park.

Golborne Fisheries W10
75 Golborne Rd 6–1A
☎ (020) 8960 3100
"An unbelievable selection" of "gorgeous fresh fish" that's "good enough to eat raw" inspires hugely enthusiastic support from fans of this family-owned fishmonger in North Kensington; no wonder it's often "crowded". / HOURS Mon 10am-4pm, Tue-Sat 8am-5.30pm CREDIT CARDS no credit cards TUBE Ladbroke Grove/Westbourne Park.

Hampstead Seafoods NW3
78 Hampstead High St 8–2A
☎ (020) 7435 3966
"Hampstead's hidden gem" (down an alley, off the High Street), this "good-quality, proper fishmonger" is worth seeking out for its "excellent fresh fish" (mainly wild) and its "knowledgeable" service. / HOURS Tue-Fri 7.30am-5pm, Sat 7.30am-4.30pm CREDIT CARDS no credit cards TUBE Hampstead.

Harrods SW1
87 Brompton Rd 5–1D
☎ (020) 7730 1234 www.harrods.com
"From the everyday to the weird and wonderful" – if you can't find your piscine pleasure among the "wonderful" selection in this Knightsbridge food hall, you probably can't find it anywhere, and it's all "top quality" too. / HOURS Mon, Tue & Sat 10am-6pm, Wed-Fri 10am-7pm SEE ALSO Big Ten; Bread; Cheese & dairy; Chocolates & sweets; Coffee & tea; Cookware; Fruit & vegetables; Grocers & delicatessens; Meat, game & poultry; Patisserie; Wine.

Fish & seafood
62

Harvey Nichols SW1
109-125 Knightsbridge   5–1D
☎ (020) 7235 5000   www.harveynichols.com
"Friendly and knowledgeable service" and "improved stock and display in recent times" make fish one of the 'destination' counters at this fifth-floor Knightsbridge food hall. / HOURS *Mon, Tue & Sat 10am-7pm, Wed-Fri 10am-8pm, Sun noon-6pm* TUBE *Knightsbridge* SEE ALSO *Big Ten; Bread; Grocers & delicatessens; Meat, game & poultry; Wine.*

MJ Hodges & Sons HA2
194 Alexandra Ave, Harrow   1–1A
☎ (020) 8422 8937
Almost half a century old, this third-generation Harrow fishmonger still displays "enthusiasm" as well as "expertise", and it's praised by locals for its "consistently fresh, high-quality fish"; smoking is carried out on the premises. / HOURS *Tue-Sat 8am-5pm, Sun 9am-1pm* CREDIT CARDS *no Amex* TUBE *Rayners Lane/South Harrow.*

Jeffreys & Son SW9
5 Market Row   10–1D
☎ (020) 7274 1883
Salmon smoked on the premises is one of the specialities of this "really sound" shop within Brixton market, whose range runs from the conventional to the exotic. / HOURS *Mon-Sat 9am-5pm, Wed 9am-1pm* CREDIT CARDS *no credit cards* TUBE *Brixton.*

HS Linwood EC3
6-7 Grand Ave   9–2D
☎ (020) 7929 0554
Reporters heap praise on this "excellent old-fashioned fishmonger" in the City, both for its "fine selection" and for its "efficient service". / HOURS *Mon-Fri 6am-3pm* TUBE *Monument & Bank.*

La Marée SW3
76 Sloane Ave   5–2C
☎ (020) 7589 8067
Brompton Cross's Poissonnerie de l'Avenue is one of the stalwarts of the Chelsea dining scene; its adjoining shop may be of much more recent vintage, but it has already made a good name for its "wide selection" of "quality" (if "quite expensive") fish and seafood. / HOURS *Mon-Sat 8am-6pm* TUBE *South Kensington.*

Northcote Fisheries SW11
14 Northcote Rd   10–2C
☎ (020) 7978 4428
A shop which sells both fish and 'ethnic' vegetables strikes some as rather "odd", but, so far as the former is concerned, this "friendly" shop is voted a "good all-rounder" by local reporters. / HOURS *Tue-Sat 9am-5.30pm* CREDIT CARDS *no Amex* TUBE *BR Clapham Junction.*

Fish & seafood

Sainsbury's
☎ (0845) 301 2020 www.sainsburys.com
BRANCHES AT:
Locations throughout London
"A brilliant variety of really good fresh fish and good service too" makes Sainsbury's fish counters (larger branches only) something of a hidden gem; especially in areas without much in the way of independent competition, they are seen by reporters as a real asset. / HOURS Some larger stores 24 hours SEE ALSO Big Ten; Bread; Cheese & dairy; Fruit & vegetables; Health & organic foods; Herbs & spices; Meat, game & poultry; Wine.

Sam Stoller & Son NW11
28 Temple Fortune Pde 1–1B
☎ (020) 8458 1429
"A great choice of fish" (but not, of course, seafood) is one of the attractions of this kosher merchant in Golders Green; fans say it offers *"good value"* too. / HOURS Mon & Sun 8am-1pm, Tue-Fri 7am-5pm (Fri 4pm or dusk), closed Sat CREDIT CARDS no Amex TUBE Golders Green.

Sandy's Fishmongers TW1
56 King St, Twickenham 1–4A
☎ (020) 8892 5788 www.sandysfish.net
It's not just that this is *"the only fish shop for miles around"* – the queues at this Twickenham fishmonger and poultryman attest to the *"wide range"* of *"brilliant"* fish on offer, and perhaps to the *"friendly advice"* that's available too. / HOURS Mon-Sat 7.30am-6pm TUBE BR Twickenham SEE ALSO Meat, game & poultry.

A Scott & Sons N2
94 High Rd 1–1C
☎ (020) 8444 7606
"A top-class local fishmonger", this East Finchley spot is praised for offering *"the best selection in the area"* – *"not cheap, but good and fresh"*. / HOURS Tue-Sat 7am-5pm CREDIT CARDS no credit cards TUBE East Finchley.

Sea Harvest SW1
16 Warwick Way 2–4B
☎ (020) 7821 5192
"Much improved display and stock" in recent times has put new spring in the step of Pimlico's only independent fish shop. / HOURS Mon-Sat 8.30am-6pm CREDIT CARDS no Amex TUBE Victoria.

Fish & seafood

Selfridges W1
400 Oxford St   3–1A
☎ (020) 7629 1234   www.selfridges.co.uk
Thanks to the "vast selection of fresh fish", and a "fantastic array of seafood" too, this was the star specialist section in our survey's most commented upon store; the Oyster Bar offers a congenial way to try-before-you-buy. / HOURS Mon-Fri 10am-8pm, Sat 9.30am-8pm, Sun noon-6pm TUBE Bond Street SEE ALSO Big Ten; Bread; Cheese & dairy; Chocolates & sweets; Cookware; Ethnic shops; Fruit & vegetables; Grocers & delicatessens; Herbs & spices; Meat, game & poultry; Wine.

FC Soper SE15
141 Elvina Rd   1–3D
☎ (020) 7639 9729
"Quality fish" (with an emphasis on wild varieties, and with some imported from distant oceans) is to be had at this family-run Nunhead business. / HOURS Tue-Fri 8am-5.30pm, Sat 8am-5.30pm, Sun 9am-2pm CREDIT CARDS no credit cards TUBE BR Nunhead/Queen's Road Peckham/Peckham Rye.

Steve Hatt N1
88-90 Essex Rd   8–3D
☎ (020) 7226 3963
By popular acclamation, this "unpretentious" Islington institution (est 1908) is simply "the best fish shop in London"; raves abound for both its range ("if it comes from the sea, it's here") and the service ("hard to beat for knowledge and helpfulness") – indeed, so excited are some reporters that they insist that "even the queue is a treat!" / HOURS Tue-Sat 7am-5pm CREDIT CARDS no credit cards TUBE Angel.

Waitrose
☎ (01344) 424680 Customer service
 www.waitrose.com
BRANCHES AT:
   Locations throughout London
"Reasonable prices" and a "wide selection" win local support for the "very good fish counters" of reporters' top-rated supermarket. / HOURS Hours vary: generally Mon-Sat 8.30am-9pm, Sun 11am-5pm SEE ALSO Big Ten; Bread; Cheese & dairy; Fruit & vegetables; Health & organic foods; Herbs & spices; Meat, game & poultry; Wine.

Walter Purkis & Sons
BRANCHES AT:
   52 Muswell Hill Broadway, N10   1–1C
   ☎ (020) 8883 4355
   17 The Broadway, N8   1–1C
   ☎ (020) 8340 6281
For its "good-quality, standard selection of fish" – "nothing exotic though" – these "always very friendly and helpful" Muswell Hill and Crouch End fishmongers have many admirers. / HOURS Tue-Sat 9am-5pm.

Fish & seafood

Willesden Fisheries NW2
1b Walm Ln   1–1A
☎ (020) 8830 2650
A self-explanatory outfit – with its mix of British and exotic fish, "it manages always to have whatever you want". / HOURS Mon-Sat 9am-6pm CREDIT CARDS no credit cards TUBE Willesden Green.

MAIL ORDER

The Fish Society GU27
Freepost, Haslemere
☎ (0800) 074 6859   www.thefishsociety.co.uk
"A huge range" – stretching all the way from the everyday to the exotic – is to be had from this mail-order supplier; fans say the products are of "superb quality".

H Forman & Son E9
6 Queens Yd, Whitepost Ln   1–1D
☎ (020) 8985 0378   www.formans.co.uk
"Britain's leading salmon smoker" – established in the East End for four generations – is the main supplier to many of the top shops, and exports all over the world; its "excellent" products – salmon wild and farmed, trout, marlin, swordfish, shark, eel and sturgeon – can be ordered direct over the web.

James Baxter & Son LA4
Thornton Rd, Morecambe
☎ (01524) 410910
"Exceptional potted shrimps", by post, with "very reliable delivery"; "best quality". / CREDIT CARDS no Amex & no Switch.

Fruit & vegetables 66

9. Fruit & vegetables

It's striking how few independent greengrocers of note there are in London, and how large in this area loom the street markets and the supermarkets. The few shops that do have a name, however, have a real 'name' – Michanicou Bros, a tiny Holland Park shop, attracted more commentary than Waitrose! A further oddity of this market sector is that it is the only one where M&S – often credited as the high-street store that led the move to quality in food shopping – attracts a particularly high level of commentary (though, even here, not quite positive enough to justify a star).

The ten most commented-upon suppliers were:

1. Marks & Spencer
2. Borough Market ★
3. Michanicou Bros ★
4. Waitrose
5. Portobello Road Market
6. Sainsbury's
7. Fry's of Chelsea ★
8. Harrods ★
9. Berwick Street Market
10. Panzer's ★

Berwick Street Market W1
Berwick St   3–2D
Best known for its 'pile it high, sell it cheap' fruit and veg stalls, this raucous Soho market is an ideal place to shop on a budget – see Chapter 13 Markets. / HOURS Mon-Sat 9am-6pm SEE ALSO *Herbs & spices; Markets.*

Bluebird SW3   ☕ S) 🚚 ★
350 King's Rd   5–3C
☎ (020) 7559 1000   🖰 www.conran.co.uk
An "incredible organic range" is among the highlights of the "very good" but "very pricey" selection of fruit and veg on offer at Conran's striking Chelsea food hall. / HOURS Mon-Wed 9am-8pm, Thu-Sat 9am-9pm, Sun 11am-5pm TUBE Sloane Square/South Kensington SEE ALSO *Big Ten; Bread; Cheese & dairy; Fish & seafood; Grocers & delicatessens.*

Fruit & vegetables

Borough Market SE1 ★
Borough High St   9–4C
🖰 www.boroughmarket.org.uk
Given its location on the site of the only remaining central London fruit and veg wholesaler, it is appropriate that of all the offerings at London's foodiest market, it is the "wide range" of such goods, including organic produce, "all reasonably priced" which attracts the greatest amount of commentary; names to look out for include Turnips (the largest outlet, and a permanent fixture) and mushroom-specialists Booths. / HOURS Fri noon-5pm, Sat 9am-4pm (wholesale fruit & veg Mon-Fri 3am-10am) CREDIT CARDS no credit cards TUBE London Bridge SEE ALSO Big Ten; Bread; Cheese & dairy; Fish & seafood; Herbs & spices; Markets; Meat, game & poultry.

Brian Lay-Jones NW3
36 Heath St   8–1A
☎ (020) 7435 5084
"Good variety and quality" and "friendly service" are among the virtues commending this Hampstead greengrocer; it carries a wide range of products, including a large selection of herbs and some organics. / HOURS Mon-Sat 8am-6pm CREDIT CARDS no credit cards TUBE Hampstead.

Brixton Market SW9
Brixton Station Rd, Popes Rd, Atlantic Rd, Electric Rd & Electric Avenue   10–2D
See Chapter 13 Markets. / HOURS Mon-Sat 8am-5.30pm, Wed 8am-1pm TUBE Brixton SEE ALSO Fish & seafood; Herbs & spices; Markets.

Chapel Street Market N1 Ⓢ
between Liverpool Road & Penton St   8–3D
See Chapter 13 Markets. / HOURS Tue, Wed, Fri & Sat 9am-5pm, Thu & Sun 9am-12.30pm TUBE Angel SEE ALSO Markets.

Clocktower Store N8 Ⓢ ☾
52 The Broadway   1–1C
☎ (020) 8348 7845
Perhaps it's the landmark position in the heart of Crouch End which helps this independent, Cypriot greengrocer to attract a particular following; it probably also has something to do with a "very wide range" of produce which is "always fresh". / HOURS Mon-Fri 8.30am-7pm, Sat 8.30am-6pm, Sun 10am-5pm CREDIT CARDS no credit cards TUBE Finsbury Park/Turnpike Lane.

TJ Ellingham & Sons N3
79 Ballards Ln   1–1B
☎ (020) 8346 1721
For local fans, this "friendly" Finchley fixture is "the best greengrocer in London" – "fresh produce, good prices, good selection". / HOURS Mon-Fri 8am-5pm, Sat 8am-4pm CREDIT CARDS no credit cards TUBE Finchley Central.

Fruit & vegetables

Fenners SE3
17 Tranquil Vale   1–4D
☎ (020) 8852 2638
"The cat is a real asset" – it's been on the staff for nearly twenty years – at this Blackheath institution (where a greengrocers has stood for a century and a half); "locals love the place", thanks in part to a range encompassing both the traditional and the exotic. / HOURS Mon-Fri 7.30am-5.30pm, Sat 7.30am-5pm, Sun 10am-2pm.

Fry's of Chelsea SW3
14 Cale St   5–2C
☎ (020) 7589 0342
"A very wide selection of produce" from which "everything is first-rate" leads many reporters to seek out this "good, old-fashioned greengrocer", hidden away on Chelsea Green; service is "pleasant' too. / HOURS Mon-Fri 5.30am-5pm, Sat 5.30am-1pm TUBE South Kensington.

Get Fresh TW1
5 London Rd, Twickenham   1–4A
☎ (020) 8288 0546
"A good serve-yourself greengrocer", praised by the locals for its "really fresh produce". / HOURS Mon-Sat 6am-6pm CREDIT CARDS no Amex TUBE BR Twickenham.

Harrods SW1
87 Brompton Rd   5–1D
☎ (020) 7730 1234   www.harrods.com
As you'd expect, if it's "variety and quality" you're looking for – or simply the esoteric and wildly expensive – this beautiful food hall is a top choice. / HOURS Mon, Tue & Sat 10am-6pm, Wed-Fri 10am-7pm SEE ALSO Big Ten; Bread; Cheese & dairy; Chocolates & sweets; Coffee & tea; Cookware; Fish & seafood; Grocers & delicatessens; Meat, game & poultry; Patisserie; Wine.

Highgate Village Fruiterers N6
3 Highgate High St   1–1C
☎ (020) 8340 0985
"Good-quality fruit" (and also flowers) commends this north London spot; range is a strength, including some "very exotic" items. / HOURS Mon-Sat 8.30am-6.30pm (Sat 6pm), Sun 10am-3.30pm CREDIT CARDS no Amex TUBE Archway/Highgate.

The Italian Fruit Company SW10
423 King's Rd   5–3B
☎ (020) 7351 5841
"Excellent and exotic fruits and vegetables", all "in peak condition", make it worth the trip to this "very nice" Chelsea greengrocer (only a small proportion of whose produce, of course, comes from Italy). / HOURS Mon-Sat 8.30am-6pm CREDIT CARDS no credit cards TUBE Sloane Square.

Fruit & vegetables

Johns N10
488 Muswell Hill Broadway   1–1C
☎ (020) 8444 9484
"Super-friendly service" – complete with *"the usual cheeky patter"* – makes this *"truly family-run"* Muswell Hill greengrocer stand out; its range is *"fresh"*, too, and offers *"good value"*. / HOURS Mon-Sat 8am-5.30pm CREDIT CARDS no credit cards TUBE Highgate.

M&C Greengrocers W4
35 Turnham Green Ter   7–2A
☎ (020) 8995 0140   www.mandcfruitandveg.co.uk
"Unusual vegetable varieties" and a *"very good choice of herbs"* are among the strengths of this Chiswick greengrocer (which does quite a lot of restaurant trade business); the butcher across the road, Macken Bros (see also), is under the same ownership. / HOURS Mon-Sat 7am-7pm (earlier closing in winter) CREDIT CARDS no Amex TUBE Turnham Green.

Marks & Spencer
☎ (0845) 609 0200   www.marksandspencer.com
BRANCHES AT:
   Locations throughout London
"Consistently superior", *"100 per cent reliable"* fruit and veg at *"reasonable prices"* are by far Marks & Sparks's leading attractions, and garner far broader support than any other aspect of its food operation; many reporters find the range *"fresh and nice"*, but some say it's *"not very varied"*. / HOURS Most stores open Mon-Sat 9am-8pm (central branches open later), Sun noon-6pm SEE ALSO Big Ten; Bread; Cheese & dairy; Meat, game & poultry.

Michanicou Bros W11
2 Clarendon Rd   6–2A
☎ (020) 7727 5191
"Absolutely the best"; it may look like a *"small village vegetable shop"*, but this *"fabulous"* greengrocer offers *"superb quality and a superb selection"* – *"fresh, fresh, fresh"*, and *"good enough even for foodie fashion shoots"* – and its staff *"really understand their stock"*; some do find shopping here *"incredibly expensive"*, but that's Holland Park for you. / HOURS Mon-Fri 9am-6.30pm, Sat 9am-5.30pm CREDIT CARDS no credit cards TUBE Holland Park.

North End Road Market SW6
North End Rd   5–3A
☎ (020) 8748 3020 ext 4936
See Chapter 13 Markets. / HOURS Mon-Sat 7am-5pm, Thu 7am-1pm TUBE Fulham Broadway SEE ALSO Cheese & dairy; Markets.

Northcote Road Market SW11
Northcote Rd   10–2C
See Chapter 13 Markets. / HOURS Mon-Sat 9am-5pm, Wed 9am-1pm TUBE BR Clapham Junction SEE ALSO Bread; Markets.

Fruit & vegetables

Panzer's NW8
13-19 Circus Rd   8–3A
☎ (020) 7722 8596 · www.panzers.co.uk
"Very strange and interesting veg and lots of mushrooms" are the sort of special attractions which draw reporters to this grand St John's Wood deli, where greengrocery is a speciality; *"prices are steep"* but the produce is *"of superb quality"*. / HOURS Mon-Fri 8am-7pm, Sat 8am-6pm, Sun 9am-2pm CREDIT CARDS no Amex TUBE St John's Wood SEE ALSO Ethnic shops; Grocers & delicatessens.

Portobello Road Market W12
Portobello Rd   6–2B
See Chapter 13 Markets. / HOURS Mon-Sat 9am-5pm TUBE Notting Hill Gate/Ladbroke Grove SEE ALSO Herbs & spices; Markets.

Sainsbury's
☎ (0845) 301 2020 · www.sainsburys.com
BRANCHES AT:
   Locations throughout London
"A large selection of produce, including a good organic range" ensures generally positive commentary for the fruit and vegetables on offer at London's largest supermarket chain. / HOURS Some larger stores 24 hours SEE ALSO Big Ten; Bread; Cheese & dairy; Fish & seafood; Health & organic foods; Herbs & spices; Meat, game & poultry; Wine.

Selfridges W1
400 Oxford St   3–1A
☎ (020) 7629 1234 · www.selfridges.co.uk
"Great variety" and *"excellent quality"* win popularity for this much commented-on food hall's array of fruit and veg; the relative paucity of commentary it attracts suggest it's not a 'destination' in quite the way many of the other sections are, though. / HOURS Mon-Fri 10am-8pm, Sat 9.30am-8pm, Sun noon-6pm TUBE Bond Street SEE ALSO Big Ten; Bread; Cheese & dairy; Chocolates & sweets; Cookware; Ethnic shops; Fish & seafood; Grocers & delicatessens; Herbs & spices; Meat, game & poultry; Wine.

Tachbrook Street Market SW1
Tachbrook St   2–4B
☎ (020) 7641 1090
See Chapter 13 Markets. / HOURS Mon-Sat 9.30am-4.30pm TUBE Pimlico/Victoria SEE ALSO Bread; Markets.

Tesco
· www.tesco.com
BRANCHES AT:
   Locations throughout London
The range *"is not exciting"*, but nevertheless a *"good selection of high-quality produce"* generally commends the fruit and veg on offer at the UK's largest supermarket chain. / HOURS Some larger stores 24 hours SEE ALSO Big Ten; Bread; Wine.

Fruit & vegetables

Two Peas in a Pod SW13
85 Church Rd   10–1A
☎ (020) 8748 0232
"Good quality for a small local greengrocer" wins praise for this "pint-sized" Barnes shop; it offers "a good range of fruit and vegetables (including organic) plus herbs, some houseplants and some dry goods". / HOURS Mon-Fri 7.30am-5.30pm, Sat 7.30am-5pm, Sun 10am-1pm CREDIT CARDS no credit cards TUBE Hammersmith.

Waitrose
☎ (01344) 424680 Customer service
www.waitrose.com
BRANCHES AT:
  Locations throughout London
"You can always get unusual fruit, reasonably priced and fresh" at the chain, which, as in so many other regards, easily outpaced all the competition; *"Waitrose always has in what Sainsbury's doesn't"*. / HOURS Hours vary: generally Mon-Sat 8.30am-9pm, Sun 11am-5pm SEE ALSO Big Ten; Bread; Cheese & dairy; Fish & seafood; Health & organic foods; Herbs & spices; Meat, game & poultry; Wine.

Grocers & delicatessens

10. Grocers & delicatessens

This section of the guide might unkindly be described as 'miscellaneous', as as – in addition to delicatessens – we have included here all the 'generalist' sources which did not attract enough comments to make it in to the Big Ten. Treating 'Delicatessen' as a speciality category in its own right, the shops most talked about by reporters were:

1. Carluccios ★
2. Luigi's ★
3. Villandry ★
4. Harrods ★
5. Selfridges ★
6. Mr Christian's
7. Mise en Place
8. Speck ★
9. Mortimer & Bennett
10. I Camisa & Son ★

Absolutely Starving SE1
51 Tooley St   9–4D
☎ (020) 7407 7417
This deli, by the entrance to the South Bank's Hay's Galleria, is not cheap, but it is one of the few food shops in the area; there's a "varied range" of dry goods and snacks (but little in the way of fruit and veg); the hot snacks and take-away range includes "great brownies". / HOURS *Mon-Fri 7am-10pm, Sat & Sun 9.30am-9pm* TUBE *London Bridge.*

Amici N2
78 High Rd East Finchley   1–1C
☎ (020) 8444 2932
This "great little Italian deli", in East Finchley (with tiny café attached) is praised for its "authentic" feel; an outside catering service is also available. / HOURS *Mon-Sat 8.30am-7pm, Sun 10am-5pm* CREDIT CARDS *no credit cards* TUBE *East Finchley.*

Asda
☎ (0500) 100055   www.asda.co.uk
BRANCHES AT:
  Locations throughout London
"Cheap, and a fairly good range" – there's a pretty consistent theme in commentary on this mega-market chain; it may be owned by the world's largest retailer (Walmart of the US), but its presence in the capital is not great (and largely confined to the outer suburbs), and survey commentary was not extensive. / HOURS *most stores Mon-Sat 7.30am-10pm (later Thu & Fri), Sun 10am-4pm.*

Grocers & delicatessens

Balthazar TW11
50 Broad St, Teddington   1–4A
☎ (020) 8943 2450
"An excellent range of Mediterranean foods" – and also from the US and the Orient – commends this Teddington delicatessen (or 'gourmet food retailer', as it prefers to be known) to local reporters. / HOURS Mon-Sat 9am-5.30pm CREDIT CARDS no Amex TUBE BR Teddington.

Bayley & Sage SW19
60 High St   10–2B
☎ (020) 8946 9904 www.bayley-sage.co.uk, www.delionline.co.uk
The scale of operations of this "pricey" Wimbledon food hall makes it "almost a supermarket", but its specialities – such as "great olives, meats and cheese" and "excellent fruit and vegetables" – attract as much commentary as its "good range of groceries"; most produce is British – hurrah! / HOURS Mon-Sun 8am-9pm CREDIT CARDS no Amex TUBE Wimbledon.

La Bella Sicilia SW1
23 Warwick Way   2–4B
☎ (020) 7630 5914
"A family-run shop with a good selection"; this popular Italian deli in Pimlico is a popular destination for those in search of something a little more authentic than Tesco (opposite); "good cooking tips" too. / HOURS Mon-Sat 9am-6pm, Sun 10am-4pm TUBE Victoria/Pimlico.

Belsize Village Delicatessen NW3
39 Belsize Ln   8–2A
☎ (020) 7794 4258
Reporters' commentary is more mixed than is the norm, but die-hard fans vaunt the "very good selection" of "excellent Jewish/Eastern European foods, cakes and so on" at this small Hampstead-fringe spot. / HOURS Mon-Fri 8.30am-7pm, Sat 8.30am-6pm, Sun 9am-2pm CREDIT CARDS no Amex TUBE Belsize Park/Swiss Cottage.

Bluebird SW3
350 King's Rd   5–3C
☎ (020) 7559 1000 www.conran.co.uk
"Everything looks delicious" and the quality is "very, very good", so when it comes to delicatessen items reporters seem willing to put up with the "high" prices of Conran's Chelsea 'gastrodrome'. / HOURS Mon-Wed 9am-8pm, Thu-Sat 9am-9pm, Sun 11am-5pm TUBE Sloane Square/South Kensington SEE ALSO Big Ten; Bread; Cheese & dairy; Fish & seafood; Fruit & vegetables.

Bon Appetit W9
73 Castellain Rd   6–1C
☎ (020) 7266 4365
They're "open seven days a week until late", but it's not just convenience which commends this Maida Vale delicatessen to local reporters – though only a small place, it manages to offer quite a wide range. / HOURS Mon-Fri 8am-10pm, Sat 8am-9pm, Sun 8am-1pm TUBE Maida Vale.

Grocers & delicatessens

Bon Vivant SW12
59 Nightingale Ln 10–2C
☎ (020) 8675 6314
True "personal service" – "they will try and track down anything for you" – commends this Clapham delicatessen to local reporters; for fruit and veg, an 'organic bag scheme', run in conjunction with Abel & Cole, is available. / HOURS Mon-Fri 8.30am-8pm, Sat 8.30am-7pm, Sun 9.30pm-12.30pm CREDIT CARDS no Amex TUBE Clapham South.

La Bottega N8
20 Crouch End Hill 1–1C
☎ (020) 8342 8181
This Crouch End deli is not very big, so its choice of (mainly Italian) produce is "necessarily limited"; fans, though, say it's of "high quality". / HOURS Tue-Sat 10am-6pm, Sun 11am-4pm CREDIT CARDS no Amex TUBE Finsbury Park.

Brindisa EC1
32 Exmouth Mkt 9–1A
☎ (020) 7713 1666 www.brindisa.com
For "everything Spanish" – including "fantastic olives, olive oils and wonderful almonds", and "excellent chorizo and hams" – the new retail outlet of this well-known importer is a popular recommendation; they also have a large stand at Borough – the queue for their chorizo sandwiches is one of the sights of the market! / HOURS Tue-Fri 10am-6pm, Sat 9am-5pm.

Brotherhood's SW18
38 Replingham Rd 10–2B
☎ (020) 8874 2138
"Friendly service, good bread, delicious ham, home-baked on the bone"; this "well-stocked, good-quality delicatessen" is a popular Southfields stand-by; any produce in the shop may be ordered in the small café. / HOURS Mon-Fri 8.30am-8pm, Sat 9am-5.30pm, Sun 9am-2pm CREDIT CARDS no Amex TUBE Southfields.

Bunces N8
10 Broadway Pde 1–1C
☎ (020) 8340 5542
"A fine selection of Italian produce" commends this "well stocked" Archway deli to local reporters; home-made pâtés and pestos a speciality. / HOURS Mon-Sun 8am-7pm TUBE Archway/Turnpike Lane.

Carluccios WC2
28 Neal St 4–2C
☎ (020) 7240 1487
"Pricey treats from an Italian celebrity chef" – Antonio Carluccio's Covent Garden deli offers a *"limited, but very good"* selection of oils, mushrooms, cured meats and chocolates, and his *"home-made pasta and sauces"* meet with particular approval; (many of the products are also available from the expanding range of Carluccio's Caffés). / HOURS Mon-Thu 11am-7pm, Fri 10am-7pm, Sat 10am-6pm SEE ALSO Bread.

Grocers & delicatessens

Chanteroy SW18
233 Wimbledon Park Rd   10–2B
☎ (020) 8874 1446
Now we understand why Southfields restaurant Le P'tit Normand has always had such a good cheeseboard! – this establishment is under the same ownership, and stocks some four dozen Gallic cheeses, as well as bread baked on-site from imported French dough; no wonder this is "a Mecca for French expats". / HOURS Mon-Sun 8am-8pm TUBE Southfields.

The Chatsworth Farm Shop SW1
54-56 Elizabeth St   2–4A
☎ (020) 7730 3033
Do they do "the best pork pies in London"? – this "lovely" Belgravia shop is better known for its butchery, but the commentary on its deli items is also very positive. / HOURS Mon-Fri 10am-6pm, Sat 10am-1pm TUBE Victoria/Sloane Square SEE ALSO Meat, game & poultry.

Christophers E9
103 Lauriston Rd   1–2D
☎ (020) 8986 2466   www.christopherscatering.co.uk
An "excellent, local deli" in the East End, near Victoria Park; "friendly staff and nearby parking" are among the features which commend it; also outside catering. / HOURS Mon-Fri 8.30am-5.30pm, Sat 9.30am-5pm, Sun 10.30am-3pm CREDIT CARDS no Amex TUBE Mile End.

Cockfosters Delicatessen EN4
19 Station Pde, Cockfosters Rd, Barnet   1–1C
☎ (020) 8441 4754
"A Greek deli, with a full range of Jewish products from dolmades to latkes"; it's a "helpful" sort of place, where hand-sliced smoked salmon is something of a speciality; small parties catered for. / HOURS Mon-Sat 8.30am-7pm, Sun 8.30am-3pm CREDIT CARDS no credit cards TUBE Cockfosters.

Comptoir Gascon EC1
63 Charterhouse St   9–1A
☎ (020) 7608 0851
It should perhaps come as no surprise that this beautifully designed "offshoot of Club Gascon" has been as immediate a hit as the nearby Smithfield restaurant was; its "high-quality" (and "surprisingly wide-ranging") product range gives "a real sense of Gascony", and fans are already hailing its traiteur dishes as "the best in the UK". / HOURS Mon-Fri 8am-8pm, Sat 9am-6pm TUBE Farringdon SEE ALSO Bread.

The Cooler N16
67 Stoke Newington Church St   1–1C
☎ (020) 7275 7266
If you wish to belong to "the Stoke Newington set", it seems that attendance at this "Aladdin's Cave" of a delicatessen is de rigueur; it offers an "awesome" variety of produce. / HOURS Mon-Fri 9am-8.30pm, Sat 9am-8pm, Sun 10am-5pm CREDIT CARDS no Amex TUBE BR Stoke Newington.

Grocers & delicatessens

Da Mario N5 ⓢ ☾
34 Highbury Pk   8–2D
☎ (020) 7226 2317
"There's often a queue" at this "old, reliable and friendly" Highbury deli, where the food – like the customers – reflects "a good range of nationalities"; a big variety of breads is a highlight, some baked on the premises. / HOURS Mon-Sat 8.30am-8pm, Sun 9am-8pm TUBE Highbury & Islington/Arsenal.

De Lieto Bakery & Delicatessen SW8 ☾ ☆
175 South Lambeth Rd   10–1D
☎ (020) 7735 1997
"Really good bread" is one of the features which wins praise for this "very reasonably priced" Italian deli in South Lambeth. / HOURS Mon-Sat 9.30am-7pm CREDIT CARDS no credit cards TUBE Stockwell.

Delizie d'Italia SW1 ☾ ☆
70 Lupus St   2–4B
☎ (020) 7834 1471
"A sumptuous selection of cheeses, oils and sausages" is the highlight at this "excellent Italian deli", in Pimlico. / HOURS Mon-Fri 9am-7pm, Sat 9am-6pm.

Du Pain Du Vin W1 ☀ ☾ 🚚
31 Paddington St   2–1A
☎ (020) 7224 1758   www.dupainduvin.co.uk
As the name suggests, if you're looking for something "very French" this Marylebone charcuterie/traiteur may be the place for you; if you're having a party, "get them to make a terrine for you". / HOURS Mon-Fri 8am-8pm, Sat 10am-6pm TUBE Baker Street.

Elizabeth King SW6 ⓢ ☾ ★
34 New Kings Rd   10–1B
☎ (020) 7736 2826   www.elizabethking.com
"Very friendly and helpful service" is something of a refrain in commentary on this "great local deli" in Fulham, which stocks a good range of all the usual items, plus "excellent" bread and organic fruit. / HOURS Mon-Fri 9am-8.30pm, Sat 9am-6pm, Sun 10am-3.30pm TUBE Parsons Green.

Europa Foods ⓢ ☀ ☾
BRANCHES AT:
   Locations throughout London
Fans say they're "always reliable", and offer the odd "unusual" item, but this slightly upmarket supermarket chain was not much commented on overall. / HOURS 17 branches, generally open Mon-Sun 8am-11pm; Trafalgar Sq branch open 24 hours.

Grocers & delicatessens

Felicitous W11
19 Kensington Park Rd   6–1A
☎ (020) 7243 4050
A "nice" modern delicatessen, in the hip and happening heart of Notting Hill; the extensive range includes bread from the trendy new Exeter Street Bakery (see also). / HOURS Mon-Fri 8.30am-9pm, Sat 8.30am-7pm, Sun 10am-5pm TUBE Notting Hill Gate/Ladbroke Grove.

Fields N5
15 Corsica St   8–2D
☎ (020) 7704 1247
This "useful" Highbury deli has quite a "small range", but the stock is of "good quality", and service is "willing". / HOURS Mon-Fri 10am-8pm, Sat 10am-6pm, Sun 10am-2pm CREDIT CARDS no Amex TUBE Highbury & Islington.

Finns of Chelsea Green SW3
4 Elystan St   5–2C
☎ (020) 7225 0733
"Prepared dinner party food" is the speciality at this Chelsea Green traiteur; the dishes – such as baked chicory in Parmesan crumbs or honey miso chicken – may display a degree of contemporary sophistication, but kitchen-cheats benefit from the fact that they also "have that home-made feel to them." / HOURS Mon-Fri 8am-5.30pm, Sat 8am-1pm CREDIT CARDS no Amex TUBE Sloane Square/South Kensington.

Flâneur EC1
41 Farringdon Rd   9–1A
☎ (020) 7404 4422
This "beautiful" new Farringdon food hall and delicatessen (with integral restaurant) has developed a reputation for pâtisserie; its other stock – stretching from Welsh lamb and Tuscan sausages to cheeses and charcuterie sourced from Paris – is thought "pricey" for what it is, though, and service can be "slow". / HOURS Mon-Fri 8am-10pm, Sat 9am-10pm, Sun 9am-6pm TUBE Farringdon SEE ALSO Patisserie.

Fortnum & Mason W1
181 Piccadilly   3–3D
☎ (020) 7734 8040   www.fortnumandmason.co.uk
'Six types of smoked salmon' (and all wild, too) are the sort of strength at the top end which distinguish the deli counter of the famous St James's store; the range also includes many imported specialities. / HOURS Mon-Sat 10am-6.30pm TUBE Piccadilly Circus/Green Park SEE ALSO Big Ten; Chocolates & sweets; Coffee & tea; Patisserie; Wine.

Grocers & delicatessens

Gallo Nero ★
BRANCHES AT:
45 Newington Grn, N16   1–1D
☎ (020) 7226 2002
75 Stoke Newington High St, N16   1–1C
☎ (020) 7254 9770

"Very good quality Italian foods at extremely competitive prices (especially compared to those in Islington and West End)" – one reporter neatly summarises the opinion of many on the attractions of these Stoke Newington delis. / HOURS Mon, Wed, Thu 8.30am-6.15pm, Tue 8.30am-2.30pm, Sat 9am-6pm CREDIT CARDS no Amex.

R Garcia & Sons W11 ★
248-250 Portobello Rd   6–1A
☎ (020) 7221 6119   www.garciafoods.co.uk

Is this "the best Spanish deli in London"?; the volume of support this "old-fashioned", "family-type" spot receives suggests it might well be; "great hams and cheeses" and "wonderful bread" are particularly approved, but you can find almost anything Hispanic ("even soap!") in this North Kensington "Aladdin's cave". / HOURS Tue-Sat 8.30am-6pm TUBE Ladbroke Grove.

La Gastronomia SE21
86 Park Hall Rd   1–4D
☎ (020) 8766 0494

A West Dulwich deli, offering "a good choice of organic foods" among a range of Italian, American and British manufacture, often from smaller operators; cakes made on the premises. / HOURS Mon-Sat 9am-5pm (Wed 7pm) TUBE Brixton/BR West Dulwich.

Gastronomia Italia SW1
8 Upper Tachbrook St   2–4C
☎ (020) 7834 2767

"Fabulous Italian quality and service" is claimed by fans of this quirky Pimlico delicatessen, whose cramped premises harbour a considerable range of stock. / HOURS Mon-Fri 9am-6pm, Sat 9am-5pm CREDIT CARDS no credit cards TUBE Victoria.

G Gazzano & Son EC1 Ⓢ ★
169 Farringdon Rd   9–1A
☎ (020) 7837 1586

"My Italian friends tell me everything is authentic, except the prices!"; this "wonderful", "very friendly" and "old-fashioned" Clerkenwell delicatessen (est 1901) offers its devotees "the complete shopping experience"; fresh pasta, sausages and olives are among the most popular items. / HOURS Mon & Sat 8am-5pm, Tue-Thu 8am-5.30pm, Fri 8am-6pm, Sun 10am-2pm CREDIT CARDS no Amex TUBE Farringdon.

Grocers & delicatessens

Gennaro SE13 ★
23 Lewis Grove 1–4D
☎ (020) 8852 1370
This "authentic" Lewisham "outpost of Italy" does indeed specialise in food from that part of the world, but it's quite "innovative" too – Polish, German, Spanish and French products also adorn its shelves. / HOURS Tue-Sat 9am-6pm CREDIT CARDS no credit cards TUBE DLR Lewisham.

Giacobazzi's NW3 ★
150 Fleet Rd 8–2A
☎ (020) 7267 7222 www.giacobazzis.co.uk
"You can watch your pasta being made" at this "great" Belsize Park deli – "a small family business" with a disproportionate local following; "Bolognese specialities" find particular favour. / HOURS Mon-Fri 9.30am-7pm, Sat 9am-6pm TUBE Belsize Park/Hampstead.

A Gold E1
42 Brushfield St 9–1D
☎ (020) 7247 2487 www.agold.co.uk
You don't get that many "British delicatessens", so John Bulls everywhere may wish to seek out this small shop near Spitalfields market, where all the food and drink celebrates indigenous British traditions. / HOURS Mon-Fri 11am-8pm, Sun 11am-6pm (closed Sat) TUBE Liverpool Street.

The Ham Pantry TW10
3 Parkleys Pde, Richmond 1–4A
☎ (020) 8549 2139
Local fans say this deli by the Cassell Hospital is "a real find"; its range – over 60 cheeses, for example, as well as charcuterie, wholefoods and health foods – is certainly quite impressive. / HOURS Mon-Fri 10am-7pm, Sat 9am-5.30pm CREDIT CARDS no credit cards TUBE Richmond.

Hampstead Food Hall NW3
23-27 Heath St 8–1A
☎ (020) 7431 0310
The combination of "range" and "convenience" distinguish this food hall in the centre of Hampstead, which offers a full range of quality fresh and preserved goods until 11pm daily; "good wine too". / HOURS Mon-Sun 7am-11pm TUBE Hampstead.

Hand Made Food SE3 ☆
40 Tranquil Vale 1–4D
☎ (020) 8297 9966 www.handmadefood.com
Careful sourcing ensures that this 'gastronomic jewel in the heart of Blackheath' (their words) pretty much lives up to its aspirations – "it's fantastic for ready-to-eat tarts, quiches, salads and the best banoffi pie ever made"; the cheeses are also approved. / HOURS Mon-Fri 9am-6pm, Sat 9am-5.30pm

Grocers & delicatessens

Harrods SW1
87 Brompton Rd   5–1D
☎ (020) 7730 1234   www.harrods.com
"An enormous variety of prepared food of all nationalities" is the general theme of commentary on the various deli counters of the famous Knightsbridge food halls. / HOURS Mon, Tue & Sat 10am-6pm, Wed-Fri 10am-7pm SEE ALSO Big Ten; Bread; Cheese & dairy; Chocolates & sweets; Coffee & tea; Cookware; Fish & seafood; Fruit & vegetables; Meat, game & poultry; Patisserie; Wine.

Hart's the Grocer
BRANCHES AT:
  248 Fulham Rd, SW10   5–3B
  ☎ (020) 7351 7031
  206 Earls Court Rd, SW5   5–2A
  ☎ (020) 7370 3967
  87-93 Gloucester Rd, SW7   5–2B
  ☎ (020) 7370 5487
  50-52 Old Brompton Rd, SW7   5–2B
  ☎ (020) 7581 1526
  82 Holland Park Ave, W11   6–2A
  ☎ (020) 7727 7332
  257 Tottenham Court Rd, W1   2–1C
  ☎ (020) 7637 0940
  40 Bernard St, WC1   2–1C
  ☎ (020) 7833 4575
  112-114 Marylebone High St, W1   2–1A
  ☎ (020) 7486 5610
Fans say they offer "good products, diversity and quality", but it's really the long, long hours – often 24/7 – which distinguish these upmarket convenience stores. / HOURS Tottenham Court Rd, SW5, both SW7 & SW10 open 24 hours; other branches generally Mon-Sun 8am-11pm

Harvey Nichols SW1
109-125 Knightsbridge   5–1D
☎ (020) 7235 5000   www.harveynichols.com
Delicatessen is one of the most commented-on departments at this Knightsbridge 'foodmarket'; there's "excellent quality and a good range, if at a price". / HOURS Mon, Tue & Sat 10am-7pm, Wed-Fri 10am-8pm, Sun noon-6pm TUBE Knightsbridge SEE ALSO Big Ten; Bread; Fish & seafood; Meat, game & poultry; Wine.

I Camisa & Son W1
61 Old Compton St   4–3A
☎ (020) 7437 7610
"A little bit of Italy in Soho", this "great old family deli" has an enormous fan club as "the best Italian store in London", with many reporters claiming it sells the "best freshly-made pasta in town". / HOURS Mon-Sat 9am 6pm CREDIT CARDS no Amex TUBE Leicester Square.

Grocers & delicatessens

I Sapori di Stefano Cavallini SW11
146 Northcote Rd   10–2C
☎ (020) 7228 2017
Even by the gentrified standards of Battersea's main foodie drag, this "excellent Italian deli" still looks rather 'Chelsea'; fans find "an obsession with quality", and, as you might hope from an operation which also does outside catering, "excellent dishes of the day" come especially recommended. / HOURS Mon-Sat 10am-7pm   CREDIT CARDS no Amex   TUBE BR Clapham Junction.

Jacobs SW7
20 Gloucester Rd   5–1B
☎ (020) 7581 9292
"Great prepared meals" and "delicious and unusual cakes" make this South Kensington deli – which offers a wide range of dishes, often using organic ingredients – a popular local stand-by; there's a "good café" too. / HOURS Mon-Sat 8am-10pm, Sun 8am-5pm   TUBE Gloucester Road.

Jeroboams
⁂ www.jeroboams.co.uk
BRANCHES AT:
   51 Elizabeth St, SW1   2–4A
   ☎ (020) 7823 5623
   96 Holland Park Ave, W11   6–2A
   ☎ (020) 7727 9359
An upmarket small group, particularly known for its cheeses, but also praised for its "hams, jams and home-made produce". / HOURS Mon-Fri 9am-7.30pm, Sat 8.30am-7pm, Sun 10am-4pm
SEE ALSO Cheese & dairy.

Kemptons of Kensington W8
1 Holland St   5–1A
☎ (020) 7376 0010
This is an "excellent new traiteur", says an early reporter on this "gourmet catering company and deli", not far from Kensington High Street. / HOURS Mon-Fri 9am-7.30pm, Sat 9am-6pm
CREDIT CARDS yes (minimum £5)   TUBE High Street Kensington.

L & D Foods N2
17 Lyttleton Rd   1–1B
☎ (020) 8455 0141   ⁂ www.totallysalmon.com
"A great local deli in Hampstead Garden Suburb"; a good range of products – well over 1000, they say, from France, Switzerland and Italy – makes this a popular destination; hand-cut smoked salmon a speciality. / HOURS Mon, Wed, Thu 8.30am-5.30pm, Tue 8.30am-1pm, Fri 7am-4pm, Sun 7am-1pm   TUBE East Finchley/Golders Green.

Grocers & delicatessens

Lina Stores W1
18 Brewer St   3–2D
☎ (020) 7437 6482
This "*great, family-owned Italian deli*" is a "*mercifully unmodernised Soho classic*", with service which is "*friendly*" (if sometimes rather "*leisurely*"); "*delicious fresh pasta*" is a highlight. / HOURS Mon-Fri 9am-6.30pm, Sat 9am-5.30pm TUBE Piccadilly Circus.

Luigi's Delicatessen SW10
349 Fulham Rd   5–3B
☎ (020) 7352 7739
"*Real Italian food*" – a "*stellar range of goodies in tins, packets and bottles*" plus "*wonderful ready-cooked dishes*" – have made this Chelsea institution one of the most popular delis in town; even some fans, though, note that it's "*expensive*" for what it is. / HOURS Mon-Fri 9am-9.30pm, Sat 9am-7pm CREDIT CARDS no Amex TUBE South Kensington/Fulham Broadway.

Maquis W6
111 Hammersmith Grove   7–1C
☎ (020) 8846 3851
Adjacent to a fashionable new Hammersmith restaurant, this chic delicatessen's eclectic range encompasses specialities from North Africa, Spain, Italy and Iran. / HOURS Mon-Fri 8am-7pm, Sat 8am-4pm CREDIT CARDS no Amex TUBE Hammersmith.

La Mediterranea W9
59 Shirland Rd   6–1C
☎ (020) 7266 1188
"*A small deli, with a very friendly café*" – this Maida Vale outfit specialises in 'all things Italian'. / HOURS Mon-Sat 8.30am-9pm, Sun 10am-5.30pm CREDIT CARDS no Amex TUBE Warwick Avenue.

Mise en Place
⌐ www.thefoodstore.co.uk
BRANCHES AT:
   21 Battersea Rise, SW11   10–2C
   ☎ (020) 7228 4392
   2 Ritherdon Rd, SW17   10–2C
   ☎ (020) 8682 0824
"*Small but reliable, very expensive but good for treats*" – one reporter speaks for the many on the charms (and the drawbacks) of these south London delicatessens. / HOURS SW11 Mon-Sun 9am-9pm; SW17 Mon-Fri 8am-8pm, Sat 8am-7pm, Sun 9am-7pm.

Monte's N1
23 Canonbury Ln   8–2D
☎ (020) 7354 4335
"*The only problem is popularity*" – this "*classic Italian deli*" is "*an absolute delight*", which stocks "*great olives and hams*" as well as a good mix of "*high street Italian brands*". / HOURS Mon-Fri 10am-7pm, Sat 10am-6pm, Sun 10am-2pm TUBE Highbury & Islington.

Grocers & delicatessens

The Moore Park Delicatessen SW6
85 Moore Park Rd   5–4A
☎ (020) 7736 2087
A "great selection" makes this Fulham-fringe spot popular with the locals; "brilliant home-made dishes" and "good olives" are among reported highlights. / HOURS Mon-Fri 8.30am-5pm CREDIT CARDS no credit cards TUBE Fulham Broadway.

Mortimer & Bennett W4
33 Turnham Green Ter   7–2A
☎ (020) 8995 4145 ⌁ www.mortimerandbennett.com
This small and "upmarket" deli near Turnham Green tube is often "very crowded" thanks to its disproportionate local following, due (in part at least) to its "careful and personal selection" of "products which no one else has"; a "great cheese selection" is a particular strength. / HOURS Mon-Fri 8.30am-6.30pm, Sat 8.30am-5.30pm CREDIT CARDS no Amex TUBE Turnham Green.

Mr Christian's W11   Ⓢ ☀ ☾
11 Elgin Cr   6–1A
☎ (020) 7229 0501
"If you don't mind paying" – quite a number of reporters say that it's just "too expensive" – this famous Notting Hill delicatessen has "the yummiest olives, gourmet foodstuffs, and deli salads around", and its many admirers also praise its "excellent cheeses, pâtés and fresh pasta". / HOURS Mon-Fri 6am-7pm, Sat 5.30am-6.30pm, Sun 7am-4pm TUBE Notting Hill Gate/Ladbroke Grove SEE ALSO Bread.

Olga Stores N1   Ⓢ ☾ ★
30 Penton St   8–3D
☎ (020) 7837 5467
"Rapid turnover" ensures that the food is always "fresh, as well as of high quality" at this Islington Italian deli; its range includes numerous types of olive, as well as fresh pasta and ready-made dishes. / HOURS Mon-Fri 9am-8pm, Sat 9am-7pm, Sun 10am-2pm CREDIT CARDS no Amex TUBE Angel.

Oliviers & Co   ☾ ☆
BRANCHES AT:
   114 Ebury St, SW1   2–4A
   ☎ (020) 7823 6770
   26a, The Market, Covent Garden, WC2   4–3D
   ☎ (020) 7240 0697
This "good-quality" specialist shop sells olives, olive oils, vinegars and tapenades in Covent Garden and Belgravia. / HOURS SW1 Mon-Fri 9.30am-6pm; WC2 Mon-Sat 10am-7pm, Sun 11am-5pm CREDIT CARDS no Amex.

Grocers & delicatessens

Outpatients W11 ⓢ) 🚚 ★
154 Notting Hill Gate   6–2B
☎ (020) 7221 9777 ⌁ www.outpatients.co.uk
"A seemingly small store that has all those things you can never find elsewhere" – the smart deli attached to Notting Hill's trendy Pharmacy restaurant *"doesn't offer a big range"*, but what it has is strongly approved; *"prepared dishes"* are a highlight. / HOURS Mon-Sat 10am-8pm, Sun 11am-5pm CREDIT CARDS no Amex TUBE Notting Hill Gate.

P de la Fuente W10
288 Portobello Rd   6–1A
☎ (020) 8960 5687
"Smaller than the famous Garcia, but cheaper too"; you can find *"all the Spanish brand names you'll ever need"* (plus the odd Italian one) at this North Kensington deli, whose specialities include biscuits, cakes and charcuterie. / HOURS Mon-Sat 9am-6pm TUBE Ladbroke Grove.

Panzer's NW8 ⓢ ☀) 🚚 ★
13-19 Circus Rd   8–3A
☎ (020) 7722 8596 ⌁ www.panzers.co.uk
"Great, hand-sliced smoked salmon" is a highlight of the *"Jewish-style"* deli section of this *"pricey"* St John's Wood institution; as far as the overall shopping experience goes, however – and you can buy most things here – the place's *"chaotic"* charms do not appeal to all. / HOURS Mon-Fri 8am-7pm, Sat 8am-6pm, Sun 9am-2pm CREDIT CARDS no Amex TUBE St John's Wood SEE ALSO Ethnic shops; Fruit & vegetables.

Partridges ⓢ ☀) ★
⌁ www.partridges.co.uk
BRANCHES AT:
  132-134 Sloane St, SW1   5–2D
  ☎ (020) 7730 0651
  17-23 Gloucester Rd, SW7   5–1B
  ☎ (020) 7581 0535
A *"very good general store"* – well, good enough for Her Majesty anyway – this long-standing Sloane Square institution (with an outpost in South Kensington) is a *"long-standing"* favourite for some reporters; some of the more plutocratic ones even say it makes *"a good alternative to supermarkets"*. / HOURS Mon-Sun 8am-10pm (SW7 11pm)

Picena SW3) ★
5 Walton St   5–1D
☎ (020) 75846573
Just behind Harrods, this *"great Italian deli"* of long standing has quite a name, especially for its *"excellent home-made dishes"*. / HOURS Mon-Fri 9am-7.30pm, Sat 9am-5.30pm CREDIT CARDS no Amex TUBE South Kensington/Knightsbridge.

Grocers & delicatessens

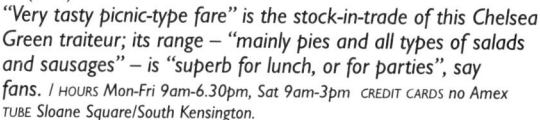

The Pie Man SW3 ☕
16 Cale St   5–2C
☎ (020) 7225 0587
"Very tasty picnic-type fare" is the stock-in-trade of this Chelsea Green traiteur; its range – "mainly pies and all types of salads and sausages" – is "superb for lunch, or for parties", say fans. / HOURS Mon-Fri 9am-6.30pm, Sat 9am-3pm CREDIT CARDS no Amex TUBE Sloane Square/South Kensington.

Platters   Ⓢ ★
BRANCHES AT:
  10 Hallswelle Pde, Finchley Rd, NW11   1–1B
  ☎ (020) 8455 7345
  83-85 Allitsen Rd, NW8   8–3A
  ☎ (020) 7722 5352
"Excellent fried fish and smoked salmon" are highlights of the "very limited range" which make these north London institutions simply the "best Jewish delis" for many reporters. / HOURS NW8 Mon-Fri 8.30am-4.30pm, Sat 8.30am-4pm, Sun 8.30am-2pm; NW11 Mon-Sat 8.30am-4.30pm, Sun 8.30am-2pm.

Rosslyn Delicatessen NW3   📧 Ⓢ ☾
56 Rosslyn Hill   8–2A
☎ (020) 7794 9210 🖳 www.delirosslyn.co.uk
"A fantastic international selection of fresh, tinned and packaged foods", including some "outstanding US imports", makes this Hampstead spot quite a local destination; some do find it "quite expensive" for what it is. / HOURS Mon-Sat 8.30am-8.30pm, Sun 8.30am-8pm TUBE Hampstead.

Safeway   📧 Ⓢ ☀ ☾
🖳 www.safeway.com
BRANCHES AT:
  Locations throughout London
A much smaller chain than Tesco (and, of course, attracting much less comment), this "good, mixed-range supermarket" is, on the quality front, rated by reporters broadly on a par with its gigantic competitor; "good, changing weekly offers" – plus some "unexpected goodies" too – were among the plusses. / HOURS Hours vary: generally Mon-Sat 8am-10pm, Sun 11am-5pm (central branches longer hours)

Salumeria Estense SW6   ☾
837 Fulham Rd   10–1B
☎ (020) 7731 7643
A small Fulham delicatessen, packed to the gunnels with traditional Italian supplies; fans insist it does "the best salami in London" (and also a "wonderful chocolate torte"). / HOURS Mon-Fri 10am-7pm, Sat 10am-5pm CREDIT CARDS no credit cards TUBE Parsons Green.

Grocers & delicatessens

Salumeria Napoli SW11
69 Northcote Rd 10–2C
☎ (020) 7228 2445
Much of the food at this family-run Battersea deli is "just like you'd find in Italy", say its supporters; pesto is the house speciality. / HOURS Mon-Sat 9am-6pm CREDIT CARDS no credit cards TUBE BR Clapham Junction.

Salusbury Foodstore NW6
56 Salusbury Rd 1–2B
☎ (020) 7328 3287
With the help of an on-site café (and pizza take-away), this "Italianate" new Queen's Park deli is already attracting quite a local following. / HOURS Mon-Sat 8.30am-8pm, Sun 9.30am-5pm CREDIT CARDS no Amex TUBE Queens Park.

Sapponara N1
23 Prebend St 8–3D
☎ (020) 7226 2771
"A good range of pasta, olives and cured meats" is among the culinary attractions which ensure continuing popularity for this "very friendly Islington institution". / HOURS Mon-Fri 8am-6pm, Sat 9am-6pm CREDIT CARDS no Amex TUBE Angel/Highbury & Islington.

Selfridges W1
400 Oxford St 3–1A
☎ (020) 7629 1234 www.selfridges.co.uk
The "really wide" and "eclectic" range makes the deli section a highlight of this popular food hall; the "best salt beef in town", "gorgeous smoked fish" and "good, fresh foie gras" are among the highlights. / HOURS Mon-Fri 10am-8pm, Sat 9.30am-8pm, Sun noon-6pm TUBE Bond Street SEE ALSO Big Ten; Bread; Cheese & dairy; Chocolates & sweets; Cookware; Ethnic shops; Fish & seafood; Fruit & vegetables; Herbs & spices; Meat, game & poultry; Wine.

Sonny's Food Shop & Cafe SW13
92 Church Rd 10–1A
☎ (020) 8741 8451
The "tiny" shop attached to the well-known Barnes restaurant sell "lots of good Italian products" (including pasta imported twice-weekly), and also a range of top-name products (such as Poilâne bread) from elsewhere. / HOURS Mon-Fri 10am-6pm, Sat 9.30am-5pm TUBE Hammersmith/BR Barnes.

Speck W11
2 Holland Park Ter 6–2A
☎ (020) 7229 7005
As long as you accept that it's "wildly expensive", reporters speak nothing but good of this small and chic Italian delicatessen in Holland Park; "amazing soups and pasta" are highlights of the home-made dishes on offer, but if you want to DIY they offer everything "from olives to fine Italian wines"; fans say that quality throughout is "excellent". / HOURS Mon-Fri 8am-8.30pm, Sat 8am-7pm TUBE Holland Park.

Grocers & delicatessens

Sutherlands W6
140 Shepherds Bush Rd 7–1C
☎ (020) 7603 5717
"A good local deli" in Hammersmith; it's moved into new ownership since our survey was conducted, and now offers an all-round Mediterranean selection, with bread and pastry something of a speciality. / HOURS Mon-Fri 7.45am-6.30pm, Sat 8.30am-5pm, Sun 8.30am-3pm CREDIT CARDS no Amex TUBE Hammersmith.

L Terroni & Sons EC1
138-140 Clerkenwell Rd 9–1A
☎ (020) 7837 1712
Established in 1878, this Clerkenwell spot claims to have been the first Italian deli in England; the combination of "lots of traditional Italian stuff" and "chaotic" organisation can make a visit here something of an "Aladdin's Cave" experience. / HOURS Tue-Fri 9am-5.45pm, Sat 9am-3pm, Sun 10.30am-2pm CREDIT CARDS no Amex TUBE Chancery Lane/Farringdon.

Tom's W11
226 Westbourne Grove 6–1B
☎ (020) 7221 8818
Shame it's so "crowded" and "badly laid out" – Tom Conran's fashionable Notting Hill deli-cum-dining room offers a "good", if rather "pricey", range of fresh and preserved produce. / HOURS Mon-Fri 8am-7pm, Sat 8am-6pm, Sun 10am-4pm TUBE Notting Hill Gate.

Tony's Deli SW8
39 South Lambeth Rd 10–1D
☎ (020) 7582 0766
"Wonderful service" helps to distinguish this "tiny corner shop in Vauxhall", which local supporters say is "packed with the best Italian produce". / HOURS Mon-Fri 6.30am-6.30pm, Sat 8.30am-5.30pm CREDIT CARDS no credit cards TUBE Vauxhall.

Tray Gourmet SW10
240 Fulham Rd 5–3B
☎ (020) 7352 7676 www.traygourmet.co.uk
Is this small spot by the Chelsea & Westminster hospital London's "best French traiteur"? – with its "very high standards" and its "highly attentive and polite staff", some reporters certainly think so. / HOURS Mon-Sat 9am-8pm CREDIT CARDS no Amex TUBE Earls Court.

Treohans SW4
56-58 Abbeville Rd 10–2D
☎ (020) 8673 2738
It's not often a shop with no more pretensions than being a well-stocked grocer figures in a world dominated by supermarkets; this Clapham shop gathers a fair degree of support, however, by offering "a better range of products than the local Sainsbury's!" / HOURS Mon-Sun 9am-9pm TUBE Clapham Common/Clapham South.

Grocers & delicatessens

Truc Vert W1
42 North Audley St   3–2A
☎ (020) 7491 9988
"Très rustique" – this Mayfair delicatessen offers ("at a price") a "small but superb" selection of Gallic cheese, charcuterie, bread, pâtisserie and wine. / HOURS Mon-Fri 7.30am-10pm, Sat 7.30am-5pm, Sun 11am-4pm TUBE Bond Street.

Valentina SW14
210 Upper Richmond Rd West   10–1A
☎ (020) 8392 9127
"Lovely ready meals" and the fact that the owners are "such nice people" contribute to enormous local popularity of this "super Italian deli", in East Sheen. / HOURS Mon-Fri 9am-7pm, Sat 9am-6pm, Sun 9.30am-3pm TUBE Richmond/Kew.

The Village Delicatessen SE3
1-3 Tranquil Vale   1–4D
☎ (020) 8852 2015
A 'traditional' wide-ranging delicatessen in Blackheath; home-cooked hams are something of a speciality. / HOURS Mon-Fri 6am-9pm, Sat & Sun 7am-7pm CREDIT CARDS no credit cards TUBE BR Blackheath.

Villandry W1
170 Gt Portland St   2–1B
☎ (020) 7631 3131
"Enticing displays" and an "eclectic selection" have made this chic and airy Marylebone deli-cum-food hall quite a destination – too much so on occasions ("20 minutes is a long time to wait"); on the deli front, specialities include smoked fish and cheeses, as well as an extensive range of home-made dishes to take away. / HOURS Mon-Sat 8am-10pm, Sun 9.30am-4pm TUBE Great Portland Street SEE ALSO Bread.

Vivian's TW10
2 Worple Way, Richmond   1–4A
☎ (020) 8940 3600
This is "a great deli", say Richmond locals; it stocks over 20 types of coffee, for example, and "a fantastic range of cheeses in tiptop condition". / HOURS Mon-Fri 9am-7pm, Sat 8.30am-6pm, Sun 8.30am-noon CREDIT CARDS no Amex TUBE Richmond.

Vom Fass W11
187 Westbourne Grove   6–1B
☎ (020) 7792 4499
Oils, vinegars and cordials (as well as wines and spirits) – all direct from the barrel – are the speciality this Notting Hill shop, which offers a bespoke bottling and wrapping service ideal for presents; after only a couple of years in business, it's been so successful that it already has an offshoot in Selfridges, and further openings are planned in Richmond and Ealing. / HOURS Mon-Sat 10.30am-7pm, Sun noon-5pm TUBE Notting Hill Gate SEE ALSO Wine.

Grocers & delicatessens

Zoran's Deli TW1
10 Crown Rd, Twickenham 1–4A
☎ (020) 8892 0001
"First-class service" and "olives to die for" are two of the features leading an early reporter to recommend this new outfit – which sells a wide range of continental goods – near St Margarets railway station; on sunny days, you can eat your purchases in the garden. / HOURS Mon & Tue 8am-4pm, Wed, Thu & Fri 8am-6pm, Sat 9am-5pm, Sun 10am-4pm TUBE BR St Margarets.

MAIL ORDER

Esperya
ITALY
☎ +39 071 7592274 www.esperya.com
For the ultimate in dinner party one-upmanship, it would seem difficult to beat this niftily-designed, next-day-delivery website, which brings a wide range of produce directly from Italy to your door; a small range of cookware and items for the table are also available. / CREDIT CARDS no Amex & no Switch.

The Food Ferry SW8
B24-B27 New Covent Garden Mkt, Nine Elms Ln 10–1D
☎ (020) 7498 0827 www.foodferry.co.uk
Eleven years in business, 'London's original grocery home-shopping company' offers some 2,500 product lines from its extensive catalogue; service is "very friendly and helpful" – you can order by phone, by fax or over the web, and take delivery on the same day in many of the more central postcodes. / CREDIT CARDS no Amex.

Fratelli Camisa WD6
Unit 3, Lismirrane Industrial Pk, Elstree Rd, Elstree, Herts
☎ (01992) 763076 www.camisa.co.uk
Unrelated to Soho's I Camisa, this is now a "very efficient" Italian mail-order service only, the brothers' shop in Charlotte Street (and, before that, in Berwick Street) now having closed; "excellent dried pasta" and Parmesan are among the products praised.

Inverawe Smokehouses PA35
Taynuilt, Argyll, Scotland
☎ (01866) 822446 www.smoked-salmon.co.uk
Suppliers of over 80 traditionally smoked products – venison, duck and chicken, as well as salmon and other fish – "all of which are beautifully packaged".

Leapingsalmon.co.uk
☎ (0870) 701 9100 www.leapingsalmon.co.uk
Time to cook, but not to think or shop? – this website, which offers same-day delivery of complete pack meals (as well as wine, and a small gift range) may well be the place for you; order by 5pm, and you can have delivery in most central postcodes that evening. / CREDIT CARDS no Amex.

Grocers & delicatessens

Olives et al BA12
Unit D2, Quarry Fields, Mere, Wiltshire
☎ (01747) 861446 www.olivesetal.co.uk
Mr and Mrs Henschel's website hints at other delights, but it's for their "excellent" olives and oil which one would be likely principally to visit it.

Portobello Food Company W6 ★
Arch 215, Trussley Rd   7–1C
☎ (020) 8748 0505 www.portobellofood.com
"Exceptional Italian food" and "great hampers" are among the strengths of this popular web and catalogue shopping service.

Simply Salmon CB11
Severals Farm, Arkesden, Essex
☎ (01799) 550143 www.simplysalmon.co.uk
Smoked salmon is of course the speciality, but this Essex-based website also offers quite a range of other delicatessen items – extending from caviar and foie gras to hams and preserves. / CREDIT CARDS no Amex.

The Weald Smokery TN5
Mount Farm, Flimwell, East Sussex
☎ (01580) 879601 www.wealdsmokery.co.uk
All manner of home-smoked produce – salmon, trout and breast of duck, for example – is to be had from this Sussex-based website, which also offers a small range of other items, including whole hams. / CREDIT CARDS no Amex & no Switch.

11. Health & organic food

Paradox: many of Londoners' most affluent food shoppers are willing to pay premium prices for health and organic foods; yet few of the specialist shops which have sprung up have truly captured reporters' hearts. And only two of the ten places most often talked about achieved the consistency of positive commentary to justify the award of a star:

1= Planet Organic
1= Fresh & Wild
3 Holland & Barrett
4 Bumblebee
5 Abel & Cole (mail order) ★
6= Spitalfields Organic Market
6= Sainsbury's
8 Waitrose
9 As Nature Intended ★
10 Simply Organic (mail order)

Alara Wholefoods WC1
58-60 Marchment St   2–1C
☎ (020) 7837 1172
A Bloomsbury shop praised by local reporters for its "wide range of high-quality cooked fare, and its vegetarian and vegan foods". / HOURS Mon-Fri 9am-6pm, Sat 10am-6pm CREDIT CARDS no Amex TUBE Russell Square.

As Nature Intended   Ⓢ ☾ ★
⌁ www.asnatureintended.uk.com
BRANCHES AT:
  201 Chiswick High Rd, W4   7–2A
  ☎ (020) 8742 8838
  270-274 Upper Richmond Rd West, SW14   10–1A
  ☎ (020) 8878 0627
"A really good organic range", "fair prices" and "supermarket-style hours" put these "nice" and "helpful" stores among the leading London's health food shops. / HOURS W4 Mon-Fri 9am-8pm, Sat 9am-6pm, Sun 11am-5.30pm; SW14 Mon-Sat 9am-7pm, Sun 11am-5.30pm CREDIT CARDS no Amex.

Balham Wholefood & Health Store SW12
8 Bedford Hill   10–2C
☎ (020) 8673 4842
A "small and friendly" shop, selling health food and supplements, and a modest range of dairy produce. / HOURS Mon-Sat 9.30am-1.30pm & 2.30pm-6pm (Tue & Thu close 7pm) CREDIT CARDS no credit cards TUBE Balham.

Health & organic food

Brixton Whole Foods SW9
59 Atlantic Rd   10–1D
☎ (020) 7737 2210
"The original hippie organic food store", still pleasing visitors to the Market (near which it is situated), and offering an extensive range of herbs, organic fruit and other goods. / HOURS Mon-Sat 8.30am-5.30pm, Wed 8am-1pm CREDIT CARDS no Mastercard & no Amex TUBE Brixton SEE ALSO Herbs & spices.

Bumblebee N7
30, 32 & 33 Brecknock Rd   8–2C
☎ (020) 7607 1936   www.bumblebee.co.uk
They strike some as *"a bit '70s"*, but *"for a non-central location"*, this mini-string of Tufnell Park health food shops offer *"a top-quality selection"* of *"everything that's wholesome and organic"*; it attract a wide north London following. / HOURS Mon-Sat 9.30am-6.30pm (Thu close 7.30pm) TUBE Kentish Town/Caledonian Road SEE ALSO Herbs & spices.

Bushwacker Wholefoods W6
132 King St   7–2C
☎ (020) 8748 2061
One reporter claims that this two-decades-old shop is *"the best place for organic vegans"*; more generally, it offers a *"good selection"*, including all-organic fruit and veg. / HOURS Mon-Sat 9.30am-6pm (Tue 10am) TUBE Hammersmith/Ravenscourt Park.

Coopers SE1
17 Lower Marsh   9–4A
☎ (020) 7261 9314
Handily-located for healthy folk passing through Waterloo, this well-stocked shop offers an extensive range of foods (including a good proportion of organics); it even has a café, which offers *"divine"* scones. / HOURS Mon-Fri 8.30am-5.30pm TUBE Waterloo.

Dandelion Health Foods SW11
120 Northcote Rd   10–2C
☎ (020) 7350 0902
"Good bread and take-aways" are among the strengths commending this shop in Battersea's premier food shopping street, where roughly half the produce is organic; staff give *"excellent advice"* too. / HOURS Mon-Sat 9am-6pm, Sun noon-3pm CREDIT CARDS no Amex TUBE BR Clapham Junction.

Farm W5
84 St Marys Rd   1–2A
☎ (020) 8566 1965
Selling British organic and farm food is the calling of this recently-established South Ealing shop, which a local reporter praises for its *"good, if not especially extensive, selection"*. / HOURS Mon noon-7pm, Tue-Fri 10am-7pm (Thu 8pm), Sat 10am-6pm, Sun 11am-4pm CREDIT CARDS no Amex TUBE South Ealing.

Health & organic food

Fresh & Wild S ☼ ☾
⌂ www.freshandwild.com
BRANCHES AT:
  69-75 Brewer St, W1 3–2D
  ☎ (020) 7434 3179
  210 Westbourne Grove, W11 6–1B
  ☎ (020) 7229 1063
  32-40 Stoke Newington Church St, N16 1–1C
  ☎ (020) 7254 2332
  49 Parkway, NW1 8–3B
  ☎ (020) 7428 7575
  305 Lavender Hill, SW11 10–2C
  ☎ (020) 7585 1488
  194 Old St, EC1 9–1C
  ☎ (020) 7250 1708
One of the two 'big names' of the organic general store world; just like its main competitor, it sometimes falls down on the service front, but its "great range of produce" sets "a high standard", putting it – in reporters' estimation – at the head of its field. / HOURS W1 Mon-Fri 7.30am-9pm, Sat 9am-9pm, Sun 11.30am-8.30pm; other shops generally slightly shorter hours SEE ALSO Bread.

Friends Organic E2
83 Roman Rd 1–2D
☎ (020) 8980 1843
Run by Buddhists ("and therefore very reasonably priced"), this Bethnal Green store offers a range of products from all over the world, about two thirds of which are organic. / HOURS Mon, Wed, Thu & Sat 10am-6.30pm, Tue 10.30am-6.30pm, Fri 10am-7pm TUBE Bethnal Green.

The Grain Shop W11
269 Portobello Rd 6–1A
☎ (020) 7229 5571
It's probably best known as a source of hot and cold take-aways to sustain visitors to Portobello Market, but this is also a well-stocked health food shop, specialising in gluten-free, yeast-free and dairy-free products. / HOURS Mon-Sat 9.30am-6pm CREDIT CARDS no Amex TUBE Ladbroke Grove/Westbourne Park.

The Haelan Clinic N8 ⌂ S
41 The Broadway 1–1C
☎ (020) 8340 1518 ⌂ www.haelen.co.uk
The appearance may strike some as "chaotic", but this "great local health food shop for Crouch End" is a popular destination, thanks in part to the "wonderful choice" it offers. / HOURS Mon-Thu & Sat 9am-6pm, Fri 9am-6.30pm, Sun noon-4pm TUBE Finsbury Park/Turnpike Lane.

Health & organic food

Here SW3
Chelsea Farmers Mkt, 125 Sydney St   5–3C
☎ (020) 7351 4321
"A good organic selection" and "free delivery" are among the strengths of this large but "friendly" Chelsea supermarket; established in 2001, it has quickly gathered a strong local following. / HOURS Mon-Sat 9.30am-8pm, Sun 10.30am-6.30pm CREDIT CARDS no Amex TUBE Sloane Square/South Kensington.

Heroes of Nature E8
20-22 Broadway Mkt   1–2D
☎ (020) 7249 1177
Locals speak very fondly of this modernistic Hackney shop, where the stock is 100% organic. / HOURS Mon-Sat 10am-7pm, Sun 11am-6pm CREDIT CARDS no Amex TUBE Bethnal Green.

The Hive Honey Shop SW11
93 Northcote Rd   10–2C
☎ (020) 7924 6233
"A large selection of honey and honey products" – "they even advised me on a perfect remedy for hay fever" – makes this unique Battersea shop well worth seeking out; this is one of London's true artisanal producers – almost all the honey comes from the owner's own hives (some of which can be seen – safely behind glass – in the shop!). / HOURS Mon-Fri 10am-5pm, Sat 10am-6pm CREDIT CARDS no Amex & no Switch TUBE BR Clapham Junction.

Holland & Barrett
☎ (0870) 606 6605 www.hollandandbarrett.com
BRANCHES AT:
   Locations throughout London
The UK's leading retailer of vitamins, minerals and herbal supplements" is "ubiquitous", and its "very wide range" of produce includes a good selection of dried fruit, nuts, teas and dry health foods; the 'joy of healthy eating' seems absent here, though – to many reporters, the shops offer a "bland" or "lifeless" experience. / HOURS general hours Mon-Sat 9am-5.30pm.

Kelly's Organic Foods SW11
46 Northcote Rd   10–2C
☎ (020) 7207 3967
"A great new organic grocer in the best tradition", say supporters of this Battersea shop, where there's "always a huge selection of fresh fruit and veg", plus "all manner of organic foods, wonderfully presented"; popular (non-organic) Fulham fish merchant Copes Seafood (see also) visits on Tue, Fri and Sat. / HOURS Mon-Thu 9am-8pm, Fri-Sat 9am-6pm TUBE BR Clapham Junction.

Health & organic food

Luscious Organic
BRANCHES AT:
  11 Fulham Broadway, SW6   5–4A
  ☎ (020) 7381 8010
  240-242 Kensington High St, W8   7–1D
  ☎ (020) 7371 6987
Recently established, these smart-looking shops aim to offer an organic take on the convenience store experience; both have juice bars on the premises (or you can take away). / HOURS Mon-Fri 8.30am-8.30pm, Sat & Sun 9.30am-6pm

Montignac Boutique SW5
160 Old Brompton Rd   5–2B
☎ (020) 7370 2010   www.montignac.co.uk
Some may think the 'Eat Yourself Slim' philosophy rather too good to be true, but the Gallic diet guru Michel Montignac's South Kensington outlet offers "good ready made-dishes" (and a small range of other produce) which are just as appealing to non-believers. / HOURS Mon-Fri 8.30am-9pm, Sat 8.30am-6pm, Sun 10am-5pm TUBE Gloucester Road/South Kensington.

Olivers Wholefood Store TW9
5 Station Approach, Kew   1–4A
☎ (020) 8948 3990
"A wide range and friendly staff" win favourable commentary for this Kew shop, whose main line is organic fruit and vegetables, but which also stocks dry health foods. / HOURS Mon-Sat 9am-7pm, Sun 10am-7pm CREDIT CARDS no Amex TUBE Kew.

The Organic Grocer W9
17 Clifton Rd   8–4A
☎ (020) 7286 1400
The name says it all about this "well stocked" Maida Vale shop, whose attractions include an almost exclusively organic range and quite long hours. / HOURS Mon-Sat 9am-8pm, Sun 11am-8pm TUBE Warwick Avenue.

Planet Organic
BRANCHES AT:
  22 Torrington Pl, WC1   2–1C
  ☎ (020) 7436 1929
  42 Westbourne Grove, W2   6–1B
  ☎ (020) 7727 2227, Deliveries 7221 1345
The style ("Sainsbury's goes hippy") can grate on non-believers, but an "excellent range" of "food that tastes as it should" makes these "health food temples" one of the survey's top two most mentioned sources of organic produce; doubters, though, complain of "comically high prices" and "poor service". / HOURS WC1 Mon-Fri 10am-8pm, Sat & Sun noon-6pm; W2 Mon-Sat 9.30am-8pm, Sun noon-6pm.

Health & organic food

Sainsbury's
☎ (0845) 301 2020 www.sainsburys.com
BRANCHES AT:
  Locations throughout London
"A fantastic choice of good food" endears Sainsbury's health and organic food range to all who comment on it; the prices are "reasonable" too. / HOURS Some larger stores 24 hours SEE ALSO Big Ten; Bread; Cheese & dairy; Fish & seafood; Fruit & vegetables; Herbs & spices; Meat, game & poultry; Wine.

Spitalfields Organic Market E1
Commercial St, Spitalfields   9–1D
The busiest of the specifically organic markets – see Chapter 13 Markets. / HOURS Mon-Fri 9am-6pm, Sun 11am-3pm (main market day) SEE ALSO Herbs & spices; Markets.

Waitrose
☎ (01344) 424680 Customer service
 www.waitrose.com
BRANCHES AT:
  Locations throughout London
A "good selection of organic fruit and vegetables" is seen as being among the healthy attractions of reporters' favourite supermarket chain. / HOURS Hours vary: generally Mon-Sat 8.30am-9pm, Sun 11am-5pm SEE ALSO Big Ten; Bread; Cheese & dairy; Fish & seafood; Fruit & vegetables; Herbs & spices; Meat, game & poultry; Wine.

MAIL ORDER

Abel & Cole SE24
Unit 8-13, MGI Estate, Milkwood Rd   10–2D
☎ (020) 7737 3648 www.abel-cole.co.uk
Reporters on this "excellent organic delivery service" – a wide range of predetermined boxes of fruit and vegetables, plus a limited à la carte meat selection – are almost all "very impressed" by its "good-value" range, by its "friendly" staff and by its "reliable" deliveries. / CREDIT CARDS no Amex.

Clearspring W3
Unit 19 Acton Park Estate   1–2A
☎ (020) 8746 0152 www.clearspring.co.uk
It generated limited feedback, but fans say this service offers an "unrivalled" range of "organic, vegetarian foods from Japan, America and Europe." / CREDIT CARDS no Amex.

Farmaround SW8
B140-143, New Covent Garden, Nine Elms Ln   10–1D
☎ (020) 7627 8066 www.farmaround.co.uk
"We love our surprise vegetable sack" – reporters are generally complimentary about this delivery service for boxes of organic fruit and vegetables, which enthusiasts say offers "excellent quality and value for money".

Health & organic food

Goodness Direct NN11
South March, Daventry, Northants
☎ (0871) 871 6611 ⌁ www.goodnessdirect.co.uk
An "informative and useful website", offering "all you need" if you have special dietary requirements; over a thousand products are on offer, and you can, for example, search for products that are dairy-free, gluten-free, wheat-free, yeast-free or low-fat. / CREDIT CARDS no Amex.

Organics Direct SW19
Olympic Hs, 196 The Broadway   10–2B
☎ (020) 8545 7676 ⌁ www.organicsdirect.co.uk
A "friendly" supplier, offering over a thousand organic products, from fruit and vegetable boxes to bread and dry goods. / CREDIT CARDS no Amex.

Simply Organic SW19
196 The Broadway   10–2B
☎ (0845) 1000 444 ⌁ www.simplyorganic.net
A 'one-stop organic shop' of the web (with a range of over 2,500 products) offers a "good choice" of organic produce; convenience, rather than any perception of premium quality, seems to be the main selling-point, so far as reporters are concerned. / CREDIT CARDS no Amex.

Herbs & spices

12. Herbs & spices

Herbs and spices seem to be something of a 'Cinderella' area so far as London's food shoppers are concerned. The ten most commented-upon suppliers were:

 1 The Spice Shop ★
 2 Sainsbury's
 3 Waitrose
 4 Culpeper ☆
 5= Borough Market ★
 5= Portobello Road Market
 5= Spitalfields Organic Market ★
 8 Selfridges ★
 9 WM Martyn ★
 10 Bumblebee ☆

Berwick Street Market W1 ★
Berwick St 3–2D
See Chapter 13 Markets. / HOURS Mon-Sat 9am-6pm SEE ALSO *Fruit & vegetables; Markets.*

Borough Market SE1 ★
Borough High St 9–4C
www.boroughmarket.org.uk
If you're looking for "big bunches" of fresh herbs which offer "really good value for money", London's favourite food market is a popular destination. / HOURS Fri noon-5pm, Sat 9am-4pm (wholesale fruit & veg Mon-Fri 3am-10am) CREDIT CARDS no credit cards TUBE London Bridge SEE ALSO *Big Ten; Bread; Cheese & dairy; Fish & seafood; Fruit & vegetables; Markets; Meat, game & poultry.*

Brixton Market SW9 ☀
Brixton Station Rd, Popes Rd, Atlantic Rd, Electric Rd & Electric Avenue 10–2D
If you're looking for some truly exotic herb or spice, it's almost certainly here ... somewhere. / HOURS Mon-Sat 8am-5.30pm, Wed 8am-1pm TUBE Brixton SEE ALSO *Fish & seafood; Fruit & vegetables; Markets.*

Brixton Whole Foods SW9 💳 ☀ ☆
59 Atlantic Rd 10–1D
☎ (020) 7737 2210
This well-established shop may be a touch "chaotic", but many find ample compensation in the value offered by its "weigh-your-own, price-your-own" selection of herbs and spices. / HOURS Mon-Sat 8.30am-5.30pm, Wed 8am-1pm CREDIT CARDS no Mastercard & no Amex TUBE Brixton SEE ALSO *Health & organic foods.*

Herbs & spices

Bumblebee N7
30, 32 & 33 Brecknock Rd   8–2C
☎ (020) 7607 1936   www.bumblebee.co.uk
This Kentish Town health food shop is "especially good for herbs and spices" – "you weigh your own", and it's "so much cheaper than the supermarkets". / HOURS Mon-Sat 9.30am-6.30pm (Thu close 7.30pm) TUBE Kentish Town/Caledonian Road SEE ALSO Health & organic foods.

Culpeper
www.culpeper.co.uk
BRANCHES AT:
  21 Bruton St, W1   3–3B
  ☎ (020) 7629 4559
  Unit 8, The Market, Covent Garden, WC2   4–3D
  ☎ (020) 7379 6698
This quaint Mayfair and Covent Garden herbalist is praised for its "excellent and pure organic herbs". / HOURS WC2 Mon-Sat 10am-7pm, Sun 10am-6pm; W1 Mon-Fri 9.30am-6pm, Sat 10am-5pm.

The Food Centre N8
68-70 Turnpike Ln   1–1C
☎ (020) 8888 1927
An Indian grocery store in north London which is "less than half supermarket prices for spices". / HOURS Mon-Thu 9.30am-7pm, Fri & Sat 9.30am-7.30pm, Sun 10am-5.30pm TUBE Turnpike Lane.

Greenfields Supermarket W1
25 Crawford St   2–1A
☎ (020) 7723 2510
This Middle Eastern supermarket in Marylebone has a good range of dried herbs and spices; its "huge bunches of fresh coriander at low prices" are especially approved. / HOURS Mon-Fri 8am-10pm, Sat & Sun 9am-10pm CREDIT CARDS no credit cards TUBE Marylebone SEE ALSO Ethnic shops.

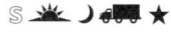

Leena SW11
58 Northcote Rd   10–2C
☎ (020) 7228 1611
"Every conceivable herb and spice" is to be found among the "phenomenal range" of this Battersea shop, most of whose stock comes from India and the Caribbean. / HOURS Mon-Thu 10am-7pm, Fri & Sat 10am-8pm CREDIT CARDS no credit cards TUBE BR Clapham Junction.

WM Martyn N10
135 Muswell Hill Broadway   1–1C
☎ (020) 8883 5642
An "excellent selection" – "all those herbs and spices you can't find elsewhere" – is one of the many aspects of this Muswell Hill grocer singled out for particular praise. / HOURS Mon-Wed, Fri 9.30am-5.30pm, Thu 9.30am-1pm, Sat 9am-5.30pm CREDIT CARDS no Amex TUBE Highgate SEE ALSO Chocolates & sweets; Coffee & tea.

Herbs & spices 100

Portobello Road Market W12
Portobello Rd 6–2B
"Big bunches of herbs at sensible prices" are a feature of some of the stalls here. / HOURS Mon-Sat 9am-5pm TUBE Notting Hill Gate/Ladbroke Grove SEE ALSO Fruit & vegetables; Markets.

Sainsbury's
☎ (0845) 301 2020   www.sainsburys.com
BRANCHES AT:
  Locations throughout London
If you're after something "interesting, rare and unusual in the way of herbs and spices", London's largest supermarket chain is – perhaps rather surprisingly – quite likely to be your handiest solution. / HOURS Some larger stores 24 hours SEE ALSO Big Ten; Bread; Cheese & dairy; Fish & seafood; Fruit & vegetables; Health & organic foods; Meat, game & poultry; Wine.

Selfridges W1
400 Oxford St 3–1A
☎ (020) 7629 1234   www.selfridges.co.uk
As so often at this department store food hall, when it comes to herbs and spices it's sheer "range" which is much of the place's attraction. / HOURS Mon-Fri 10am-8pm, Sat 9.30am-8pm, Sun noon-6pm TUBE Bond Street SEE ALSO Big Ten; Bread; Cheese & dairy; Chocolates & sweets; Cookware; Ethnic shops; Fish & seafood; Fruit & vegetables; Grocers & delicatessens; Meat, game & poultry; Wine.

The Spice Shop W11
1 Blenheim Cr 6–1A
☎ (020) 7221 4448   www.thespiceshop.co.uk
This "tiny", "aromatic" Notting Hill shop is "packed with every spice", and enjoys a disproportionate following thanks to its "huge range" and its "very, very knowledgeable service"; "it stocks everything you can't find anywhere else", and "you can buy small quantities" too. / HOURS Mon-Sat 9.30am-6pm, Sun 11am-3pm CREDIT CARDS no Amex TUBE Ladbroke Grove/Notting Hill Gate.

Spitalfields Organic Market E1
Commercial St, Spitalfields 9–1D
"Loads of brilliant fresh herb stalls" are one of the particular attractions of this popular City-fringe market. / HOURS Mon-Fri 9am-6pm, Sun 11am-3pm (main market day) SEE ALSO Health & organic foods; Markets.

Taj Stores E1
112-114 Brick Ln 1–2D
☎ (020) 7377 0061   www.cuisinenet.co.uk/tajstores
"Every herb and spice under the sun" – in "vast quantities for small prices" – provide a special reason to visit this East End Indian supermarket. / HOURS Mon-Sun 9am-9pm TUBE Aldgate East SEE ALSO Ethnic shops.

Herbs & spices

Talad Thai SW15
326 Upper Richmond Rd   10–2A
☎ (020) 8789 8084
A *"good range of unusual herbs and spices at great prices"* is one of the attractions of this Putney oriental supermarket. / HOURS Mon-Sat 9am-8pm, Sun 10am-8pm CREDIT CARDS no credit cards TUBE East Putney SEE ALSO Ethnic shops.

Tooting Market SW17
Upper Tooting Rd, between Mitcham Rd, Upper Tooting Rd & Totterdam St   10–2C
"Unsophisticated, but plenty of choice, and cheap" – the attractions of this largely ethnic market are particularly in evidence on the herb and spice front. / HOURS Mon-Sat 9.30am-5pm, Wed 9.30am-1pm TUBE Tooting Broadway SEE ALSO Ethnic shops; Markets.

Waitrose
☎ (01344) 424680 Customer service
www.waitrose.com
BRANCHES AT:
  Locations throughout London
The range is perhaps a touch on the "usual" side, but reporters' favourite supermarket offers quite a "wide" range of herbs, of "consistent" quality. / HOURS Hours vary: generally Mon-Sat 8.30am-9pm, Sun 11am-5pm SEE ALSO Big Ten; Bread; Cheese & dairy; Fish & seafood; Fruit & vegetables; Health & organic foods; Meat, game & poultry; Wine.

MAIL ORDER

Fox's Spices CV37
Units J-K, Masons Rd Industrial Estate, Stratford upon Avon
☎ (01789) 266420
If you're having difficulty finding fenugreek seeds, sumac powder or trassi – if you need it, you'll know what it is – you might like to check out this mail order operator which prides itself on having most herbs and spices, and quite a number of other things besides; order by phone or fax (01789 267737). / CREDIT CARDS no Amex.

Markets 102

13. Markets

As markets have been in existence since time immemorial, it must be a sign of some dynamism that of the ten which attracted the most attention from reporters, as set out in the following list, four have come into existence over the past decade:

1. Borough ★
2. Portobello Road
3. Berwick Street
4. Spitalfields Organic
5. Northcote Road
6. Notting Hill Farmers ★
7. North End Road
8. Islington Farmers ★
9. Brixton
10. Tachbrook Street

Berwick Street Market W1
Berwick St   3–2D
An atmospheric Soho street market, sandwiched between record shops, fabric warehouses and strip clubs; the twenty or so stalls offer cheap fruit and vegetables – probably best eaten or cooked the same day – plus bread, cheese, olives, fish, some household goods, flowers and dry goods. / HOURS Mon-Sat 9am-6pm SEE ALSO *Fruit & vegetables; Herbs & spices.*

Billingsgate E14
Trafalgar Way   11–1C
☎ (020) 7987 1118 ⌂ fis.com/billingsgate/
See Chapter 8 Fish & seafood. / HOURS Tue-Sat 5am-8.30am TUBE DLR West India Quay SEE ALSO *Fish & seafood.*

Blackheath Farmers Market SE3   S ☆
Blackheath Station Car Pk, 2 Blackheath Village   1–4D
⌂ www.lfm.org.uk
"Small but very fresh" – a visit to this diverse but modestly-scaled market has become a "Sunday morning ritual" for some reporters, but it does not generate a huge amount of feedback. / HOURS Sun 10am-2pm.

Borough Market SE1   ★
Borough High St   9–4C
⌂ www.boroughmarket.org.uk
The ne plus ultra of market food shopping in London – see Big Ten. / HOURS Fri noon-5pm, Sat 9am-4pm (wholesale fruit & veg Mon-Fri 3am-10am) CREDIT CARDS no credit cards TUBE London Bridge SEE ALSO *Big Ten; Bread; Cheese & dairy; Fish & seafood; Fruit & vegetables; Herbs & spices; Meat, game & poultry.*

Markets

Brick Lane Market E1
Brick Ln, at junction of Cheshire & Sclater Streets   1–2D
The market of this famous East End street is now "better known for junk than for food", but there are some decent fruit and veg stalls, especially near the Brick Lane Beigel Bake, and a few cheap fish stalls too. / HOURS Sun 6am-2pm TUBE Shoreditch/Liverpool Street.

Brixton Market SW9
Brixton Station Rd, Popes Rd, Atlantic Rd, Electric Rd & Electric Avenue   10–2D
"Fun", "funky" and "exotic" – such are the "exciting" charms of this enormous (300-stall) and "truly ethnic" market, which offers a "fantastic" profusion of ingredients for "West Indian, African, European and many other cuisines"; and the food, of course, is just the beginning … / HOURS Mon-Sat 8am-5.30pm, Wed 8am-1pm TUBE Brixton SEE ALSO Fish & seafood; Fruit & vegetables; Herbs & spices.

Chapel Street Market N1
between Liverpool Road & Penton St   8–3D
"A local no-nonsense street market" near Islington's Sainsbury's – it's "best on Friday and Saturday"; fruit and veg are the speciality – "generally fair quality, but mixed" – and there's also a fish stall. / HOURS Tue, Wed, Fri & Sat 9am-5pm, Thu & Sun 9am-12.30pm TUBE Angel SEE ALSO Fruit & vegetables.

Church Street Market NW1
between Edgware Rd & Lisson Grove   8–4A
Some reporters find "lovely fruit" and "exotic vegetables" at this wide-ranging street market. / HOURS Tue-Sat 9am-5pm TUBE Edgware Road.

Inverness Street Market NW1
Inverness St   8–3B
☎ (020) 7413 6917
A small market in Camden Town; "cheap, good-quality vegetables" are the highlight. / HOURS Mon-Sat 9am-5pm, Thu 9am-1pm TUBE Camden Town.

Islington Farmers Market N1
Essex Rd, opposite Islington Green   8–3D
www.lfm.org.uk
"A small, but well-stocked farmers' market", near Islington Green; it can get "horribly crowded". / HOURS Sun 10am-2pm TUBE Angel.

Leadenhall Market EC3
Whittington Ave, off Gracechurch & Leadenhall St   9–2D
This wonderfully atmospheric Victorian landmark isn't nowadays really a market at all in the general sense, but rather a collection of quality food shops which sell their wares straight on to the covered street; see entries for Butcher & Edmonds (Meat, game & poultry) and HS Linwood (Fish & seafood). / HOURS Mon-Fri 7am-4pm TUBE Bank/Monument.

Markets

Lower Marsh Market SE1
Lower Marsh 9–4A
☎ (020) 7926 2530
Though handy for commuters through Waterloo, this street market that doesn't generate much in the way of feedback; fruit 'n' veg and good deals in kitchenware would be the main reasons to seek it out. / HOURS Mon-Sat 10am-2pm TUBE Waterloo.

North End Road Market SW6
North End Rd 5–3A
☎ (020) 8748 3020 ext 4936
"A total bargain, if you can bear the crowds" – it's the "good value and good atmosphere" which make Fulham's large street market such a popular destination; "cheap fruit and veg" are the lead attraction, but the Gallic cheese stall also has its followers. / HOURS Mon-Sat 7am-5pm, Thu 7am-1pm TUBE Fulham Broadway SEE ALSO Cheese & dairy; Fruit & vegetables.

Northcote Road Market SW11
Northcote Rd 10–2C
As you might expect, the market in South London's foodiest street is one which attracts particular attention, and the quality level – of "everything from fruit and veg to good bread and olives" – is notably higher than the norm. / HOURS Mon-Sat 9am-5pm, Wed 9am-1pm TUBE BR Clapham Junction SEE ALSO Bread; Fruit & vegetables.

Notting Hill Farmers Market W8 ★
in car park behind Waterstones on Notting Hill Gate (access from Kensington Place) 6–2B
🌐 www.lfm.org.uk
It may be Saturday mornings only (and parking may be "appalling"), but the handy location helps make this a popular shopping destination; some find variety a touch lacking – the bread and fruit 'n' veg stalls, however, attract particular praise. / HOURS Sat 9am-1pm.

Palmers Green Farmers Market N13 Ⓢ
Palmers Green Railway Station Car Park 1–1C
🌐 www.lfm.org.uk
"Great atmosphere" and "a lovely range of food" commend this Southgate market to a small number of reporters. / HOURS Sun 10am-2pm TUBE BR Palmers Green.

Portobello Road Market W12
Portobello Rd 6–2B
For "street theatre" (especially "on a sunny Saturday"), it's difficult to beat this famous west London market, where the food section is but one part of a mile of stalls selling pretty much anything and everything; on the food front, fruit and veg are to the fore – "quality varies, but prices are great". / HOURS Mon-Sat 9am-5pm TUBE Notting Hill Gate/Ladbroke Grove SEE ALSO Fruit & vegetables; Herbs & spices.

Markets

Ridley Road Market E8
13-15 Ridley Rd 1–1D
☎ (020) 7923 0666
Some reporters proclaim the "wonderful atmosphere" of this East End carnival, whose stalls offer "anything and everything under the sun" (including a huge choice for those cooking Afro-Caribbean or à la turque); "quality and service vary from great to appalling". / HOURS Mon-Sat 9am-5pm TUBE BR Dalston Junction.

Roman Road Market E2
Roman Rd 1–2D
Not much feedback on this East End market – such as it is tips the "fine fish and greengrocery stalls, near Globe Road". / HOURS Tue, Thu & Sat 8.30am-5.30pm TUBE Mile End.

Shepherd's Bush Market W12
Uxbridge Rd 7–1C
There was perhaps surprisingly little survey commentary on this extensive west London market, whose "great range" includes meat, fruit and vegetables, and lots of choice of African and Asian foods. / HOURS Mon-Sat 9am-5pm, Thu 9am-1pm TUBE Goldhawk Road/Shepherd's Bush.

Smithfield Market EC1 ☀ ★
Charterhouse St 9–2A
☎ (020) 7248 3151
See Chapter 14, Meat, game & poultry. / HOURS Mon-Fri approx 4.30am-noon TUBE Farringdon/Barbican SEE ALSO Meat, game & poultry.

Spitalfields Organic Market E1 Ⓢ
Commercial St, Spitalfields 9–1D
"Good-quality, fresh organic produce" and an "excellent Sunday excursion", too; reporters speak only well of the food area at this large and atmospheric market, in a covered hall on the fringe of the City; the only reservation is that "the selection is not quite as good as at Borough". / HOURS Mon-Fri 9am-6pm, Sun 11am-3pm (main market day) SEE ALSO Health & organic foods; Herbs & spices.

Swiss Cottage Farmers Market NW3 ★
02 Centre Car Park, Finchley Rd 8–2A
🌐 www.lfm.org.uk
"Only open on Wednesdays, so not easy to get to" – notwithstanding the accessibility problem, reporters are complimentary about the "all very fresh" fare of this varied farmers' market; if you're planning a visit do note that some fear it's "doomed by re-development". / HOURS Wed 10am-2pm TUBE Swiss Cottage.

Markets

Tachbrook Street Market SW1
Tachbrook St   2–4B
☎ (020) 7641 1090
"Small but interesting", this street market, just off the Vauxhall Bridge Road, is mainly dedicated to food; a large fruit 'n' veg stall is the linchpin, but the fish and bread stalls also have their fans. / HOURS Mon-Sat 9.30am-4.30pm TUBE Pimlico/Victoria SEE ALSO Bread; Fruit & vegetables.

Tooting Market SW17
Upper Tooting Rd, between Mitcham Rd, Upper Tooting Rd & Totterdam St   10–2C
Especially if you're looking for "Indian traditional food", you won't do much better than this "unpretentious" and "cheap" covered market. / HOURS Mon-Sat 9.30am-5pm, Wed 9.30am-1pm TUBE Tooting Broadway SEE ALSO Ethnic shops; Herbs & spices.

Twickenham Farmers Market TW1
Holly Rd Car Park, Off King St, Twickenham   1–4A
🌐 www.lfm.org.uk
"A good range of meat, cheese, fruit, vegetables and juices served by the farmers themselves" – not a market which generated a huge amount of feedback, but all favourable, such as it is. / HOURS Sat 9am-1pm.

Walthamstow Market E17
High St   1–1D
This distant-East End market may claim to be the longest street market in Britain, but it incited little commentary from reporters, mainly to the effect that it's "good for ethnic vegetables". / HOURS Mon-Sat 9am-5pm TUBE Walthamstow Central.

West Ealing Farmers Market W13
Leeland Rd   1–2A
🌐 www.lfm.org.uk
Both organic and conventional farmers sell meat, vegetables, cheese, apple juices, fish, seafood, plants and flowers, honey, bread, pies and much more at this Saturday-only west London market. / HOURS Sat 9am-1pm.

14. Meat, game & poultry

Butchers' ranks may have been depleted in recent years, but the roast beef of Old England isn't done for yet: London still has a number of superlative shops, amongst which almost all are independents. This is an area where it seems that there's just no substitute for age, and most of the top firms have generations of experience behind them. The ten most commented-upon suppliers were:

1. C Lidgate ★
2. Randall's ★
3. Harrods ★
4. A Dove ★
5. M Moen & Son ★
6. Allen & Co ★
7. Kingsland ★
8. Selfridges ★
9. Frank Godfrey ★
10. Macken Bros ★

Allen & Co W1
117 Mount St   3–3B
☎ (020) 7499 5831
Butchers just don't come grander than this august centenarian and, for its supporters, this is simply "the best butcher in the country", never mind Mayfair; "brilliant lamb" and "the best grouse in the south of England" are among reported highlights. / HOURS Mon-Fri 6am-4pm, Sat 6am-noon CREDIT CARDS no credit cards at present TUBE Bond Street/Green Park.

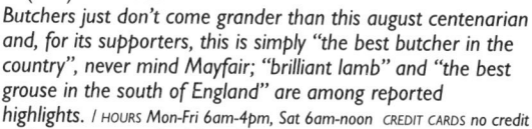

FT Barrett NW3
40 Englands Ln   8–2B
☎ (020) 7722 1131
These "real old-fashioned butchers" in Hampstead "really know their work"; local fans proclaim "superb quality" and "very reasonable prices". / HOURS Mon-Fri 8.30am-5.30pm TUBE Belsize Park.

GH Baxter W7
330 Greenford Ave   1–2A
☎ (020) 8578 1728
This half-centenarian Hanwell operation cooks its own hams, and makes its own sausages and burgers. / HOURS Mon-Sat 6.30am-5.30pm, Sun 7am-1pm TUBE Ealing Broadway.

Meat, game & poultry

Bifulco NW2
182 Cricklewood Ln   1–1B
☎ (020) 8452 2674
A "friendly" Cricklewood family business that's a real local hero, thanks to the consistent quality of its meat and its range of home-made pre-prepared dishes. / HOURS Mon-Sun 7am-5.30pm (Sat closes 1pm) CREDIT CARDS no credit cards TUBE Golders Green/Kilburn.

Biggles W1
66 Marylebone Ln   2–1A
☎ (020) 7224 5937   www.ebiggles.co.uk
"Home-made varieties of every description" are a highlight of this Marylebone 'gourmet sausage maker' (est 1989), which prides itself on offering over 40 varieties of banger – including a wheat-free version, and one type for veggies. / HOURS Mon & Sat 9.30am-4.30pm, Tue-Fri 9.30am-6pm CREDIT CARDS no Amex TUBE Bond Street.

Borough Market SE1
Borough High St   9–4C
www.boroughmarket.org.uk
"Amazing choice and quality" makes Londoners' favourite foodie market as popular for meat – from "best-quality venison and ostrich" to "scrummy sausages" – as it is for almost everything else; among the stallholders, Northfield Farm (see mail order) and Ginger Pig are two of the bigger stalls to look out for. / HOURS Fri noon-5pm, Sat 9am-4pm (wholesale fruit & veg Mon-Fri 3am-10am) CREDIT CARDS no credit cards TUBE London Bridge SEE ALSO Big Ten; Bread; Cheese & dairy; Fish & seafood; Fruit & vegetables; Herbs & spices; Markets.

Butcher & Edmonds EC3
1-3 Grand Ave   9–2D
☎ (020) 7626 5816
With a history stretching back a quarter of a millennium, this City game specialist must be presumed to be doing something right; out of season, they sell a range of quality meat and poultry. / HOURS Mon-Fri 5am-3pm TUBE Monument.

Chadwicks SW12
208 Balham High Rd   10–2C
☎ (020) 8772 1895
www.chadwicksorganicbutchers.com
This Balham shop – a partnership between a butcher with a vision and his wife who's a cook – only opened in 2000, but locals already proclaim it "great for free-range and organic" produce; and it's not just for meat – also eggs, home-made pies, and so on. / HOURS Mon-Fri 9am-7pm (Wed early closing), Sat 9am-5pm TUBE Balham.

Meat, game & poultry

The Chatsworth Farm Shop SW1
54-56 Elizabeth St   2–4A
☎ (020) 7730 3033
"The London branch of the Duchess of Devonshire's farm" brings a taste of the country to deepest Belgravia, and it offers "a fresh and unusual variety of game and meat", plus "chicken that tastes the way it ought to"; sausages – including the special recipe which graces their Graces' breakfast table – are also a feature. / HOURS Mon-Fri 10am-6pm, Sat 10am-1pm TUBE Victoria/Sloane Square SEE ALSO Grocers & delicatessens.

City Meat SW10
421 King's Rd   5–3B
☎ (020) 7352 9894
This Chelsea spot is "a small Spanish butcher with a surprisingly wide selection of high-quality meats" (including "well-hung beef"); and is one of the few places in town to seek out for continental cuts; in season, there's a "wide selection of prepared game" too. / HOURS Mon-Sat 7am-6pm CREDIT CARDS no Amex TUBE Fulham Broadway.

Cooksleys Butchers NW7
12 The Broadway   1–1A
☎ (020) 8959 1374   www.cooksleys.com
Everything is free-range at this small, traditional family butcher in Mill Hill, in business for half a century. / HOURS Mon-Sat 8.30am-5pm TUBE Mill Hill East.

Coppin Bros SW17
276 Mitcham Rd   10–2C
☎ (020) 8672 6053
Over a century in business, this Tooting butcher can still prepare such Victorian specialities as a goose stuffed with a chicken stuffed with a pheasant stuffed with a quail; the 21st-century shopper, however, is likely to focus on such attractions as home-cooked meats and the high proportion of organics. / HOURS Tue-Sat 7am-5pm CREDIT CARDS no Amex TUBE Tooting Broadway.

A Dove SW11
71 Northcote Rd   10–2C
☎ (020) 7223 5191
This small but "very busy" Battersea butcher (est 1889) has a big name south of the river for its "classy", all-free-range selection, including "excellent beef", "a wide range of game" and "good home-made pies"; a number of reporters do find shopping here "quite pricey", but few seem to doubt that it's worth it. / HOURS Mon 8am-4pm, Tue-Sat 8am-5.30pm CREDIT CARDS no Amex TUBE BR Clapham Junction.

Meat, game & poultry

Frank Godfrey N5
7 Highbury Pk 8–2D
☎ (020) 7226 2425
"An unequalled range of poultry" is a highlight of the "fabulous" meat selection – mainly free-range, and including some rare breeds – available at this century-old Highbury Park butcher; "slow service" can contribute to a queuing problem at peak times. / HOURS Mon-Fri 8am-6pm, Sat 8am-5pm CREDIT CARDS no Amex TUBE Highbury & Islington.

Freeman's Butchers N8
9 Topsfield Pde 1–1C
☎ (020) 8340 3100
"Good-quality game" is a highlight of the selection at this Crouch End butcher, whose range includes quite a lot of organics; "if they don't stock what you want, they'll order it in for you". / HOURS Mon-Fri 7am-6pm, Sat 7am-5.30pm TUBE Finsbury Park.

Graham's Butchers N2
134 East End Rd 1–1C
☎ (020) 8883 6187
East Finchley is perhaps not the most obvious source of South African meat, but if you're looking for the likes of biltong and boerewors, this is the place (though, for the faint-hearted, organic Scottish beef, and so on, is also available); "very experienced and friendly staff" are on hand to guide those in need of instruction. / HOURS Tue-Fri 8.30am-5.30pm, Sat 8.30am-4pm, Sun 9am-1pm CREDIT CARDS no credit cards TUBE East Finchley SEE ALSO Ethnic shops.

Harrods SW1
87 Brompton Rd 5–1D
☎ (020) 7730 1234 www.harrods.com
The hall of the Knightsbridge store housing the butchery counters is perhaps the most impressive food retail space in London; the "wonderful range of produce" does not let it down – "top prices, but first-class quality". / HOURS Mon, Tue & Sat 10am-6pm, Wed-Fri 10am-7pm SEE ALSO Big Ten; Bread; Cheese & dairy; Chocolates & sweets; Coffee & tea; Cookware; Fish & seafood; Fruit & vegetables; Grocers & delicatessens; Patisserie; Wine.

Hart's of Victoria SW1
39 Tachbrook St 2–4C
☎ (020) 7821 6341
"A good neighbourhood butcher"; "nice, friendly service" helps to distinguish this Pimlico operation, that's been in the same family for a couple of decades; occasional organics. / HOURS Tue-Sat 8.30am-5pm CREDIT CARDS no credit cards TUBE Victoria.

Meat, game & poultry

Harvey Nichols SW1
109-125 Knightsbridge 5–1D
☎ (020) 7235 5000   www.harveynichols.com
"Knowledgeable butchers" who "will prepare special cuts" are one of the attractions of the (quite small) butchery counter of this elevated Knightsbridge food hall. / HOURS Mon, Tue & Sat 10am-7pm, Wed-Fri 10am-8pm, Sun noon-6pm TUBE Knightsbridge SEE ALSO Big Ten; Bread; Fish & seafood; Grocers & delicatessens; Wine.

Hesters SE11
344 Kennington Ln 10–1D
☎ (020) 7735 9121
"A small shop, but a proper butcher"; this "charming" and "unpretentious" Kennington operation, which was established in 1862, wins strong local support for its "top-quality" meat and its "friendly" service; game is a speciality. / HOURS Tue-Sat 7.30am-6pm CREDIT CARDS no credit cards TUBE Vauxhall.

Highgate Butchers N6
76 Highgate High St 1–1C
☎ (020) 8340 9817
"A small, friendly, family business", this self-explanatory outfit offers "good quality and a good selection of game, beef and pork", plus 18 varieties of free-range sausages"; service is "very helpful" too. / HOURS Mon-Fri 7.30am-5.30pm, Sat 7am-5pm CREDIT CARDS no credit cards TUBE Archway.

Husseys E1
64 Wapping Ln 11–1A
☎ (020) 7488 3686
This Wapping butcher – the family also has a greengrocers up the street – has been in business for fifty years, and gets nothing but approval from local reporters; home-cooked hams are something of a feature. / HOURS Mon-Sat 6am-6pm TUBE Wapping.

Jago Butchers SW3
9 Elystan St 5–2C
☎ (020) 7589 5531
If you're looking for a "good, old-fashioned butcher", you won't do much better than this "friendly" Chelsea Green stalwart, in business for half a century; "very good steak" and "great sausages" are particularly approved. / HOURS Mon-Fri 8.30am-5.30pm, Sat 8am-1pm TUBE Sloane Square/South Kensington.

James Elliott N1
96 Essex Rd 8–3D
☎ (020) 7226 3658
"Fine produce and jokes" win much support for this "excellent traditional butchers" in Islington, all aspects of whose operation are unanimously approved by reporters. / HOURS Mon-Sat 6.30am-5.30pm CREDIT CARDS no credit cards TUBE Angel.

Meat, game & poultry   112

Kent & Sons NW8
59 St John's Wood High St   8–3A
☎ (020) 7722 2258   www.kent-butchers.co.uk
The "good variety" of meats, all free-range – plus quite a range of what they call 'kitchen-ready products' – wins universal praise for this St John's Wood butcher. / HOURS Mon-Sat 8am-5.45pm CREDIT CARDS no Amex TUBE St John's Wood.

AA King SW6
30 New Kings Rd   10–1B
☎ (020) 7736 4004
It doesn't attract the same degree of support as the more celebrated Randall's, nearby, but some Parsons Green locals say that this is a "better butcher, and offers better value too". / HOURS Mon-Fri 8am-5.30pm, Sat 8am-4pm CREDIT CARDS no Amex TUBE Parsons Green.

Kingsland W11   ★
140 Portobello Rd   6–2B
☎ (020) 7727 6067
"Be prepared for old-fashioned banter" when you visit this popular Notting Hill butcher, which boasts "every cut of meat you could want" (including a lot from organic herds) and "more awards than you can shake a stick at"; "prices are lower than Lidgates, too". / HOURS Mon-Sat 7.30am-6pm TUBE Notting Hill Gate/Ladbroke Grove.

C Lidgate W11   ★
110 Holland Park Ave   6–2A
☎ (020) 7727 8243
"Awesome quality, and awesomely expensive, but the best in London"; this "outstanding" fourth-generation Holland Park butcher is "always crowded" (and there "are often queues out into the street"), thanks to its "superior organic meat" (often from royal estates), its "superlative pies" and its "fantastic sausages". / HOURS Mon-Sat 7.30am-6pm (Sat 5pm) CREDIT CARDS no Amex TUBE Holland Park SEE ALSO Cheese & dairy.

Macken Bros W4   ★
44 Turnham Green Ter   7–2A
☎ (020) 8994 2646
For its widespread west London fan club, this "knowledgeable" and "really friendly" Chiswick butcher is "London's best by far" and "totally reliable"; the range includes quite a lot of organics. M&C Greengrocers (see also), over the road, is owned by the same people. / HOURS Mon-Fri 7am-6pm, Sat 7am-5.30pm CREDIT CARDS no Amex TUBE Turnham Green.

Meat, game & poultry

Marks & Spencer
☎ (0845) 609 0200 www.marksandspencer.com
BRANCHES AT:
  Locations throughout London
M&S's butchery range attracted surprisingly little survey comment, but such as there was spoke unanimously of "high standards". / HOURS Most stores open Mon-Sat 9am-8pm (central branches open later), Sun noon-6pm SEE ALSO Big Ten; Bread; Cheese & dairy; Fruit & vegetables.

Meat City EC1
507 Central Markets, Farringdon Rd 9–2A
☎ (020) 7253 9606 www.meatcity.uk.com
The proprietor of this Smithfield butcher has something of a self-proclaimed mission: to bring carefully sourced organic fare to the consumer at reasonable prices – aims which reporters find are broadly achieved. / HOURS Mon-Fri 8.30am-6.15pm CREDIT CARDS no Amex TUBE Farringdon.

M Moen & Son SW4
24 The Pavement, Clapham Common 10–1D
☎ (020) 020 7622 1624 www.moen.co.uk
This "old-school but friendly" butcher gets nothing but praise, down Clapham way, for its "excellent meat, game and poultry" (and there's also quite a deli range) – this is a shop which prides itself on offering meat products that are difficult to find elsewhere. / HOURS Mon-Fri 8.30am-6.30pm, Sat 8.30am-5pm CREDIT CARDS no Amex TUBE Clapham Common.

Olympia Butchers W14
70 Blythe Rd 7–1C
☎ (020) 7602 4843
"Quality meat" and "friendly service" make this 40-year-old firm something of a find. / HOURS Wed-Fri 7.30am-6.30pm, Sat 6.30am-7.30pm CREDIT CARDS no Amex TUBE Olympia.

Organic World TW10
23 Friars Stile Rd, Richmond 1–4A
☎ (020) 8940 0414
A dozen years old (but trading as the Natural Meat Company for the first ten), this Richmond butcher offers exclusively organic meat, often from rare breeds, and also fish; it generated little survey commentary, to the effect that it's "pricey, but offers great quality". / HOURS Mon-Sat 7.30am-5.30pm CREDIT CARDS no Amex TUBE Richmond.

Pethers TW9
16 Station Pde, Kew 1–4A
☎ (020) 8940 0163
A "good local butcher" in Kew, whose range includes quite a large free-range element; "delicious home-made sausages are especially approved", and they do lots of deli-type items too, such as pies and spit-roasted chickens. / HOURS Mon-Fri 7.30am-6.30pm, Sat 7.30am-5pm CREDIT CARDS no Amex TUBE Kew Gardens.

Meat, game & poultry

Porterford Meats EC4
6 Bow Ln 9–2B
☎ (020) 7248 1396
Quite a find in the heart of the City (near St Mary-le-Bow), this "cramped" but welcoming shop is a "very fine", "classic" butchers (complete with "old-fashioned courtesy"); "excellent sausages", in flavours conventional and modern, are a highlight, and there's also quite a range of pre-prepared dinner-party dishes; also exotic meats. / HOURS Mon-Thu 6.30am-6.30pm, Fri 6.30am-7.30pm CREDIT CARDS no Amex TUBE Mansion House.

Portwine & Son WC2
24 Earlham St 4–2B
☎ (020) 7836 2353
"They'll tell me what to buy, how to cook it and what wine to drink too!"; you certainly don't want for service at this "consistently good" and "knowledgeable Covent Garden-fringe butcher, which was established in 1760, and claims to be the capital's oldest; "excellent meat" is a theme of many reports. / HOURS Mon & Sat 7.30am-2pm, Tue-Thu 7.30am-5pm, Fri 7.30am-5.30pm TUBE Leicester Square.

Randall's Butchers SW6
113 Wandsworth Bridge Rd 10–1B
☎ (020) 7736 3426
"Exceptional meat and super service" make a winning combination for this "great" Fulham butcher; it's "simply the best" for many reporters (even if you do need to take out a "small mortgage" for some of their organic selections); cheese and cookbooks are also available. / HOURS Mon-Fri 7am-5.30pm, Sat 7am-4.30pm CREDIT CARDS no Amex TUBE Fulham Broadway.

Richardson's W13
88 Northfield Ave 1–2A
☎ (020) 8567 1064
"Queues outside on a Saturday morning" attest to the popularity of this Barnes butcher; some reporters single out the "home-prepared cooked meats" for particular praise, but "very good beef" and "the best sausages" also find approval. / HOURS Mon-Sat 8am-5.30pm CREDIT CARDS no Amex TUBE Northfields.

Robert Edwards SW19
19 Leopold Rd 10–2B
☎ (020) 8946 5834
This Wimbledon butcher is pricey by local standards, but local reporters reckon it's "worth it" for the "excellent meat" and "good service" too. / HOURS Mon-Fri 7am-5pm, Sat 7am-3.30pm TUBE Wimbledon.

Meat, game & poultry

Sainsbury's
☎ (0845) 301 2020 www.sainsburys.com
BRANCHES AT:
Locations throughout London
"A great selection of organic meat" (larger stores only), is the highlight of Sainsbury's butchery range; overall, the shops attracted only a modest level of survey commentary, though it was mainly complimentary. / HOURS Some larger stores 24 hours SEE ALSO Big Ten; Bread; Cheese & dairy; Fish & seafood; Fruit & vegetables; Health & organic foods; Herbs & spices; Wine.

Sandy's Fishmongers TW1
56 King St, Twickenham 1–4A
☎ (020) 8892 5788 www.sandysfish.net
Don't be fooled by the name – "excellent poultry and game, as well as fish" commend this old-style Twickenham 'fishmonger and poultryman'. / HOURS Mon-Sat 7.30am-6pm TUBE BR Twickenham SEE ALSO Fish & seafood.

J Seal SW13
7 Barnes High St 10–1A
☎ (020) 8876 5118
"Very competent" standards characterise this popular Barnes butcher, for which the queue *"sometimes stretches down the street"*. / HOURS Mon & Tue 6.30am-5.30pm, Wed 6.30am-1pm, Sat 6.30am-4pm CREDIT CARDS no Amex TUBE BR Barnes.

Selfridges W1
400 Oxford St 3–1A
☎ (020) 7629 1234 www.selfridges.co.uk
Lots of positive survey ratings but little in the way of explanation from reporters as to why they like the butchery section of London's favourite food hall – the usual combination of quality and range, presumably? / HOURS Mon-Fri 10am-8pm, Sat 9.30am-8pm, Sun noon-6pm TUBE Bond Street SEE ALSO Big Ten; Bread; Cheese & dairy; Chocolates & sweets; Cookware; Ethnic shops; Fish & seafood; Fruit & vegetables; Grocers & delicatessens; Herbs & spices; Wine.

Simply Sausages EC1
Harts Corner, 341 Central Markets, Farringdon St 9–2A
☎ (020) 7329 3227
"Still the leader in gourmet sausages", this authentically-located (fringe-of-Smithfield) operation was *"one of the original banger revivalists"*; it offers an *"excellent variety"* of some two dozen recipes, *"including flavours of the month"*, and, perhaps rather surprisingly, *"a good veggie selection"*. / HOURS Mon-Fri 8am-6pm, Sat 9.30am-2.30pm CREDIT CARDS no Amex TUBE Farringdon.

Meat, game & poultry

Smithfield Market EC1 ★
Charterhouse St   9–2A
☎ (020) 7248 3151
"Can't be bettered in price or quality, but you need to get there early"; London's historic meat market – 800 years old, and the only one of the capital's trade markets still on its original site – is as open to the discerning retail customer as it is to the restaurants and butchers which account for most of its trade; thanks to the local licensing laws, you can finish your expedition with a refreshing pint (plus meaty breakfast), in one of the nearby pubs. / HOURS Mon-Fri approx 4.30am-noon
TUBE Farringdon/Barbican   SEE ALSO Markets.

GG Sparkes SE3 ★
24 Old Dover Rd   1–3D
☎ (020) 8355 8597
www.ggsparkesorganicbutchers.com
"Meat like it used to taste" and "very good service" make this "fine butcher" – in business for half a century, and mainly organic for the past decade – very popular down Blackheath way; "organic eggs and delicatessen items" are also commended. / HOURS Mon, Tue, Thu & Fri 8.30am-5.30pm, Sat 8am-5pm
TUBE BR Blackheath.

JA Steele NW3 ★
8 Flask Walk   8–1A
☎ (020) 7435 3587
"Fabulous quality meat, poultry and game" commend this family-run (and "family-orientated") Hampstead butchers to all who comment on them. / HOURS Mon-Thu 7.30am-5pm, Fri 7am-5pm, Sat 7am-4.30pm   TUBE Hampstead.

Stenton Family Butcher W6 ☆
55 Aldensley Rd   7–1C
☎ (020) 8748 6121
"First-class organic meats of outstanding quality" – and from a wide range of suppliers – are a highlight of the range at this "very friendly", family-owned butchers, in the heart of 'Brackenbury Village'. / HOURS Tue-Sat 8am-6.30pm (Thu till 1pm).

Thorogoods W13
113 Northfield Ave   1–2A
☎ (020) 8567 0339
"Good-value organic meat" – including "orgasmic chicken", apparently – is the star attraction at this "helpful" Barnes butcher. / HOURS Tue-Sat 8am-5pm   CREDIT CARDS no credit cards
TUBE Northfields/West Ealing.

Meat, game & poultry

Waitrose S) 🚚 ★
☎ (01344) 424680 Customer service
🖱 www.waitrose.com
BRANCHES AT:
  Locations throughout London
"For the price, very good"; reporters are very positive about Waitrose's meat range – both pre-packed, and from the counters – and its *"skilled"* and *"always helpful"* staff. / HOURS Hours vary: generally Mon-Sat 8.30am-9pm, Sun 11am-5pm
SEE ALSO Big Ten; Bread; Cheese & dairy; Fish & seafood; Fruit & vegetables; Health & organic foods; Herbs & spices; Wine.

HG Walter W14 ☀) 🚚 ★
51 Palliser Rd   7–2C
☎ (020) 7385 6466
"The best butcher in town, and with more smiles than Coco the clown" – fans do not stint in their praise of this shop near Barons Court tube, whose *"good selection"* of organic meats inspires a high degree of satisfaction; *"great sausages"*, too. / HOURS Mon-Fri 8am-7pm, Sat 8am-5.30pm TUBE Barons Court.

MAIL ORDER

Donald Russell AB51 📬 ☆
Harlaw Rd, Inverurie, Aberdeenshire
☎ (01467) 629666 🖱 www.donaldrussell.co.uk
"Fantastic beef" (hung for three weeks) and *"very efficient service"* are among the plusses reported in buying from this Scottish supplier, which is a major supplier to the top end of the restaurant trade; also Scottish seafood. / CREDIT CARDS no Amex.

Heal Farm EX37 📬
Kings Nympton, Umberleigh, North Devon
☎ (01769) 574341 🖱 www.healfarm.co.uk
Meat and poultry produced in 'high welfare' conditions have been the rule at this North Devon farm for over a quarter of a century; their produce is now available from an easy-to-use website; also other local specialities, such as clotted cream.

Northfield Farm LE15 📬
Whissendine Lane, Cold Overton, Rutland
☎ Mail order (01664) 474271 🖱 www.northfieldfarm.com
Naturally-reared beef, lamb and pork (plus game, geese and turkeys) – if you can't get to their 'cage' in Borough Market, you can place a phone order directly with the farm. / HOURS see Borough Market for stall hours

The Pure Meat Company PL15 📬
Home Place Farm, Northcott, Launceston, Cornwall
☎ (01409) 211127 🖱 www.puremeatdirectonline.co.uk
An online supplier of organic and additive-free meat; the range stretches all the way from standard pre-selected packs to such esoteric delights as a five-bird roast. / CREDIT CARDS no Amex.

Meat, game & poultry

Richard Woodall LA19
Lane End, Waberthwaite, Cumbria
☎ (01229) 717237 ◦ www.richardwoodall.co.uk
Her Majesty's supplier of Traditional Cumberland Sausage is a family firm in business for over half a century; from their website, you can also order hams and home-cured bacon. / CREDIT CARDS no Amex.

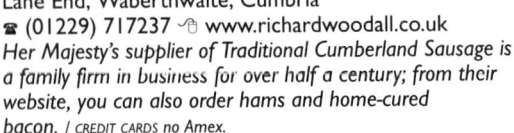

Seldom Seen Farm LE7
Billesdon, Leicester, Leicestershire
☎ (01162) 596742
Geese – especially for Christmas – are the speciality of this farm near Rugby, the majority of whose output ends up in London and the Home Counties; three-bird (goose, chicken and pheasant) roasts are a speciality of which they apparently sell upwards of a thousand a year; customers wishing to check out the produce can visit the company's stall at Borough Market. / CREDIT CARDS no credit cards.

Swaddles Green Farm TA20 ★
Hare Lane, Buckland St Mary, Chard, Somerset
☎ (01460) 234387 ◦ www.swaddles.co.uk
"Great organic meat that's always delivered on time" wins enthusiastic support for this pioneer among out-of-town meat suppliers, which offers a wide range, (including "great ready-made dishes"); some, though, can't help noting that goods from here are "enormously expensive".

15. Pâtisserie

When it comes to quality cakes, tarts and pastries, reporters are pretty evenly divided in their support between the more modern operators and the traditionalists (whose roots go back half a century or more). It's approriate that, standing well clear of the rest of the field, reporters' top two choices – Pâtisserie Valerie (which claims to have brought the croissant to London in the '30s) and Maison Blanc (a chain established, in Oxford, in 1979) – include one representative from each camp.

The ten most commented-upon suppliers were:

1 Pâtisserie Valerie ★

2 Maison Blanc ★

3 Paul ★

4 Baker & Spice ★

5 Konditor & Cook ★

6 Maison Bertaux ★

7 Louis Patisserie

8 Harrods ★

9= &Clarke's ★

9= Lisboa Patisserie ★

Amato W1
14 Old Compton St 4–2A
☎ (020) 7734 5733 www.amato.co.uk
It's perhaps better known for an eat-in coffee and a cake, but this Soho pâtisserie is praised for the take-away possibilities of its "gorgeous tarts and gâteaux", both French and Italian. / HOURS Mon-Sat 8am-10pm, Sun 10am-8pm TUBE Tottenham Court Road/Leicester Square.

Bagatelle Boutique SW7
44 Harrington Rd 5–2B
☎ (020) 7581 1551 www.bagatelle.co.uk
Perhaps this Gallic pâtisserie in South Kensington is just a touch too authentic – fans say its "beautiful" and "elegant" products offer "a taste of Paris", but some also find them a touch "conventional". / HOURS Mon-Sat 8am-8pm, Sun 8am-6pm TUBE South Kensington SEE ALSO Bread.

Patisserie

120

Baker & Spice

BRANCHES AT:
46 Walton St, SW3   5–1D
☎ (020) 7589 4734
75 Salusbury Rd, NW6   1–2B
☎ (020) 7604 3636

"Nirvana in a pain au chocolat" is the sort of experience which wins universal praise from reporters for the "absolutely decadent" pâtisserie of this famous Knightsbridge bakery; "fantastic fruit tarts" are a further highlight of its "expensive but wonderful" range. / HOURS Mon-Sat 7am-7pm (NW6 Mon-Fri 7am-8pm), Sun 8.30am-2pm CREDIT CARDS no Amex SEE ALSO Bread.

Botticelli SW13

74 Church Rd, The Blue Door Yd   10–1A
☎ (020) 87414230

"Delectable flans and pastries" are hailed at this "tiny" Barnes pâtisserie – it's mainly a trade supplier, accounting for the rather limited opening times. / HOURS Fri & Sat 9.30am-4.30pm CREDIT CARDS no credit cards TUBE Hammersmith/BR Barnes.

Café Mozart N6

17 Swains Ln   8–1B
☎ (020) 8348 1384

"Authentic Austrian pastries" – no mean claim, given that the correct term for what we call French pastry is 'viennoiserie' – are the highlight at this café-cum-pâtisserie by Hampstead Heath. / HOURS Mon-Sun 9am-10pm CREDIT CARDS no Amex
TUBE Archway/Kentish Town.

&Clarke's W8

122 Kensington Church St   6–2B
☎ (020) 7229 2190   www.sallyclarke.com

Sally Clarke's Kensington bakery is much better known for bread, but its "terrific tarts, both sweet and savoury" have quite a following in their own right. / HOURS Mon-Fri 8am-8pm, Sat 9am-4pm TUBE Notting Hill Gate SEE ALSO Bread; Cheese & dairy; Chocolates & sweets.

Euphorium Bakery N1

202 Upper St   8–2D
☎ (020) 7704 6905

"A limited range, but super" – the "best croissants in town" are a highlight of the "excellent" pâtisserie range on offer at this modernistic Islington bakery. / HOURS Mon-Fri 7am-7pm, Sat 8am-6pm, Sun 9am-3.30pm CREDIT CARDS no Amex TUBE Highbury & Islington SEE ALSO Bread.

Fileric SW7

57 Old Brompton Rd   5–2C
☎ (020) 7584 2967

"Excellent croissants" are a highlight of the "quality pâtisserie" on offer at this modestly furnished South Kensington cake and coffee shop. / HOURS Mon-Sat 8am-8pm, Sun 9am-8pm TUBE South Kensington.

Patisserie

Flâneur EC1
41 Farringdon Rd   9–1A
☎ (020) 7404 4422
"Very good tarts and cakes" are a particular highlight at this attractive new Farringdon food hall. / HOURS Mon-Fri 8am-10pm, Sat 9am-10pm, Sun 9am-6pm TUBE Farringdon SEE ALSO Grocers & delicatessens.

Fortnum & Mason W1
181 Piccadilly   3–3D
☎ (020) 7734 8040   www.fortnumandmason.co.uk
The famous St James's store's *"small but perfectly formed"* pâtisserie counter has a similarly small-scale following among reporters; almost all of them, however, speak in terms of the *"excellence"* of its range. / HOURS Mon-Sat 10am-6.30pm TUBE Piccadilly Circus/Green Park SEE ALSO Big Ten; Chocolates & sweets; Coffee & tea; Grocers & delicatessens; Wine.

Frankonia SW19
79 High St   10–2B
☎ (020) 8947 9911
"Delicious tarts and cakes" are a highlight at this *"great German bakery"* (and delicatessen), in Wimbledon. / HOURS Mon-Fri 9am-6pm, Sat 8.30am-6pm, Sun 10am-5pm TUBE Wimbledon.

Harrods SW1
87 Brompton Rd   5–1D
☎ (020) 7730 1234   www.harrods.com
"Amazing, freshly-made cakes" – in the profusion of styles which is the hallmark of this landmark Knightsbridge store – make its pâtisserie counters a destination of some note in their own right. / HOURS Mon, Tue & Sat 10am-6pm, Wed-Fri 10am-7pm SEE ALSO Big Ten; Bread; Cheese & dairy; Chocolates & sweets; Coffee & tea; Cookware; Fish & seafood; Fruit & vegetables; Grocers & delicatessens; Meat, game & poultry; Wine.

Jane Asher Party Cakes SW3
22-24 Cale St   5–2C
☎ (020) 7584 6177   www.jane-asher.co.uk
If you're celebrating something special, and are looking for a baker that's *"full of ideas"*, check out this bespoke party cake-maker in Chelsea; absolutely everything is made to order – they have no cakes for sale on spec; the adjoining shop offers every cake-making and decorating aid you could ever want. / HOURS Mon-Sat 9.30am-5.30pm TUBE Sloane Square/South Kensington.

Kastner & Ovens WC2
52 Floral St   4–2D
☎ (020) 7836 2700
A *"fantastic selection of cakes and biscuits"* is to be found in the Tardis-like setting of this recently-opened shop by the Royal Opera House; their range is really designed for putting together a quick and easy lunch – perhaps some quiche and a slice of exotic cheesecake. / HOURS Mon-Fri 8am-5pm CREDIT CARDS no credit cards TUBE Covent Garden.

Patisserie

Konditor & Cook ☀ ☽ ★
BRANCHES AT:
66 The Cut, SE1   9–4A
☎ (020) 7261 0465
22 Cornwall Rd, SE1   9–4A
☎ (020) 7261 0456
10 Stoney St, SE1   9–4C
☎ (020) 7407 5100

"Traditional" cakes with an "inventive" (or even "camp") twist have made a big name for this string of trendy South Bank bakeries. / HOURS Mon-Fri 7.30am-6.30pm, Sat 8.30am-2.30pm; The Cut Mon-Fri 8.30am-11pm, Sat 10.30am-11pm SEE ALSO Bread.

Lisboa Patisserie W10 ☕ S ☀ ☽ ★
57 Golborne Rd   6–1A
☎ (020) 8968 5242

"Custard tarts sold by the thousands" – "the cheapest and the best" – have made a heady reputation for this inauspicious-looking Portuguese cake and coffee shop, in North Kensington; "hot from the oven, from 8am onwards, is best". / HOURS Mon-Sun 8am-8pm TUBE Ladbroke Grove.

Louis Patisserie NW3 ☕ S
32 Heath St   8–1A
☎ (020) 7435 9908

This crowded, Hungarian-owned Hampstead pâtisserie and tearoom has been packing 'em in for 40 years; "the bread and pastries aren't bad" but its cosy ambience is much of its appeal. / HOURS Mon-Sun 9am-6pm TUBE Hampstead.

Maison Bertaux W1 ☕ S ☽ ★
28 Greek St   4–2A
☎ (020) 7437 6007

London's oldest pâtisserie-cum-coffee shop (est 1871) occupies characterful Soho premises, and has a wide fan club for its "terrific" cakes and pastries; the house speciality – 'croque-en-bouche' profiterole towers – can be seen in the window display. / HOURS Mon-Sat 8.30am-9pm, Sun 9am-8.30pm CREDIT CARDS no credit cards TUBE Leicester Square.

Patisserie

Maison Blanc S★
⌐ www.maisonblanc.co.uk
BRANCHES AT:
62 Hampstead High St, NW3   8–2A
☎ (020) 7431 8338
37 St John's Wood High St, NW8   8–3A
☎ (020) 7586 1982
303 Fulham Rd, SW10   5–3B
☎ (020) 7795 2663
11 Elystan St, SW3   5–2C
☎ (020) 7584 6913
102 Holland Park Ave, W11   6–2A
☎ (020) 7221 2494
7 Thayer St, W1   2–1A
☎ (020) 7224 0228
26 Turnham Green Terr, W4   7–2A
☎ (020) 8995 7220
7a Kensington Church St, W8   5–1A
☎ (020) 7937 4767

A "wide choice" of "fabulous", "inventive" and "elegantly presented" French pâtisserie" makes this growing chain a big hit with reporters; "exquisite lemon tarts" win particular praise. / HOURS *usual hours Mon-Sat 8am-7pm (SW3 5.30pm), Sun 9am-6pm (SW3 3.30pm)* CREDIT CARDS *no Amex* SEE ALSO *Bread; Chocolates & sweets.*

Patisserie Bliss EC1 ☕ S 🌅 ☆
428 St John St   8–3D
☎ (020) 7837 3720

Does this inauspicious-looking Islington bakery offer "the best croissants this side of Paris"? – there's certainly a vocal local fan club to that effect, and the other pastries ("both sweet and savoury") are also approved. / HOURS *Mon-Fri 8am-6pm, Sat 9am-6pm, Sun 9am-4pm* CREDIT CARDS *no credit cards* TUBE *Angel.*

Pâtisserie Valerie S 🌅 ☽ ★
⌐ www.patisserie-valerie.co.uk
BRANCHES AT:
105 Marylebone High St, W1   2–1A
☎ (020) 7935 6240
44 Old Compton St, W1   4–2A
☎ (020) 7437 3466
8 Russell St, WC2   4–3D
☎ (020) 7240 0064
215 Brompton Rd, SW3   5–2C
☎ (020) 7823 9971

"An institution much copied but never bettered" – this "naughty, but really nice", "ultra-consistent" Gallic pâtisserie chain has a huge following for "cakes that are a work of art to look at and taste divine"; the original Soho branch claims to have introduced croissants to England, and they still win many votes as "the best in town". / HOURS *Times vary, but generally open by 7.30am until early evening*

Patisserie

Paul   S ☀ ☾ ★
BRANCHES AT:
   115 Marylebone High St, W1   2–1A
   29 Bedford St, WC2   4–3C
   ☎ (020) 7836 3304
Covent Garden's "real French bakery", now with a branch in Marylebone, has – rightly, in our view – a fractionally bigger name with reporters for its "gorgeous tarts and pastries" than it has for its bread. / HOURS *WC2 Mon-Fri 7.30am-9pm, Sat & Sun 9am-9pm; W1 still to open as we go to press* SEE ALSO *Bread.*

Pierre Pechon   S ☀ ☾
BRANCHES AT:
   127 Queensway, W2   6–2C
   ☎ (020) 7229 0746
   4 Chepstow Rd, W2   6–1B
   ☎ (020) 7229 5289
   27 Kensington Church St, W8   5–1A
   ☎ (020) 7937 9574
They've "been there for ever" (well, the original has been around since 1925 anyway), and this small chain of Kensington and Bayswater pâtisseries remains a "dependable" and "unfussy" choice for "unbeatable butter croissants" and the like; continental-style celebration cakes are something of a speciality. / HOURS *W2 Sun-Wed 7am-7pm, Thu-Sat 7am-8pm; W8 shorter hours* SEE ALSO *Bread.*

16. Wine

'Connoisseurship' in England is a term still perhaps more likely to be associated with wine than with food. London, as a – some would say *the* – great centre of the world wine trade, has a huge variety of merchants offering 'strength in depth'. Is there any area of food supply of which the same could truly be said?

The wine merchants that reporters comment on are an interesting mixture of chains and supermarkets on the one hand and the specialist operators on the other. Reporters are generally quite satisfied with the better high street multiples, but as the 'stars' of the list confirm, for real quality you just can't beat the independents. The top ten most commented on by reporters were:

1. Oddbins
2. Majestic Wine
3. Nicolas
4. Berry Bros. & Rudd ★
5. Lea & Sandeman ★
6. Waitrose
7. The Wine Society (mail order) ★
8= Jeroboams ★
8= Bibendum Wines (mail order) ★
10 Handford ★

Berry Bros. & Rudd SW1 ★
3 St James's St   3–4D
☎ (020) 7396 9600   www.bbr.com
"The best all-round merchant" (and by quite a margin), the "grande dame" of the London wine scene – established in 1698 – wows reporters with its "stunning selection of fine wines", its "very knowledgeable staff" and its "old-fashioned courtesy and quality"; the list is wide-ranging (with a leaning to the Old World) but "whether you spend £5 or £500, you can expect the highest standards"; bbr.com – the company's web-based service – has quite a following in its own right. / HOURS Mon-Fri 9am-5.30pm, Sat 10am-4pm TUBE Green Park SEE ALSO Coffee & tea.

Bottoms Up
www.bottomsup.co.uk
BRANCHES AT:
   Locations throughout London
Supporters say the range is "full of surprises", but reports on the upmarket end of the First Quench group (which also owns Victoria Wine and Threshers) were quite thin on the ground. / HOURS Hours vary: generally Mon-Sat 10am-10pm, Sun noon-9pm.

Wine

Corney & Barrow W11
194 Kensington Park Rd 6–1A
☎ (020) 7221 5122 www.corneyandbarrow.com
"Old-fashioned service" and *"informative and friendly advice"* are oft-commented-on virtues of this By Appointment merchant, established in 1780; the Notting Hill shop attracted most attention from reporters – if you're looking for Old World bottles with a bit of age, it's a browsers' delight. / HOURS Mon-Sat 10.30am-9pm.

Davy's SE10
161-165 Greenwich High Rd 1–3D
☎ (020) 8858 6014
It is rather *"out of the way"* (in distant Greenwich), which perhaps explains why this famous wine bar chain's sole retail outlet is relatively little known; fans say it's an *"atmospheric"* place though (suitably housed in a cellar), and it attracts praise for its *"good range at the top and bottom of the market"* – the former comprises the Davy's house selections, the latter an extensive range strong in claret, port and Madeira. / HOURS Mon-Fri 10am-7pm, Sat 10am-5pm TUBE Greenwich BR.

Farr Vintners SW1
19 Sussex St 2–4B
☎ (020) 7821 2000 www.farr-vintners.com
Presumably it's the £500 minimum order which discourages a wider range of reports on this discreet Pimlico 'shop', which is in fact a 'front' for the UK's largest wine broker (whose wine turnover is four times that of Sotheby's and Christie's combined!); one fan who is prepared to pay the 'entry fee' exalts in the *"fantastic list"*, and at *"good prices"* too. / HOURS Mon-Fri 9am-6pm.

Fortnum & Mason W1
181 Piccadilly 3–3D
☎ (020) 7734 8040 www.fortnumandmason.co.uk
Given that the famous St James's store offers a *"wonderful selection of the best wines"* it attracted remarkably little attention from reporters; if you're looking for something rare and special, though – perhaps an unusual spirit or a difficult-to-find vintage of claret or Burgundy – their list is well worth checking out; gift business is something of a speciality. / HOURS Mon-Sat 10am-6.30pm TUBE Piccadilly Circus/Green Park SEE ALSO Big Ten; Chocolates & sweets; Coffee & tea; Grocers & delicatessens; Patisserie.

Friarwood SW6
26 New Kings Rd 10–1B
☎ (020) 7736 2628 www.friarwood.com
A *"good selection"* – *"ranging from very pricey to perfectly affordable"* – and *"excellent service and delivery"* makes this Parsons Green shop a consistently popular local recommendation. / HOURS Mon-Sat 10am-7pm.

Wine

Gerry's W1
74 Old Compton St   4–3A
☎ (020) 7734 4215
*It's the "amazing selection of spirits and liqueurs" –
150 vodkas, 50 rums and 40 tequilas, for example – which
leads people from all over the UK (and even abroad,
apparently) to seek out this extraordinary Soho shop; if you're
looking for an array of intriguing bottles for your new bar, this is
the place.* / HOURS Mon-Fri 9am-6.30pm, Sat 9am-5.30pm CREDIT CARDS no credit cards TUBE Piccadilly Circus.

The Grape Shop SW11
135 Northcote Rd   10–2C
☎ (020) 7924 3638
*"Very friendly and knowledgeable staff" and a "good range of
wines and prices" are among the features which endear this
enthusiastically-run Battersea shop to locals; France provides
the backbone of the stock, which, says the management,
is chosen with an emphasis on readiness for
drinking.* / HOURS Mon-Sat 10.30am-9pm, Sun 11.30am-2pm TUBE BR Clapham Junction.

The Grogblossom NW6
253 West End Ln   1–1B
☎ (020) 7794 7808
*"Good, independent wine merchants" don't seem to come
much more popular than Paul O'Connor's "friendly and
welcoming local shop", where "dessert wines are something of
a speciality".* / HOURS Mon-Thu 4pm-10pm, Fri-Sun noon-10pm TUBE West Hampstead.

Handford W11
12 Portland Rd   6–2A
☎ (020) 7221 9614
*James Handford MW may have the appearance of being
a "small" operator, but his "exceptionally helpful" and
"knowledgeable" service helps make his "very personal"
Holland Park outlet the only one-shop operation to make it into
reporters' top ten – a visit to the impressively wide-ranging and
easy-to-use website (which can accept orders) helps one
understand why.* / HOURS Mon-Sat 10am-8.30pm.

Harrods SW1
87 Brompton Rd   5–1D
☎ (020) 7730 1234   www.harrods.com
*The wine department of the 'Knightsbridge grocer' offers
"a very wide selection of French wines" (not to mention many
other choice champagnes, wines and spirits) and "very helpful"
service; like all the department store wine outlets, however,
it attracted surprisingly little commentary from
reporters.* / HOURS Mon, Tue & Sat 10am-6pm, Wed-Fri 10am-7pm SEE ALSO Big Ten; Bread; Cheese & dairy; Chocolates & sweets; Coffee & tea; Cookware; Fish & seafood; Fruit & vegetables; Grocers & delicatessens; Meat, game & poultry; Patisserie.

Wine

Harvey Nichols SW1
109-125 Knightsbridge 5–1D
☎ (020) 7235 5000 www.harveynichols.com
The comments on Harrods (see previous entry) are all equally applicable to this more modernistic wine hall – there is a similar inconsistency between the positive nature of the commentary, and the low apparent level of patronage by reporters; the stock emphasis here is more Italian and New World than up the road. / HOURS *Mon, Tue & Sat 10am-7pm, Wed-Fri 10am-8pm, Sun noon-6pm* TUBE *Knightsbridge* SEE ALSO *Big Ten; Bread; Fish & seafood; Grocers & delicatessens; Meat, game & poultry.*

Haynes Hanson & Clark SW1
25 Eccleston St 2–4B
☎ (020) 7259 0102
This "small" and "personal" Belgravia corner shop is the public face of an enterprise (established in 1978) that's quite a big noise in the Burgundy world and does most of its business from its list (which also includes Bordeaux, and some top-end Kiwis); though not hugely commented on, the shop was unanimously praised by reporters, in particular for its "good value". / HOURS *Mon-Fri 9am-7pm.*

Jeroboams
 www.jeroboams.co.uk
BRANCHES AT:
  6 Pont St, SW1
  ☎ (020) 7235 1612
  50-52 Elizabeth St, SW1
  ☎ (020) 7730 8108
  20 Davies St, W1
  ☎ (020) 7499 1015
  77-78 Chancery Ln, WC2 2–1D
  ☎ (020) 4705 0552
These smart shops allied to the delicatessens of the same name offer a "quality selection" of vintages (with an Old World preponderance, plus a "careful selection" from the New); "knowledgeable" and "helpful" service is often praised. / HOURS *Mon-Fri all shops open at least 10am-6.30pm; Sat Elizabeth St 10am-4pm, Pont St 10am-7pm.*

Justerini & Brooks SW1
61 St James's St 3–4D
☎ (020) 7493 8721
Why does this augustly-housed St James's merchant attract so little commentary? – it was mentioned by only a tenth as many reporters as Berry Bros. (sited across the road, and similarly graced with a brace of royal warrants), yet such few reports as there were unanimously speak of a "great 'Old' list", "very helpful service" and "good prices". / HOURS *Mon-Fri 9am-7pm* TUBE *Piccadilly Circus/Green Park.*

Wine

Lea & Sandeman 📧 ☾ ★
🌐 www.londonfinewine.co.uk
BRANCHES AT:
 170 Fulham Rd, SW10   5–3B
 ☎ (020) 7244 0522
 211 Kensington Church St, W8   6–2B
 ☎ (020) 7221 1982
 206 Haverstock Hill, NW3   8–2A
 ☎ (020) 7431 4412
 51 Barnes High St, SW13   10–1A
 ☎ (020) 8878 8643
This "adventurous" chain (established in 1988) is some way behind Berry Bros. in terms of volume of commentary, but snapping at its heels in terms of quality; "good, personal service" is much praised, but the highlight is the "wonderful" range, in which Italy is a highlight – "some expensive wines, but some very affordable ones too". / HOURS Mon-Sat 10am-8pm.

Majestic Wine Warehouses   📧 Ⓢ ☾
☎ (020) 7485 0478 🌐 www.majestic.co.uk
BRANCHES AT:
 Locations throughout London
Some reporters do find it "irritating" to have to buy at least a dozen bottles at a time, but many find ample compensation in the "broad range" ("good for all but the priciest wines"), good quality and "friendly and knowledgeable" service of the capital's most popular wine warehouse chain by far. / HOURS Mon-Sat 10am-8pm, Sun 10am-5pm.

Nicolas   ☾ 🚚
🌐 www.nicolas-wines.com
BRANCHES AT:
 Locations throughout London
"Helpful and knowledgeable staff" are a much-commented-on plus of shopping at the London outlets of France's biggest multiple merchant (established in Paris in 1822); no surprise that the list is "mainly French", but there's a rare dichotomy in reporters comments on pricing – some find the selection "a bit pricey", whereas others note it as "particularly good for simple or budget wines". / HOURS Mon-Fri 10am-7.30pm, Sat 11am-6pm.

Oddbins   ☾ 🚚
☎ (0800) 328 2323 🌐 www.oddbins.com
BRANCHES AT:
 Locations throughout London
"Good selection, good prices, generally high quality" – the attractions which have made omnipresent Oddbins the default choice for London's wine-buyers are well-known; the reporter who pronounced them "infinitely better than other 'high street' wine merchants" had the support of many. / HOURS Hours vary: generally Mon-Sat 10am-8pm (central branches open later, some open Sun).

Wine

Philglas & Swiggot SW11
21 Northcote Rd   10–2C
☎ (020) 7924 4494
Mike and Karen Rogers's Battersea wine shop must be doing something right, as it was trebling in size as we went to press; "they clearly care about what they sell" – in recent years, this had included Australian and Italian selections of unusual depth, but France is apparently to get first call on some of the new space. / HOURS Mon-Sat 11am-7.30pm, Sun noon-5pm   TUBE BR Clapham Junction.

La Reserve
www.la-reserve.co.uk
BRANCHES AT:
56 Walton St, SW3   5–1D
☎ (020) 7589 2020
29 Heath St, NW3   8–1A
☎ (020) 7435 6845
"Very knowledgeable staff who obviously have a taste for their great stock" win a small but vociferous following for these Chelsea and Hampstead merchants; France is the backbone of the list – in particular, "they know their Burgundies backwards". / HOURS SW3 Mon-Fri 9.30am-9pm, Sat 9.30am-6pm; NW3 Mon-Sat 10am-8pm, Sun noon-3pm.

Roberson W14
348 Kensington High St   7–1D
☎ (020) 7371 2121
"A good range of fine wines" makes this "friendly" merchant – which has unusually spacious and well laid out premises, at the Olympia end of Kensington – a consistently popular recommendation. / HOURS Mon-Sat 10am-8pm.

Sainsbury's
☎ (0845) 301 2020   www.sainsburys.com
BRANCHES AT:
Locations throughout London
"Good-value offers and knowledgeable staff" – Sainsbury's wine and spirit 'offer' (as they say in the trade) attracts consistently positive reports, although not in great numbers. / HOURS Some larger stores 24 hours   SEE ALSO Big Ten; Bread; Cheese & dairy; Fish & seafood; Fruit & vegetables; Health & organic foods; Herbs & spices; Meat, game & poultry.

Selfridges W1
400 Oxford St   3–1A
☎ (020) 7629 1234   www.selfridges.co.uk
"Many rare bottles" add interest to a visit to the (surprisingly thinly commented-on) wine section of Londoners' most commented-on food hall; when it comes to more everyday drinking, Italy and Spain are highlights, and "knowledgeable staff" are praised for their "good guidance". / HOURS Mon-Fri 10am-8pm, Sat 9.30am-8pm, Sun noon-6pm   TUBE Bond Street   SEE ALSO Big Ten; Bread; Cheese & dairy; Chocolates & sweets; Cookware; Ethnic shops; Fish & seafood; Fruit & vegetables; Grocers & delicatessens; Herbs & spices; Meat, game & poultry.

Wine

The Soho Wine Company W1
18 Percy St   2–1C
☎ (020) 7636 8490
A "wonderful imported vodka selection" (plus liqueurs and other spirits in profusion) and "helpful" staff are among the attractions of this old Soho merchant, which decamped over the Oxford Street divide in 1977; on the wine front, they offer quite a range, with France the linchpin. / HOURS Mon-Fri 9am-7pm (Thu 7.30pm), Sat 9am-6pm TUBE Tottenham Court Road/Goodge Street.

Tesco
www.tesco.com
BRANCHES AT:
   Locations throughout London
Given the scale of Tesco's operations, reports are surprisingly sparse, but loyal supporters applaud the "amazing prices and range" of wines on offer at the UK's largest supermarket chain. / HOURS Some larger stores 24 hours SEE ALSO Big Ten; Bread; Fruit & vegetables.

Thresher
www.victoriawine.co.uk
BRANCHES AT:
   Locations throughout London
They hardly set the world on fire, but these classic 'high street' off-licences are reckoned by reporters to be "good all-rounders" – "reliable" and "consistent". / HOURS Hours vary: generally Mon-Sat 10am-10pm, Sun noon-9pm.

Uncorked EC2
Exchange Arcade, Broadgate   9–2D
☎ (020) 7638 5998 www.uncorked.co.uk
This discreet three-man operation in a smart little shop in the Broadgate centre makes a thing of knowing its producers as individuals; as you might guess, they specialise in pricier bottles for local Masters of the Universe, but all price-brackets are served. / HOURS Mon-Fri 10am-6.30pm.

Unwins
☎ (020) 7485 3341 www.unwins.co.uk
BRANCHES AT:
   Locations throughout London
They are certainly "not posh", but if you're looking for a "standard chain store with a good selection", these unassuming-looking off-licences have a better range than you might perhaps expect. / HOURS Mon-Sat 9am-10pm, Sun 11am-9pm.

Wine

La Vigneronne SW7
105 Old Brompton Rd   5–2B
☎ (020) 7589 6113   www.lavigneronne.co.uk
Mike and Liz Berry, owners of this South Kensington merchant, live in the South of France and their on-the-spot researches no doubt contribute to the "rare selection" – specialising in the Rhône and Languedoc – which makes it an extremely popular enthusiasts' destination; much of their wine comes in small quantities, so early birds should sign up for e-mail notifications. / HOURS Mon-Fri 10am-8pm, Sat 10am-6pm.

Vinopolis SE1
1 Bank End   9–3C
☎ (0870) 4444 777   www.vinopolis.co.uk
"Quality and choice are very good", say supporters of this Bermondsey wine shop, which benefits from "a lovely location", attached to a wine museum; although management is franchised to Majestic Wine, there is no requirement to buy by the case; "an extensive range of balsamic vinegars, olive oils and so on" completes the range of liquid offerings (and there are also cheeses from Neal's Yard Dairy). / HOURS Mon 11am-9pm, Tue-Fri & Sun 11am-6pm, Sat 11am-8pm.

Vintage Cellars SW1
33 Churton St   2–4B
☎ (020) 7630 6254
Formerly called Pimlico Dozen, this small shop is run by the "knowledgeable" Mr Heiko Vermeulen, who can speak with authority on the shop's wide (but not especially deep) Old and New World ranges. / HOURS Mon-Fri 10am-8pm, Sat 10am-6.30pm TUBE Pimlico/Victoria.

Vom Fass W11
187 Westbourne Grove   6–1B
☎ (020) 7792 4499
Products from the cask – basic wines and more interesting spirits – are the speciality of this Notting Hill shop, which now also has an offshoot in Selfridges; gift presentation a speciality. / HOURS Mon-Sat 10.30am-7pm, Sun noon-5pm TUBE Notting Hill Gate SEE ALSO Grocers & delicatessens.

Waitrose
☎ (01344) 424680 Customer service
  www.waitrose.com
BRANCHES AT:
  Locations throughout London
"Always dependable, sometimes surprising" – the "wide selection of cheap-to-reasonably expensive wines" makes Waitrose the most nominated supermarket wine supplier by far; "staff are always helpful" too. / HOURS Hours vary: generally Mon-Sat 8.30am-9pm, Sun 11am-5pm SEE ALSO Big Ten; Bread; Cheese & dairy; Fish & seafood; Fruit & vegetables; Health & organic foods; Herbs & spices; Meat, game & poultry.

Wine

The Waterloo Wine Company SE1
6 Vine Yd, Lant St 9–4B
☎ (020) 7403 7967
A bit of a hidden gem, not far from Borough tube station, this is the warehouse of a firm that's an importer first, and a retailer second; sourcing is largely from smaller, family-owned vineyards, so it's a good destination for those in search of something a little out-of-the-ordinary. / HOURS Mon-Fri 10am-6.30pm, Sat 10am-5pm TUBE Borough.

Wimbledon Wine Cellar SW19
1 Gladstone Rd 10–2B
☎ (020) 8540 9979 www.wimbledonwinecellar.com
"Independent, helpful, knowledgeable" – it's the staff who really make this a *"good local wine store"* and, of course, the *"good value and excellent choice of wine"*; Andrew Pavli's shop won the Best Small Independent Wine Merchant 2001 in the International Wine Challenge Awards. / HOURS Mon-Sat 10am-9pm.

Wine Cellar
 www.winecellar.co.uk
BRANCHES AT:
  41 Horseferry Rd, SW1 2–4C
  ☎ (020) 7834 2189
  294 High Rd, W4
  ☎ (020) 8987 9502
It seems rather odd at first that though this large Westminster shop (also in Chiswick) has 'chain' written all over it, you don't see other similarly-named establishments around town – everything becomes clear when you realise that this is the sole central London outpost of a North Western chain (NW England, that is); as a result the range (though it includes many mass-market brands) seems just that bit different – certainly worth a look if you're in the area. / HOURS Mon-Sat 8am-10pm, Sun 10am-10pm

The Wine Library EC3
43 Trinity Sq 9–3D
☎ (020) 7481 0415
The classic "try-before-you-buy" venue – you choose your bottle, pay £3.50 corkage, and quaff your wine with a picnic-type buffet (£11.95 a head) in aged City cellars; some say the place "is really a restaurant", but it's the wine side of the business – with a traditional bent, and strong in France – which is run "with passion and interest". / HOURS Mon-Fri 11am-8pm.

Wine

The Winery W9
4 Clifton Rd   8–4A
☎ (020) 7286 6475
Maida Vale's "lovely local wine shop" offers "intelligent, independently-sourced wines" — mainly from Burgundy, the Rhône, Italy and California — and "great advice"; proprietor David Motion "just could not be more helpful". / HOURS *Mon-Sat 11am-9pm, Sun noon-8pm.*

MAIL ORDER

A&B Vintners TN12
Little Tawsden, Spout Ln, Brenchley, Kent
☎ 01892 724977   www.abvintners.co.uk
Two ex-City types run this expanding business, which specialises in domaine-bottlings from Burgundy, the Rhône Valley and southern France. / CREDIT CARDS *no Amex.*

Adnams IP18
Sole Bay Brewery, Southwold, Suffolk
☎ (01502) 727222   www.adnams.co.uk
Adnams' famous Southwold brewery is also home to a wine operation; it doesn't take itself too seriously — the wacky website certainly stands out but, wacky or not, feedback from reporters, though modest in scale, was all positive.

Beerbarons.co.uk
☎ (0800) 085 5496   www.beerbarons.co.uk
Beer-lovers in search of a brew that's a little bit different will find much of interest in this well-organised website — it offers a veritable fund of information, whether or not you have a purchase in mind.

Bibendum Wines NW1
113 Regent's Park Rd   8–2B
☎ (020) 7916 7706   www.bibendum-wine.co.uk
For the past couple of years or so, this Primrose Hill-based merchant (which does quite a lot of restaurant business) has foregone a 'walk-in' retail presence, and now sells from its list by phone and mail, and through its website; reporters heap praise on its "very good choice of wines at all price brackets" and its "helpful staff".

Chateauonline
☎ (0800) 169 2736   www.chateauonline.co.uk
This claims to be Europe's leading online wine merchant, but — so far as least — it has established only a modest following among reporters; its operations are based in Paris and Bordeaux, so Gallic wines are, unsurprisingly, to the fore.

Wine

Domaine Direct
☎ (0800) 7837 1142 ⌘ www.domainedirect.co.uk
This "very helpful" supplier, two decades in business, boasts both a well-organised website and a clear sense of purpose – to offer 'the widest and most thoroughly-researched selection of domaine-bottled Burgundy available in Britain'; the site is well structured and has depth – given the complexities of the region with which it is principally concerned, it's quite approachable too.

John Armit Wines W11 ★
5 Royalty Studios, 105 Lancaster Rd   6–1A
☎ (020) 7908 0600
"A very good selection, especially from Alsace and Burgundy" is part of the "very fine" choice on offer at this fashionable merchant (which is presented on an extremely elegantly produced list); Mr Armit was for many years one of the backers of that linchpin of Notting Hill life, the restaurant 192.

Laithwaites RG7
New Aquitaine Hs, Exeter Way, Theale, Reading
☎ (0870) 444 8383 ⌘ www.laithwaites.co.uk
Formerly known as Bordeaux Direct, this "good-value" supplier offers a nice balance between everyday wines and collectors' items (and one enthusiast speaks of "some real gems"); a money-back guarantee offers protection for those who simply don't like their purchases.

Lay & Wheeler CO2
Gosbecks Park, Colchester, Essex
☎ (0845) 330 1855 ⌘ www.layandwheeler.co.uk
We were surprised how little this well-reputed Colchester merchant (est 1854) figured in the survey – perhaps it was to address this lack of 'profile' that a 'flagship' wine bar was recently opened in the City; their extensive list can be viewed on – but not at the time of writing directly purchased from – their website.

Morris & Verdin SE1
10 The Leathermarket, Weston St
☎ (020) 7357 8866 ⌘ www.morris-verdin.co.uk
If you're interested in Burgundy or California, in particular, it would be worth getting a copy of the retail list offered by this highly-reputed importer.

The Sunday Times Wine Club RG7
New Aquitaine House, Exeter Way, Theale, Berkshire
☎ (0870) 220 0010 ⌘ www.sundaytimeswineclub.co.uk
"Brilliant research from small vineyards" is – perhaps rather surprisingly – a highlight of the service branded with the name of the biggest-selling quality Sunday; all aspects of the operation were favourably rated.

Wine

Swig SW6
5-6 Roxby Pl   5–3A
☎ (020) 7903 8311   ⌁ www.swig.co.uk
This wine shop formerly located in Belsize Park recently acquired the Fulham premises of the South African Wine Centre, and now offers a mail order (only) service specialising in Italy, the Rhône and, of course, South Africa; sourcing a difficult-to-find wine you're particularly looking for is something of a speciality.

Virginwines
☎ (0845) 603 63 63   ⌁ www.virginwines.com
"Ease of use" – the site combines a number of interesting features, but not at the expense of clarity – and "good variety and special offers" are among the plusses which reporters see in this website service; "evening delivery within the M25" is another.

Waitrose Wine Direct
☎ (0800) 188881   ⌁ www.waitrosedirect.co.uk
"No duds", says one user of Waitrose's mail order operation; it attracted relatively little commentary, though, presumably because Waitrose's many London supporters prefer to buy from the shelves.

The Wine Society   ★
☎ (01438) 741177   ⌁ www.thewinesociety.com
"A class act"; this "outstanding mail order service" – run as a co-operative since 1874 – earns nothing but praise from its members (of whom there are over 90,000); plusses include a "comprehensive and reliable selection", a "very good delivery service" and "competitive prices".

Wine Wine Wine SE1
2 Bedale St   9–4C
☎ (020) 7407 2724   ⌁ www.winewinewine.co.uk
A mail order service with its heart firmly in France – foie gras features in an ancillary range of food items; the company is also to be found at Borough Market.

Yapp Brothers BA12   ☆
The Old Brewery, Water St Mere, Warminster
☎ (01747) 860423
This idiosyncratic Wiltshire merchant has a tiny (among reporters) but ecstatic following as "the best French wine seller in the world", and some say that it's "unbeatable for the Loire and the Rhône"; the history – on the website – of one enthusiast's transition from dentist to wine merchant is well worth reading.

Maps

MAP 1 – LONDON OVERVIEW

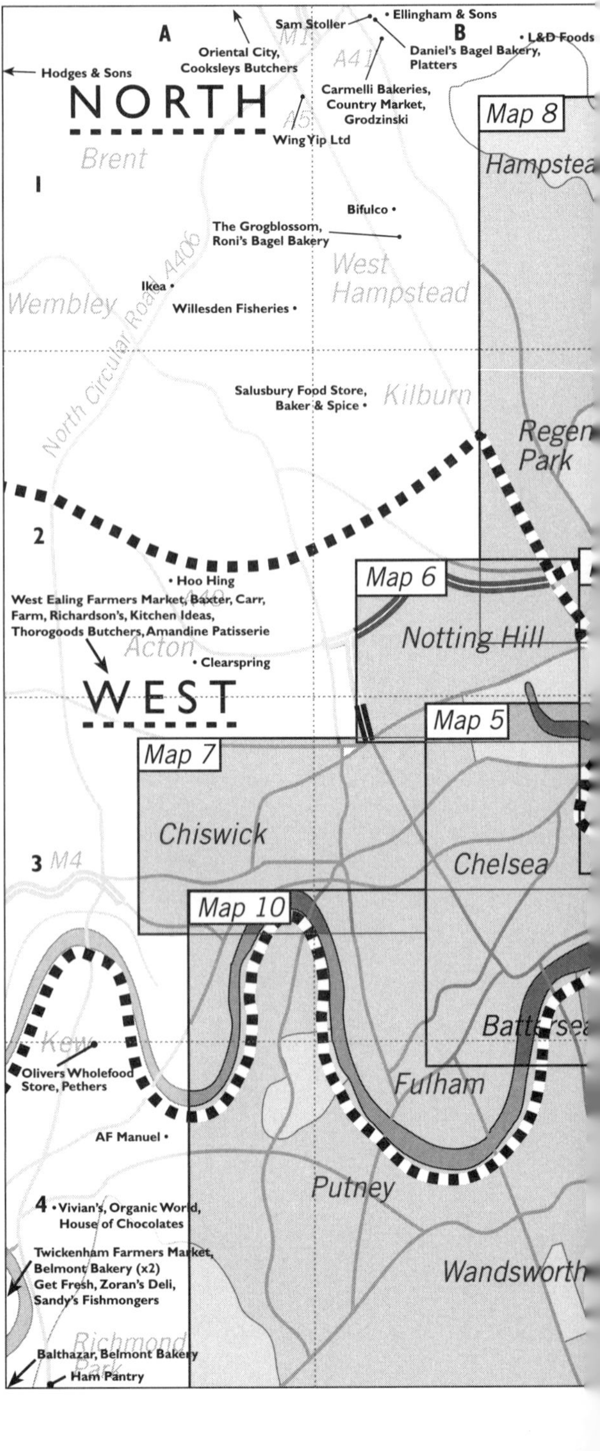

NORTH

- Hodges & Sons
- Sam Stoller
- Ellingham & Sons
- Oriental City, Cooksleys Butchers
- Daniel's Bagel Bakery, Platters
- L&D Foods
- Carmelli Bakeries, Country Market, Grodzinski
- Wing Yip Ltd

Brent — *Hampstead* — Map 8

- The Grogblossom, Roni's Bagel Bakery
- Bifulco
- Ikea
- Willesden Fisheries

Wembley — *West Hampstead*

- Salusbury Food Store, Baker & Spice

Kilburn — *Regents Park*

North Circular Road A406

- Hoo Hing
- West Ealing Farmers Market, Baxter, Carr, Farm, Richardson's, Kitchen Ideas, Thorogoods Butchers, Amandine Patisserie
- Clearspring

Acton — Map 6 — *Notting Hill* — Map 5

WEST

Map 7 — *Chiswick* — *Chelsea*

M4 — Map 10 — *Battersea* — *Fulham*

Kew
- Olivers Wholefood Store, Pethers
- AF Manuel

Putney — *Wandsworth*

- Vivian's, Organic World, House of Chocolates
- Twickenham Farmers Market, Belmont Bakery (x2), Get Fresh, Zoran's Deli, Sandy's Fishmongers
- Balthazar, Belmont Bakery
- Ham Pantry

Richmond

MAP 1 – LONDON OVERVIEW

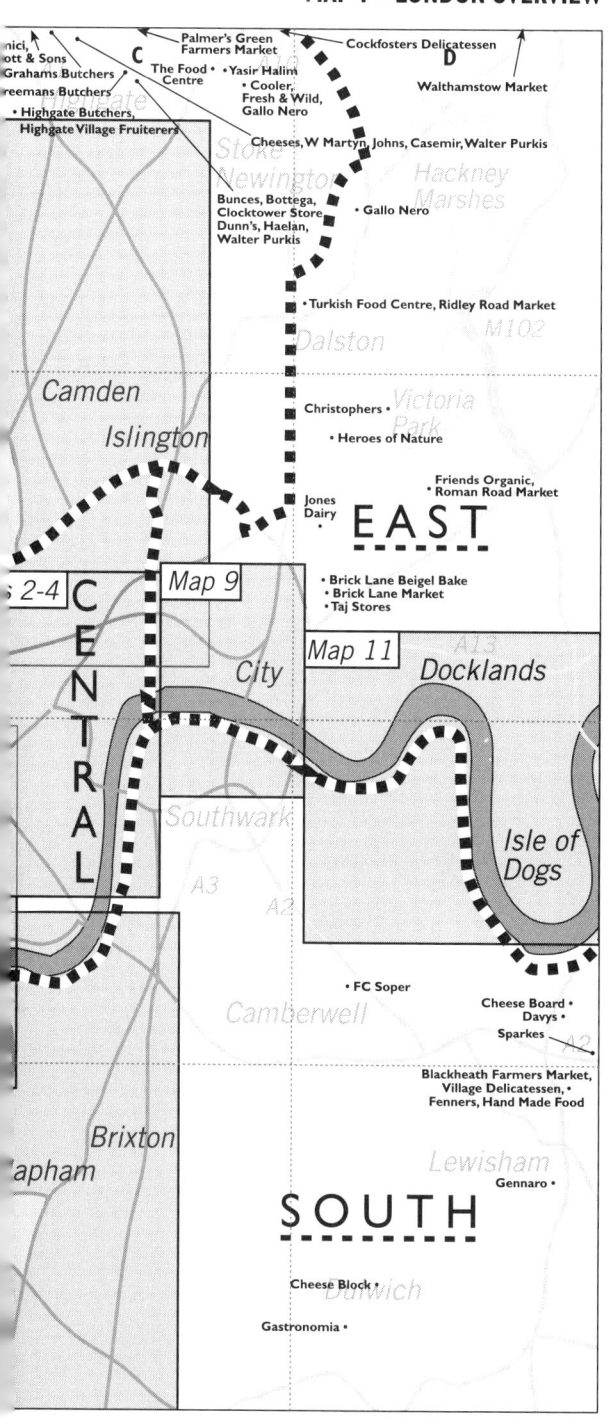

nici,
ott & Sons
Grahams Butchers
reemans Butchers
- Highgate Butchers,
Highgate Village Fruiterers

Palmer's Green Farmers Market
Cockfosters Delicatessen

C D

The Food Centre • Yasir Halim
• Cooler, Fresh & Wild, Gallo Nero

Walthamstow Market

Cheeses, W Martyn, Johns, Casemir, Walter Purkis

Stoke Newington

Hackney Marshes

Bunces, Bottega, Clocktower Store
Dunn's, Haelan, Walter Purkis

• Gallo Nero

• Turkish Food Centre, Ridley Road Market

Dalston M102

Camden

Islington

Christophers • Victoria Park
• Heroes of Nature

Friends Organic,
• Roman Road Market

Jones Dairy EAST

2-4 C Map 9

E
N
T
R
A
L

City

Southwark

A3

• Brick Lane Beigel Bake
• Brick Lane Market
• Taj Stores

Map 11 Docklands

Isle of Dogs

• FC Soper

Camberwell

Cheese Board •
Davys •
Sparkes •

Blackheath Farmers Market,
Village Delicatessen,
Fenners, Hand Made Food

Brixton
apham

Lewisham
Gennaro •

SOUTH

Cheese Block •
Dulwich

Gastronomia •

MAP 2 – WEST END OVERVIEW

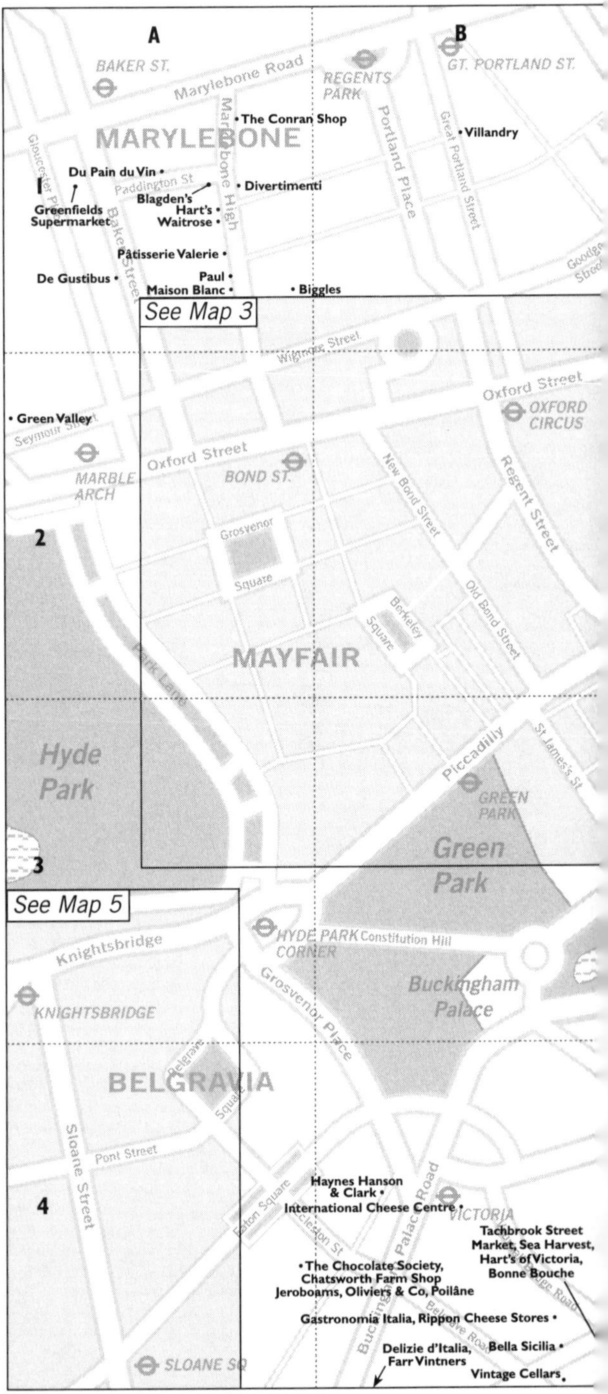

A

BAKER ST.

Marylebone Road

REGENTS PARK

B

GT. PORTLAND ST.

• The Conran Shop

MARYLEBONE

• Villandry

Du Pain du Vin •
Paddington St
Blagden's
Greenfields   Hart's
Supermarket   Waitrose •

• Divertimenti

Pâtisserie Valerie •

De Gustibus •   Paul •
Maison Blanc •   • Biggles

See Map 3

Wigmore Street

Oxford Street

• Green Valley
Seymour
MARBLE ARCH

Oxford Street   BOND ST.

OXFORD CIRCUS

New Bond Street

Regent Street

Grosvenor Square

Berkeley Square

Old Bond Street

2

MAYFAIR

Hyde Park

Piccadilly   St James's St

GREEN PARK

3

Green Park

See Map 5

Knightsbridge

HYDE PARK CORNER   Constitution Hill

KNIGHTSBRIDGE

Grosvenor Place

Buckingham Palace

BELGRAVIA

Pont Street

Sloane Street

4

Haynes Hanson & Clark •
International Cheese Centre •

VICTORIA

Tachbrook Street Market, Sea Harvest, Hart's of Victoria, Bonne Bouche

• The Chocolate Society,
Chatsworth Farm Shop
Jeroboams, Oliviers & Co, Poilâne •

Gastronomia Italia, Rippon Cheese Stores •

Delizie d'Italia, Farr Vintners

• Bella Sicilia

SLOANE SQ

Vintage Cellars

MAP 2 – WEST END OVERVIEW

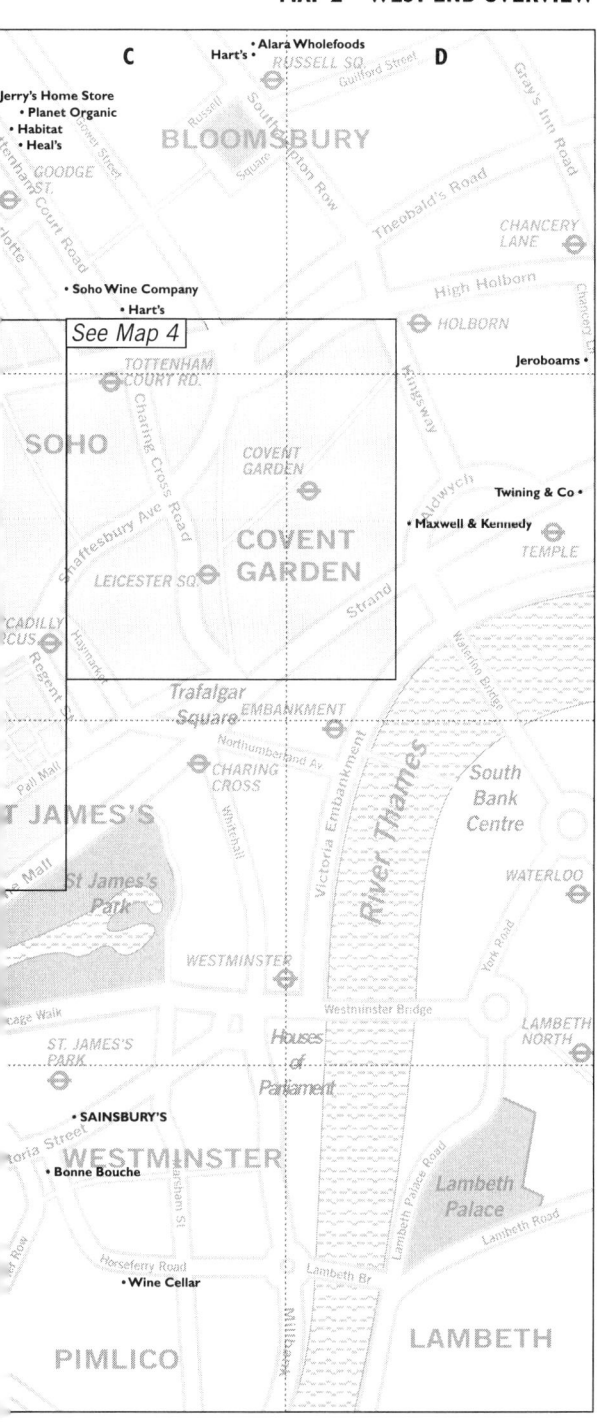

C | **D**

Alara Wholefoods
Hart's
RUSSELL SQ.
Guilford Street
Gray's Inn Road

Jerry's Home Store
• Planet Organic
• Habitat
• Heal's

BLOOMSBURY

Russell Square
Southampton Row
Theobald's Road

GOODGE ST.

CHANCERY LANE

• Soho Wine Company
• Hart's

High Holborn

HOLBORN

Jeroboams •

See Map 4

TOTTENHAM COURT RD.

SOHO

Charing Cross Road

COVENT GARDEN

Kingsway

Twining & Co •
• Maxwell & Kennedy

TEMPLE

Shaftesbury Avenue

COVENT GARDEN

LEICESTER SQ.

Strand

PICCADILLY CIRCUS

Regent St.

Haymarket

Trafalgar Square

EMBANKMENT

Northumberland Av.

CHARING CROSS

Whitehall

Victoria Embankment

River Thames

South Bank Centre

WATERLOO

Pall Mall

ST JAMES'S

The Mall

St James's Park

WESTMINSTER

Westminster Bridge

York Road

LAMBETH NORTH

Birdcage Walk

ST. JAMES'S PARK

Houses of Parliament

• SAINSBURY'S

Victoria Street

WESTMINSTER

• Bonne Bouche

Marsham St

Lambeth Palace Road

Lambeth Palace

Lambeth Road

Horseferry Road

• Wine Cellar

Lambeth Br.

Millbank

PIMLICO

LAMBETH

MAP 3 – MAYFAIR, ST JAMES'S & WEST SOHO

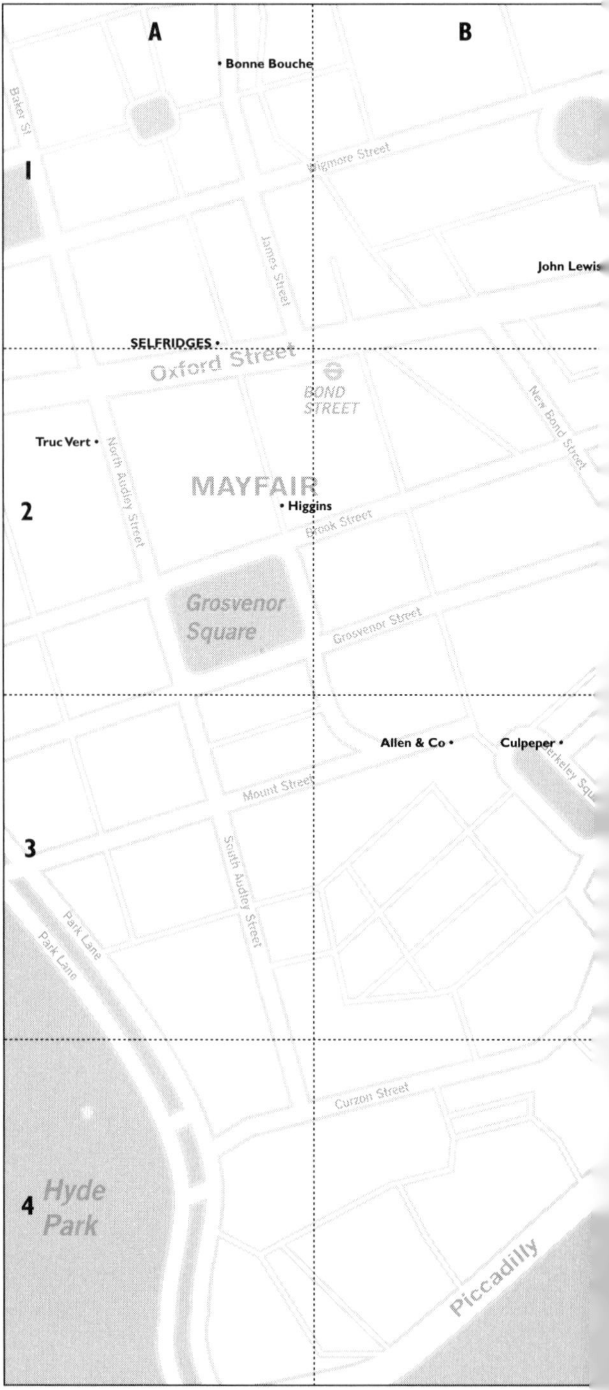

MAP 3 – MAYFAIR, ST JAMES'S & WEST SOHO

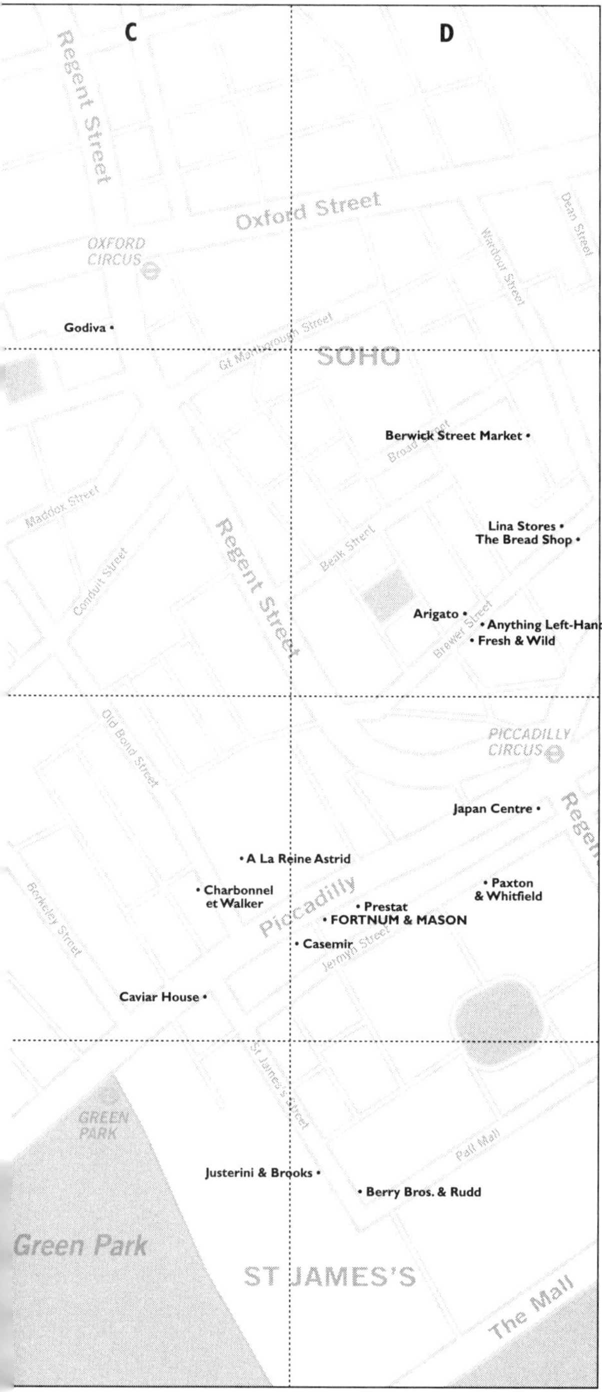

C | **D**

Regent Street

Oxford Street

OXFORD CIRCUS

Dean Street

Godiva

Gt Marlborough Street

Wardour Street

SOHO

Berwick Street Market

Broadwick Street

Maddox Street

Regent Street

Beak Street

Lina Stores
The Bread Shop

Conduit Street

Arigato • Anything Left-Handed
• Fresh & Wild

Brewer Street

PICCADILLY CIRCUS

Old Bond Street

Japan Centre

Regent Street

• A La Reine Astrid

• Charbonnel et Walker

Piccadilly

• Prestat
• FORTNUM & MASON

• Paxton & Whitfield

Berkeley Street

• Casemir

Jermyn Street

Caviar House

St James's Street

GREEN PARK

Justerini & Brooks •

Pall Mall

• Berry Bros. & Rudd

Green Park

ST JAMES'S

The Mall

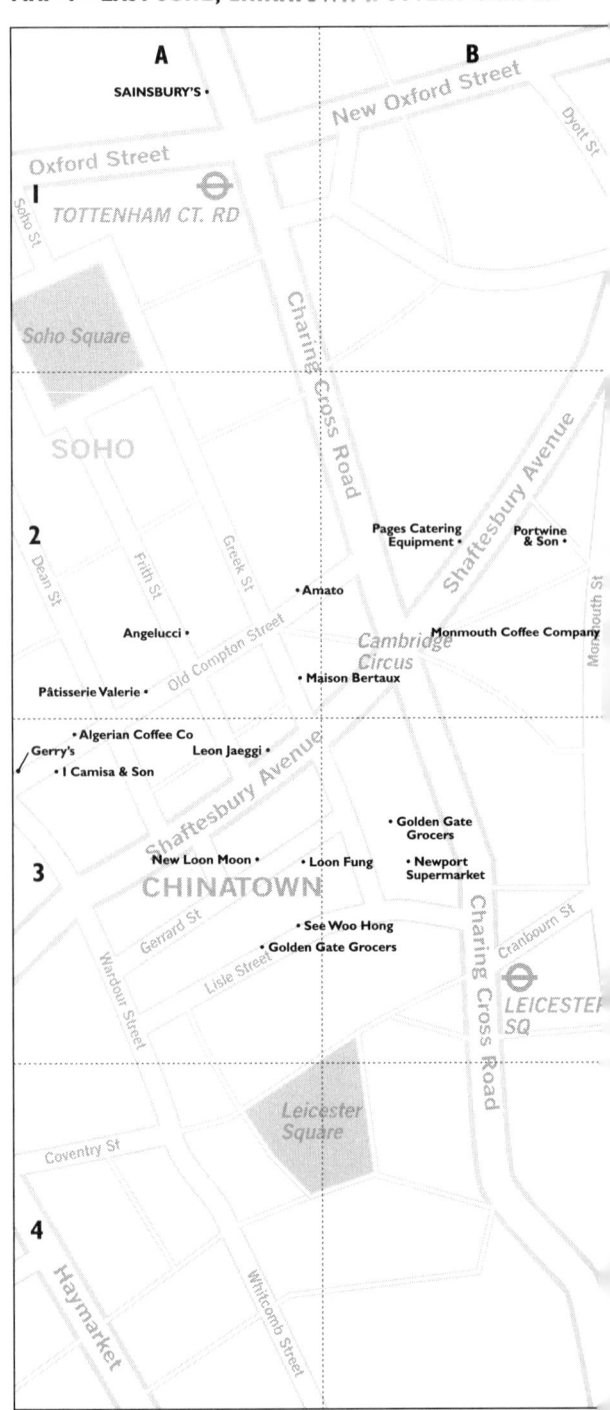

MAP 4 – EAST SOHO, CHINATOWN & COVENT GARDEN

A

SAINSBURY'S

Oxford Street

1 TOTTENHAM CT. RD

Soho Square

SOHO

Charing Cross Road

2

Dean St
Frith St
Greek St

• Amato

Angelucci •

Old Compton Street

Pâtisserie Valerie •

• Maison Bertaux

• Algerian Coffee Co
Gerry's   Leon Jaeggi •
• I Camisa & Son

Shaftesbury Avenue

3 New Loon Moon •   • Loon Fung
CHINATOWN

Gerrard St   • See Woo Hong
           • Golden Gate Grocers
Lisle Street

Wardour Street

Coventry St

4

Haymarket

B

New Oxford Street

Dyott St

Pages Catering
Equipment •   Portwine
                    & Son •

Shaftesbury Avenue

Cambridge   Monmouth Coffee Company
Circus

                           Monmouth St

• Golden Gate
  Grocers
• Newport
  Supermarket

Charing Cross Road

Cranbourn St

LEICESTER
SQ

Leicester
Square

Whitcomb Street

MAP 4 – EAST SOHO, CHINATOWN & COVENT GARDEN

C · D

High Holborn
Drury Lane
Gt Queen St

Neal St · Carluccio's
· Neal's Yard Bakery
Neal's Yard Dairy ·
Shelton Street
Endell Street

Tea House · COVENT GARDEN
MARKS & SPENCER ·
Long Acre
· Kastner & Ovens
Royal Opera House
Bow Street

COVENT GARDEN

Covent Garden Market
· Pâtisserie Valerie
Exeter Street Bakery ·
· Oliviers & Co
· Culpeper
Wellington St

Garrick St
TESCO ·
Sainsbury's
· Paul
· Australia & New Zealand Shop
Bedford St

Strand

Coliseum
William IV Street

Victoria Emb.

MAP 5 – KNIGHTSBRIDGE, CHELSEA & SOUTH KENSINGTON

A

Kensington Ch St

KENSINGTON

- Kemptons of Kensington
- Pierre Pechon
- Maison Blanc
- Habitat

1
- Exeter Street Bakery
- Safeway
- MARKS & SPENCER

HIGH ST. KENSINGTON

Kensington High Street

B

Kensington Gardens

Gloucester Road

Jacobs

Royal Albert Hall

- Partridges

- SAINSBURY'S
Cromwell Road
TESCO •
- WAITROSE
GLOUCESTER RD
- Hart's
- Bagatelle Boutique
- Bonne Bouche

2
- Hart's
EARLS COURT

Warwick Road
Earl's Court Road

Hart's

Vigneronne

EARL'S COURT

- Montignac Boutique
Old Brompton Road
- Amandine Patisserie

Earl's Court Exhibition Centre

Safeway
Lillie Road
WEST BROMPTON

3
- Swig

Finborough Road
Redcliffe Gardens

Brompton Cemetery

- Lea & Sandeman
Fulham Road
- Maison Bl

← North End Road Market
- Tray Gourmet, Hart's
- Luigi's Delicatessen

Rococo Chocola

City Mea
Italian Fruit Company —

FULHAM BROADWAY

- Luscious Organic
Fulham Road

- Moore Park Delicatessen

4 FULHAM

New King's Road

Chelsea Harbour

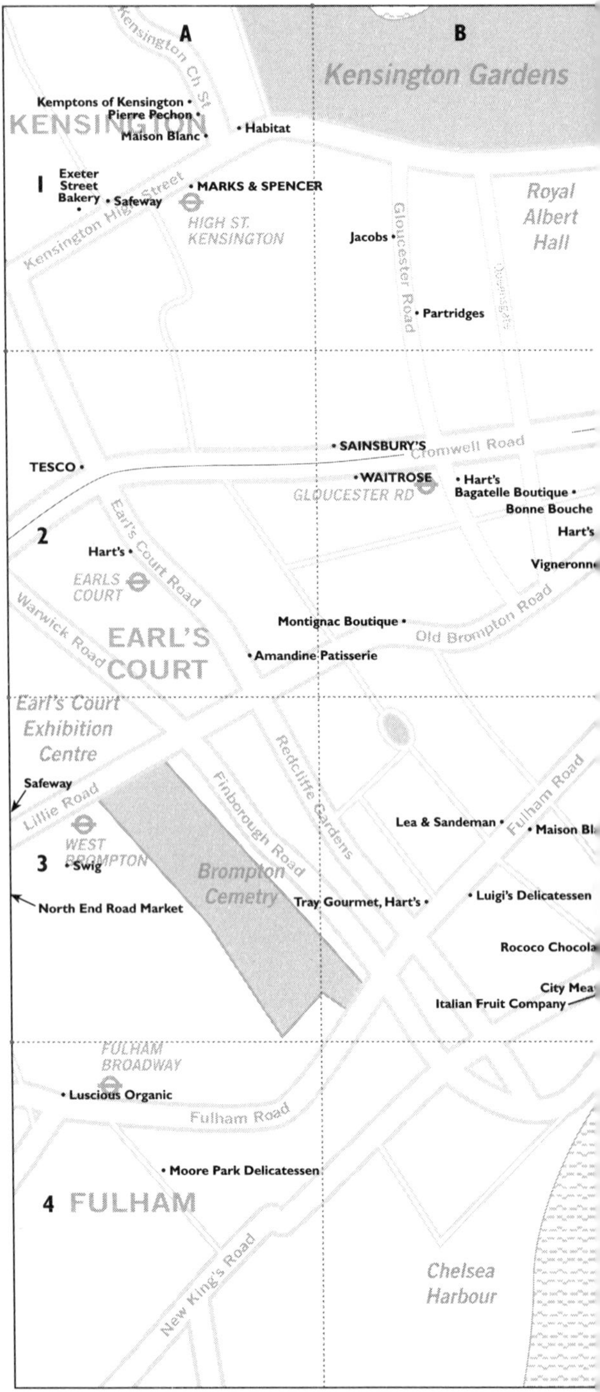

MAP 5 – KNIGHTSBRIDGE, CHELSEA & SOUTH KENSINGTON

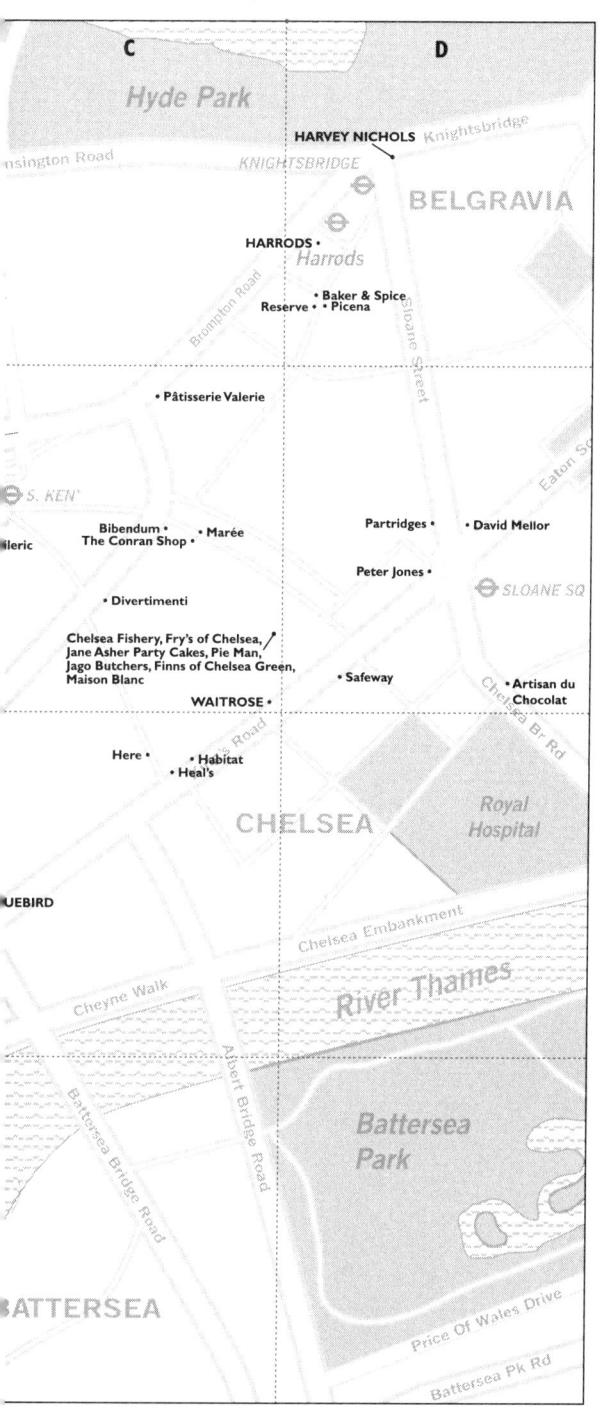

C | **D**

Hyde Park

HARVEY NICHOLS Knightsbridge
KNIGHTSBRIDGE
BELGRAVIA
ensington Road

HARRODS • Harrods
Brompton Road
• Baker & Spice
Reserve • • Picena

• Pâtisserie Valerie

S. KEN'
Bibendum • • Marée
The Conran Shop •
lleric

Partridges • • David Mellor

Peter Jones •
SLOANE SQ

• Divertimenti

Chelsea Fishery, Fry's of Chelsea,
Jane Asher Party Cakes, Pie Man,
Jago Butchers, Finns of Chelsea Green,
Maison Blanc
• Safeway
• Artisan du Chocolat
Chelsea Br Rd
WAITROSE •

Here • • Habitat
• Heal's

CHELSEA

Royal Hospital

UEBIRD

Cheisea Embankment

Cheyne Walk
River Thames

Battersea Bridge Road
Albert Bridge Road

Battersea Park

BATTERSEA

Price Of Wales Drive

Battersea Pk Rd

MAP 6 – NOTTING HILL & BAYSWATER

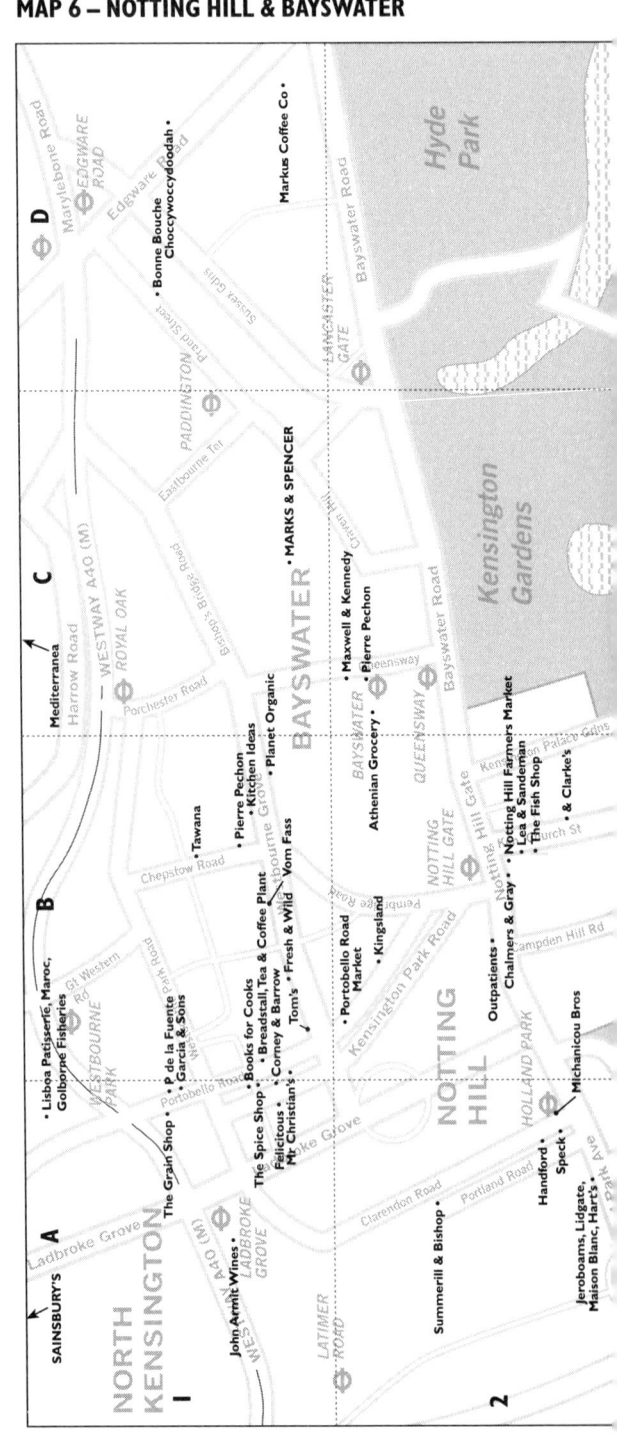

MAP 7 – HAMMERSMITH & CHISWICK

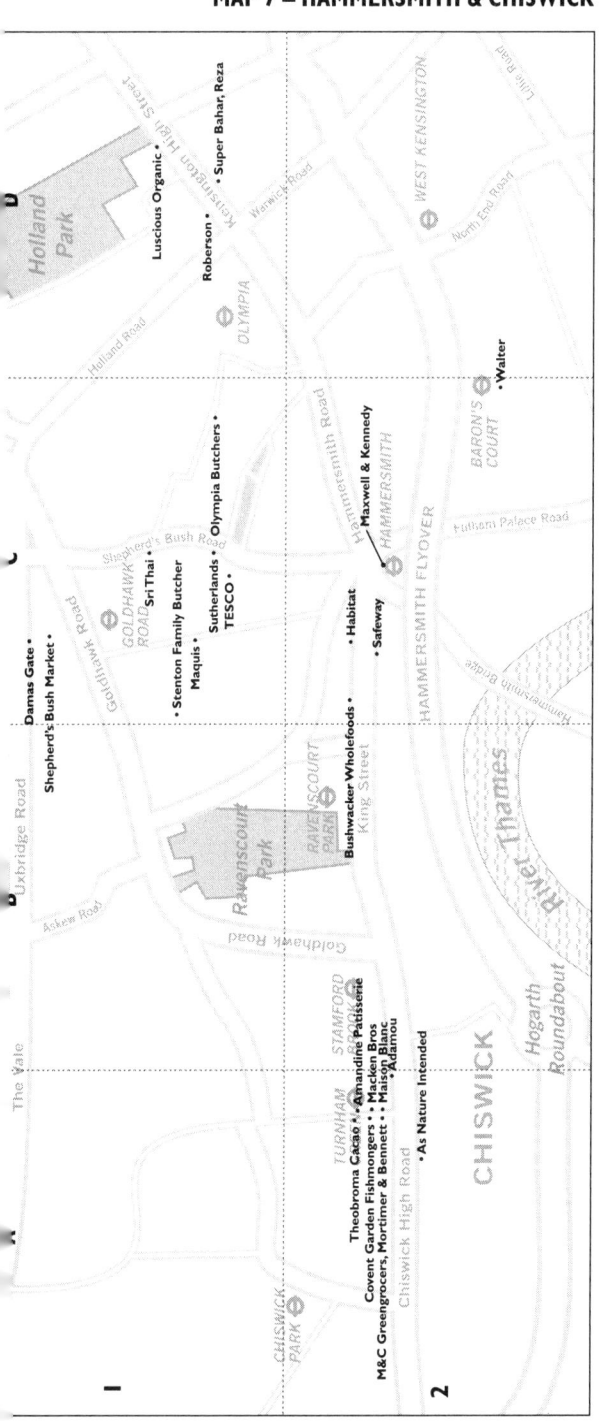

- Luscious Organic
- Super Bahar, Reza
- Roberson
- Damas Gate
- Shepherd's Bush Market
- Sri Thai
- Stenton Family Butcher
- Maquis
- Sutherlands
- Olympia Butchers
- TESCO
- Bushwacker Wholefoods
- Habitat
- Safeway
- Maxwell & Kennedy
- Walter
- Theobroma Cacao
- Amandine Patisserie
- Macken Bros
- Covent Garden Fishmongers
- M&C Greengrocers, Mortimer & Bennett
- Maison Blanc
- Adamou
- As Nature Intended

Holland Park
Kensington High Street
Holland Road
OLYMPIA
Warwick Road
WEST KENSINGTON
Lisle Road
North End Road
BARON'S COURT
Hammersmith Road
HAMMERSMITH
Fulham Palace Road
HAMMERSMITH FLYOVER
Hammersmith Bridge
River Thames
Shepherd's Bush Road
GOLDHAWK ROAD
Goldhawk Road
Uxbridge Road
Askew Road
Ravenscourt Park
RAVENSCOURT PARK
King Street
The Vale
TURNHAM STAMFORD
Chiswick High Road
CHISWICK
Hogarth Roundabout
CHISWICK PARK

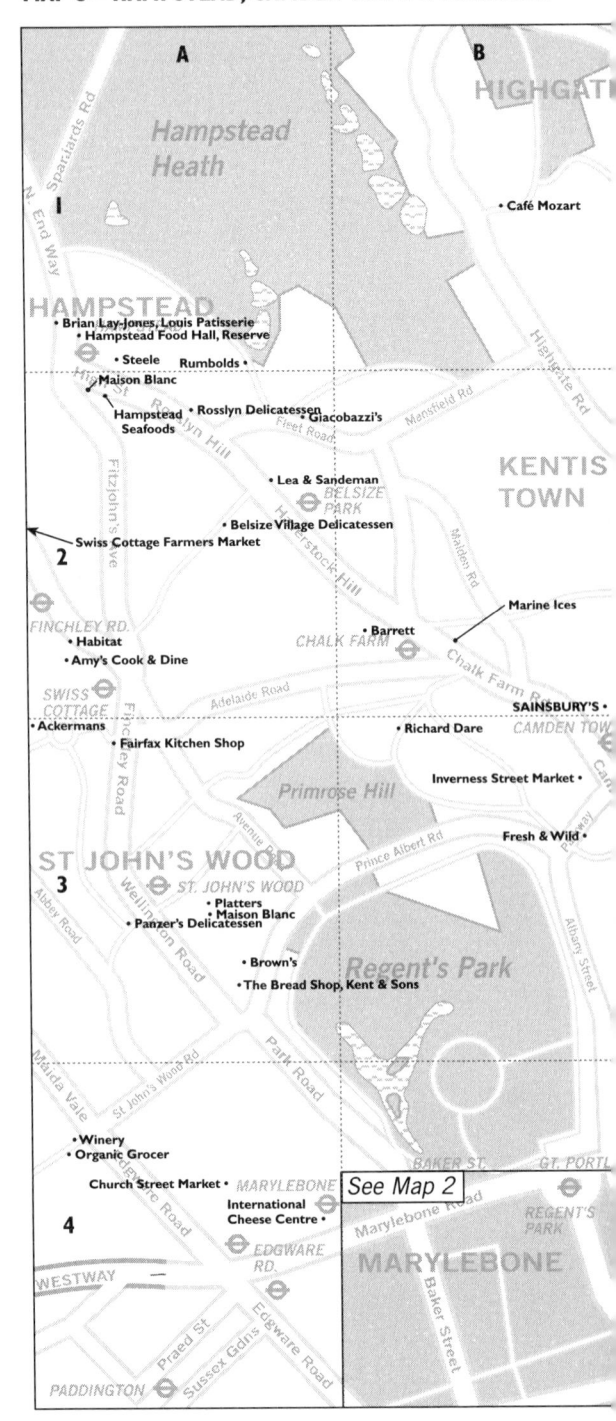

MAP 8 – HAMPSTEAD, CAMDEN TOWN & ISLINGTON

MAP 8 – HAMPSTEAD, CAMDEN TOWN & ISLINGTON

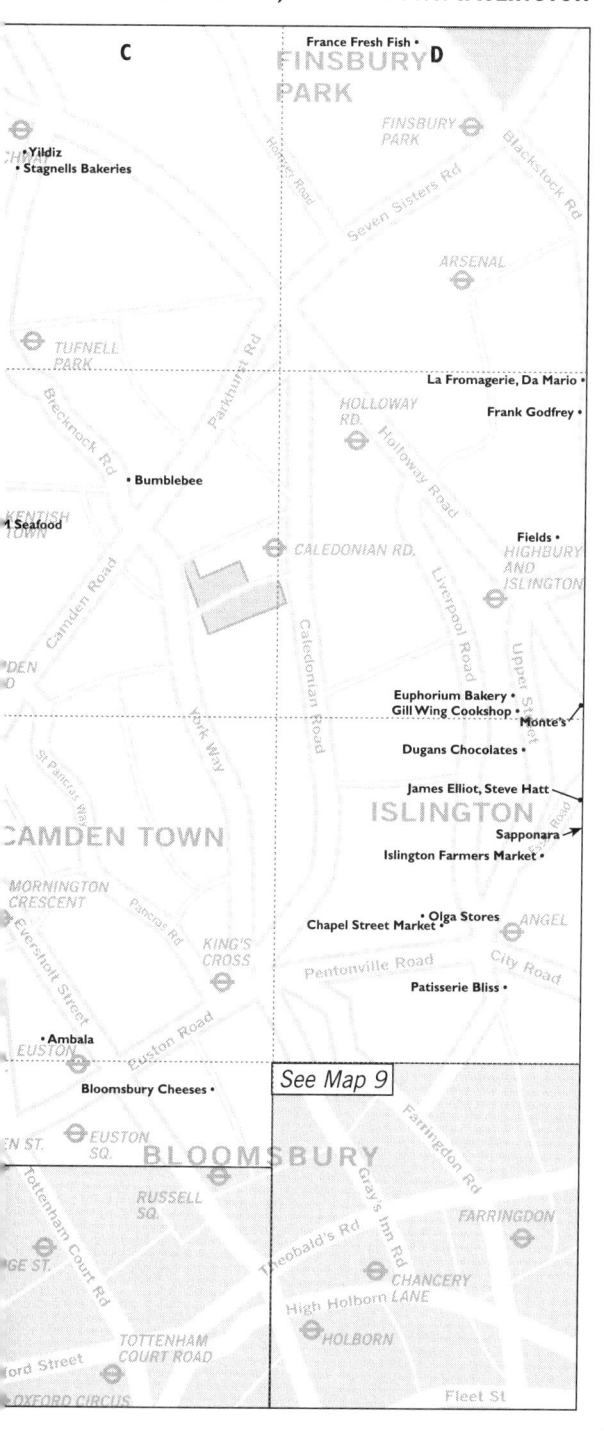

C **D**

- France Fresh Fish
- FINSBURY PARK
- FINSBURY PARK
- Yildiz
- Stagnells Bakeries
- ARSENAL
- TUFNELL PARK
- La Fromagerie, Da Mario
- HOLLOWAY RD.
- Frank Godfrey
- Bumblebee
- Seafood
- KENTISH TOWN
- CALEDONIAN RD.
- Fields
- HIGHBURY AND ISLINGTON
- Euphorium Bakery
- Gill Wing Cookshop
- Monte's
- Dugans Chocolates
- James Elliot, Steve Hatt
- ISLINGTON
- Sapponara
- CAMDEN TOWN
- MORNINGTON CRESCENT
- Islington Farmers Market
- Chapel Street Market • Olga Stores
- ANGEL
- KING'S CROSS
- Pentonville Road
- City Road
- Patisserie Bliss
- Ambala
- EUSTON
- Bloomsbury Cheeses
- See Map 9
- EUSTON SQ.
- BLOOMSBURY
- RUSSELL SQ.
- FARRINGDON
- Theobald's Rd
- CHANCERY LANE
- High Holborn
- HOLBORN
- TOTTENHAM COURT ROAD
- OXFORD CIRCUS
- Fleet St

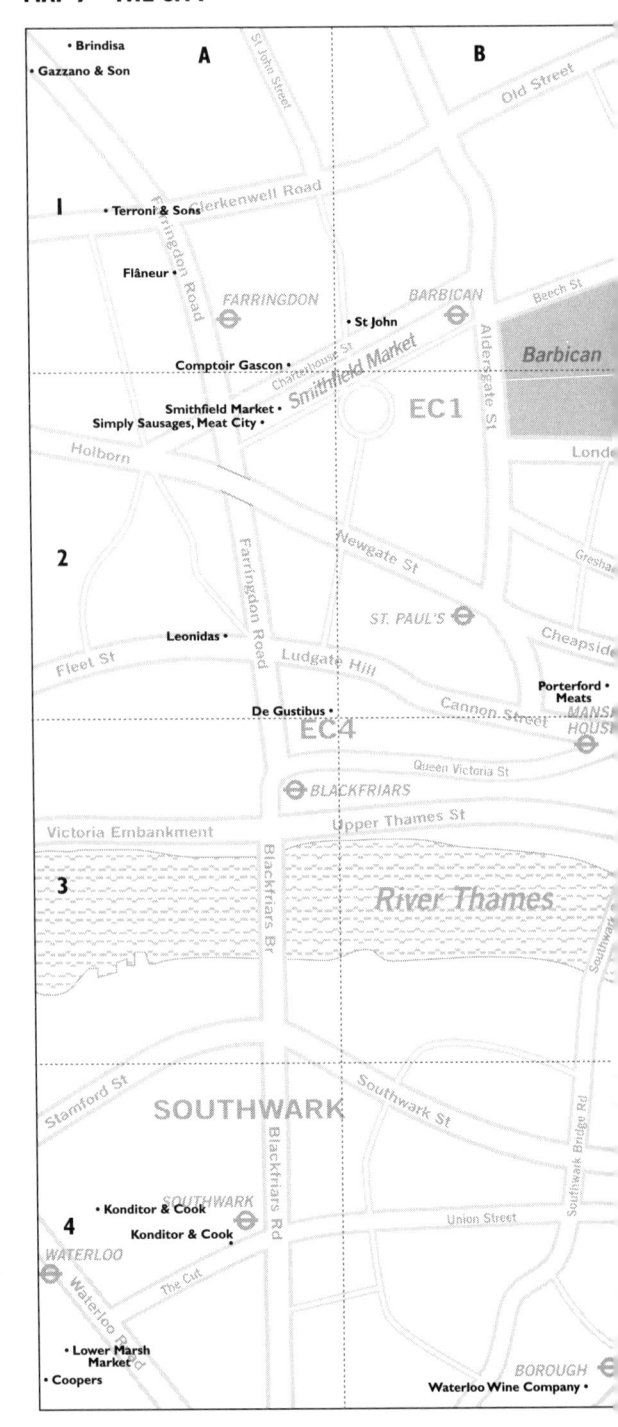

MAP 9 – THE CITY

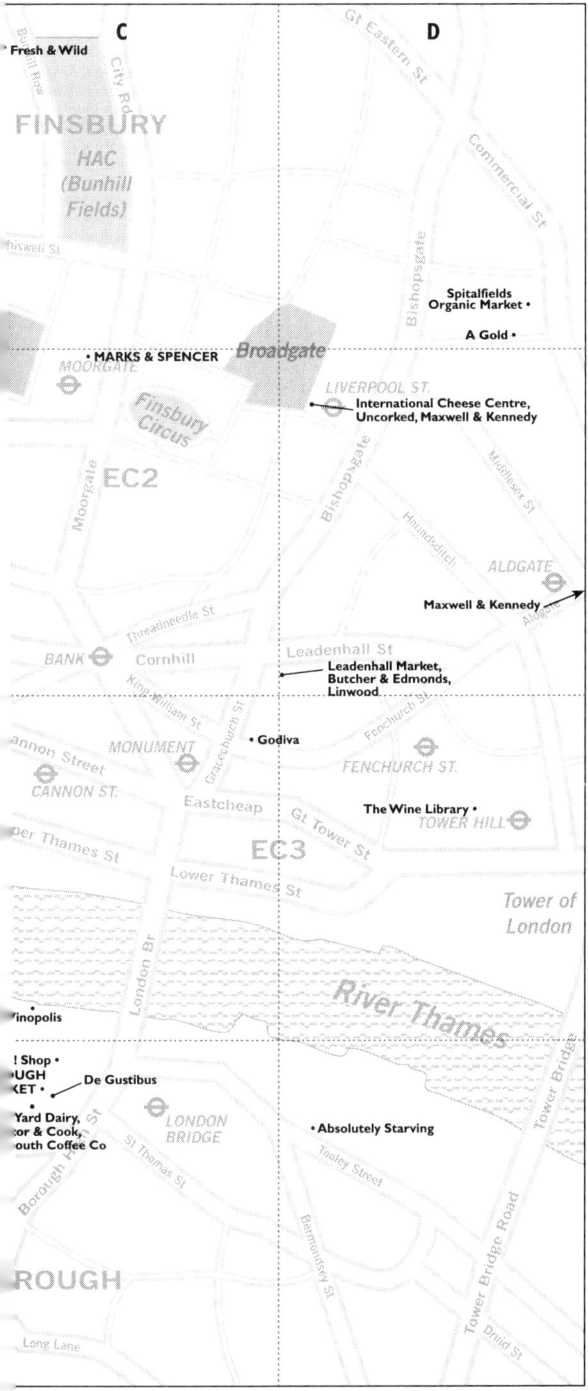

MAP 9 – THE CITY

MAP 10 – SOUTH LONDON (& FULHAM)

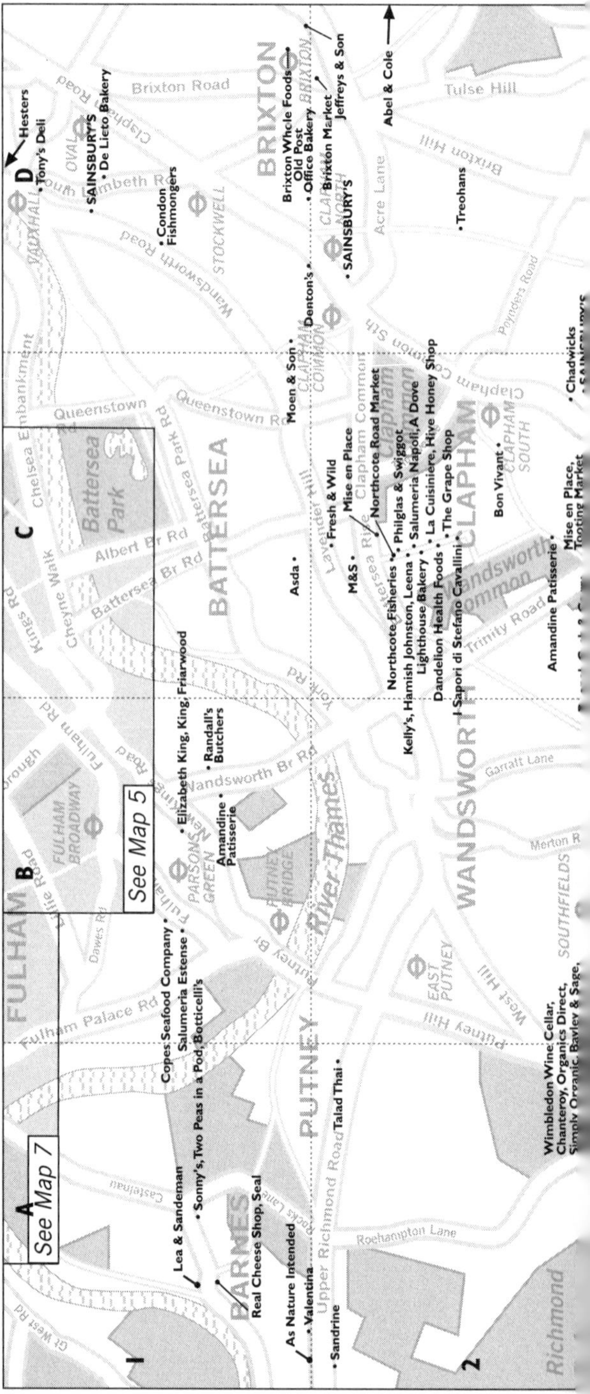

- Hesters
- Tony's Deli
- De Lieto Bakery
- SAINSBURY'S
- VAUXHALL
- OVAL
- Condon Fishmongers
- STOCKWELL
- Brixton Whole Foods
- Old Post Office Bakery
- Brixton Market
- Jeffreys & Son
- BRIXTON
- CLAPHAM NORTH
- SAINSBURY'S
- Abel & Cole
- Treohans
- Denton's
- CLAPHAM COMMON
- Moen & Son
- Fresh & Wild
- Mise en Place
- Philglas & Swiggot
- Northcote Road Market
- Kelly's, Hamish Johnston, Leena
- Salumeria Napoli, A Dove
- Lighthouse Bakery, Hive Honey Shop
- La Cuisinière
- Dandelion Health Foods
- The Grape Shop
- I Sapori di Stefano Cavallini
- Ada
- M&S
- CLAPHAM SOUTH
- Bon Vivant
- Chadwicks
- Amandine Patisserie
- Mise en Place, Tooting Market
- Copes Seafood Company
- Salumeria Estense
- Botticelli's
- FULHAM BROADWAY
- Elizabeth King, King, Friarwood
- Randall's Butchers
- Amandine Patisserie
- PARSONS GREEN
- PUTNEY BRIDGE
- EAST PUTNEY
- SOUTHFIELDS
- Lea & Sandeman
- As Nature Intended
- Valentina
- Sonny's, Two Peas in a Pod
- Sandrine
- Real Cheese Shop, Seal
- Talad Thai
- BARNES
- Wimbledon Wine Cellar, Chanteroy, Organics Direct, Simply Organic, Bayley & Sage,
- See Map 5
- See Map 7
- Battersea Park
- BATTERSEA
- WANDSWORTH
- CLAPHAM
- PUTNEY
- FULHAM
- Richmond

MAP 11 – EAST END & DOCKLANDS

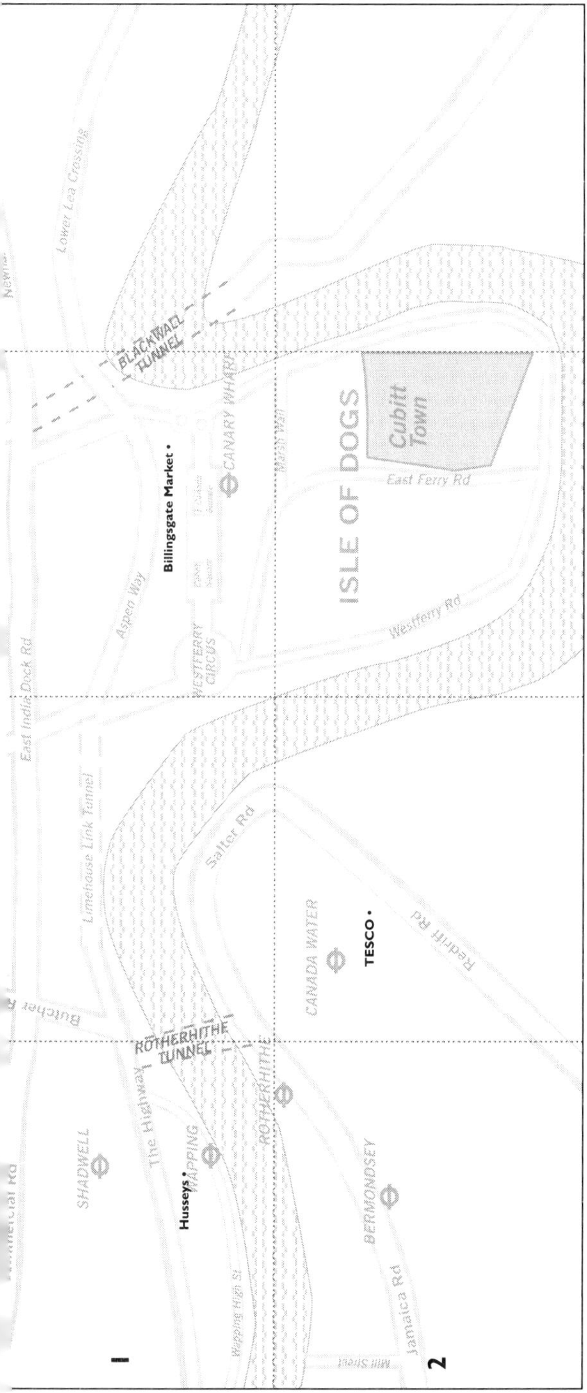

Area overviews

Large supermarket chains and mail-order-only companies are not listed in this section.

Area overviews

CENTRAL

Soho, Covent Garden & Bloomsbury
(Parts of W1, all WC2 and WC1)

Alara Wholefoods
(HEALTH & ORGANIC FOODS)

Algerian Coffee Stores
(COFFEE & TEA)

Amato
(PATISSERIE)

Angelucci
(COFFEE & TEA)

Anything Left-Handed
(COOKWARE)

Arigato
(ETHNIC)

The Australia & NZ Shop
(ETHNIC)

Berwick Street Market
(FRUIT & VEG; HERBS & SPICES; MARKET)

Bloomsbury Cheeses
(BREAD; CHEESE & DAIRY)

The Bread Shop
(BREAD)

Carluccios
(BREAD; GROCERS AND DELICATESSENS)

Culpeper
(HERBS & SPICES)

Drurys
(COFFEE & TEA)

Exeter Street Bakery
(BREAD)

Fresh & Wild
(BREAD; HEALTH & ORGANIC FOODS)

Gerry's
(WINE)

Godiva
(CHOCOLATES & SWEETS)

Golden Gate Grocers
(ETHNIC)

Hart's the Grocer
(GROCERS AND DELICATESSENS)

I Camisa & Son
(GROCERS AND DELICATESSENS)

Jeroboams
(WINE)

Kastner & Ovens
(PATISSERIE)

Leon Jaeggi
(COOKWARE)

Lina Stores
(GROCERS & DELIS)

Loon Fung Supermarket
(ETHNIC)

Maison Bertaux
(PATISSERIE)

Monmouth Coffee Company
(COFFEE & TEA)

Neal's Yard Bakery
(BREAD)

Neal's Yard Dairy
(CHEESE & DAIRY)

New Loon Moon
(ETHNIC)

Newport Supermarket
(ETHNIC)

Oliviers & Co
(GROCERS & DELIS)

Pages Catering Equipment
(COOKWARE)

Pâtisserie Valerie
(PATISSERIE)

Paul
(BREAD; PATISSERIE)

Planet Organic
(HEALTH & ORGANIC FOODS)

Portwine & Son
(MEAT, GAME & POULTRY)

See Woo Hong
(ETHNIC)

The Soho Wine Company
(WINE)

The Tea House
(COFFEE & TEA)

R Twining & Co
(COFFEE & TEA)

Mayfair & St James's
(Parts of W1 & SW1)

A La Reine Astrid
(CHOCOLATES & SWEETS)

Allen & Co
(MEAT, GAME & POULTRY)

Caviar House
(FISH & SEAFOOD)

Charbonnel et Walker
(CHOCOLATES & SWEETS)

Choccywoccydoodah
(CHOCOLATES & SWEETS)

Culpeper
(HERBS & SPICES)

Fortnum & Mason
(BIG TEN; CHOCOLATES & SWEETS; COFFEE & TEA; GROCERS & DELIS; PATISSERIE; WINE)

Godiva
(CHOCOLATES & SWEETS)

Green Valley
(ETHNIC)

Greenfields Supermarket
(ETHNIC; HERBS & SPICES)

HR Higgins (Coffee-Man)
(COFFEE & TEA)

Japan Centre
(ETHNIC)

Jeroboams
(WINE)

Truc Vert
(GROCERS & DELIS)

Fitzrovia & Marylebone
(Part of W1)

Biggles
(MEAT, GAME & POULTRY)

JF Blagden's
(FISH & SEAFOOD)

Bonne Bouche
(BREAD)

The Conran Shop
(COOKWARE)

De Gustibus
(BREAD)

Divertimenti
(COOKWARE)

Du Pain Du Vin
(GROCERS & DELIS)

Habitat
(COOKWARE)

Hart's the Grocer
(GROCERS & DELIS)

Heal's
(COOKWARE)

Jerry's Home Store
(COOKWARE)

John Lewis
(COOKWARE)

Maison Blanc
(BREAD; CHOCOLATES & SWEETS; PATISSERIE)

Pâtisserie Valerie
(PATISSERIE)

Paul
(BREAD; PATISSERIE)

Selfridges
(BIG TEN; BREAD; CHEESE & DAIRY; CHOCOLATES & SWEETS; COOKWARE; ETHNIC; FISH & SEAFOOD; FRUIT & VEG; GROCERS & DELIS; HERBS & SPICES;

Area overviews

MEAT, GAME & POULTRY; WINE)

Villandry
(BREAD; GROCERS & DELIS)

Belgravia, Pimlico, Victoria & Westminster (SW1, except St James's)

L'Artisan du Chocolat
(CHOCOLATES & SWEETS)

La Bella Sicilia
(GROCERS & DELIS)

Berry Bros. & Rudd
(COFFEE & TEA; WINE)

Bonne Bouche
(BREAD)

Casemir
(CHOCOLATES & SWEETS)

The Chatsworth Farm Shop
(GROCERS & DELIS; MEAT, GAME & POULTRY)

The Chocolate Society
(CHOCOLATES & SWEETS)

David Mellor
(COOKWARE)

Delizie d'Italia
(GROCERS & DELIS)

Farr Vintners
(WINE)

Gastronomia Italia
(GROCERS & DELIS)

Harrods
(BIG TEN; BREAD; CHEESE & DAIRY; CHOCOLATES & SWEETS; COFFEE & TEA; COOKWARE; FISH & SEAFOOD; FRUIT & VEG; GROCERS & DELIS; MEAT, GAME & POULTRY; PATISSERIE; WINE)

Hart's of Victoria
(MEAT, GAME & POULTRY)

Harvey Nichols
(BIG TEN; BREAD; FISH & SEAFOOD; GROCERS & DELIS; MEAT, GAME & POULTRY; WINE)

Haynes Hanson & Clark
(WINE)

International Cheese Centre
(CHEESE & DAIRY)

Jeroboams
(CHEESE & DAIRY; GROCERS & DELIS;

Jeroboams
(WINE)

Justerini & Brooks
(WINE)

Oliviers & Co
(GROCERS & DELIS)

Partridges
(GROCERS & DELIS)

Paxton & Whitfield
(CHEESE & DAIRY)

Peter Jones
(COOKWARE)

Poilâne
(BREAD)

Prestat
(CHOCOLATES & SWEETS)

Rippon Cheese Stores
(CHEESE & DAIRY)

Sea Harvest
(FISH & SEAFOOD)

Tachbrook Street Market
(BREAD; FRUIT & VEG; MARKET)

Vintage Cellars
(WINE)

Wine Cellar
(WINE)

WEST

Chelsea, South Kensington, Kensington, Earl's Court & Fulham (SW3, SW5, SW6, SW7, SW10 & W8)

L'Amandine Patisserie
(BREAD)

Bagatelle Boutique
(BREAD; PATISSERIE)

Baker & Spice
(BREAD; PATISSERIE)

Bibendum
(FISH & SEAFOOD)

Bluebird
(BIG TEN; BREAD; CHEESE & DAIRY; FISH & SEAFOOD; FRUIT & VEG; GROCERS & DELIS)

Bonne Bouche
(BREAD)

Chelsea Fishery
(FISH & SEAFOOD)

City Meat
(MEAT, GAME & POULTRY)

&Clarke's
(BREAD; CHEESE & DAIRY; CHOCOLATES & SWEETS; PATISSERIE)

The Conran Shop
(COOKWARE)

Copes Seafood Company
(FISH & SEAFOOD)

Divertimenti
(COOKWARE)

Elizabeth King
(GROCERS & DELIS)

Exeter Street Bakery
(BREAD)

Fileric
(PATISSERIE)

Finns of Chelsea Green
(GROCERS & DELIS)

The Fish Shop
(FISH & SEAFOOD)

Friarwood
(WINE)

Fry's of Chelsea
(FRUIT & VEG)

Habitat
(COOKWARE)

Hart's the Grocer
(GROCERS & DELIS)

Heal's
(COOKWARE)

Here
(HEALTH & ORGANIC FOODS)

The Italian Fruit Company
(FRUIT & VEG)

Jacobs
(GROCERS & DELIS)

Jago Butchers
(MEAT, GAME & POULTRY)

Jane Asher Party Cakes
(PATISSERIE)

Jerry's Home Store
(COOKWARE)

Kemptons of Kensington
(GROCERS & DELIS)

AA King
(MEAT, GAME & POULTRY)

Lea & Sandeman
(WINE)

Luigi's Delicatessen
(GROCERS & DELIS)

Luscious Organic
(HEALTH & ORGANIC FOODS)

Maison Blanc
(BREAD; CHOCOLATES & SWEETS; PATISSERIE)

La Marée
(FISH & SEAFOOD)

Area overviews

Montignac Boutique (HEALTH & ORGANIC FOODS)
The Moore Park Delicatessen (GROCERS & DELIS)
North End Road Market (CHEESE & DAIRY; FRUIT & VEG; MARKET)
Notting Hill Farmers Market (MARKET)
Partridges (GROCERS & DELIS)
Pâtisserie Valerie (PATISSERIE)
Picena (GROCERS & DELIS)
The Pie Man (GROCERS & DELIS)
Pierre Pechon (BREAD; PATISSERIE)
Randall's Butchers (MEAT, GAME & POULTRY)
La Reserve (WINE)
Reza (ETHNIC)
Rococo Chocolates (CHOCOLATES & SWEETS)
Salumeria Estense (GROCERS & DELIS)
Super Bahar (ETHNIC)
Tray Gourmet (GROCERS & DELIS)
La Vigneronne (WINE)

Notting Hill, Holland Park, Bayswater, N Kensington & Maida Vale (W2, W9, W10 & W11)

Athenian Grocery (ETHNIC)
Bon Appetit (GROCERS & DELIS)
Bonne Bouche (BREAD)
Books for Cooks (COOKWARE)
The Breadstall (BREAD)
Chalmers & Gray (FISH & SEAFOOD)
Corney & Barrow (WINE)
Felicitous (GROCERS & DELIS)
Fresh & Wild (BREAD; HEALTH & ORGANIC FOODS)
R Garcia & Sons (GROCERS & DELIS)
Golborne Fisheries (FISH & SEAFOOD)
The Grain Shop (HEALTH & ORGANIC FOODS)
Handford (WINE)
Hart's the Grocer (GROCERS & DELIS)
Jeroboams (CHEESE & DAIRY; GROCERS & DELIS)
Kingsland (MEAT, GAME & POULTRY)
Kitchen Ideas (COOKWARE)
C Lidgate (CHEESE & DAIRY; MEAT, GAME & POULTRY)
Lisboa Patisserie (PATISSERIE)
Maison Blanc (BREAD; CHOCOLATES & SWEETS; PATISSERIE)
Markus Coffee Co (COFFEE & TEA)
Le Maroc (ETHNIC)
Maxwell & Kennedy (CHOCOLATES & SWEETS)
La Mediterranea (GROCERS & DELIS)
Michanicou Bros (FRUIT & VEG)
Mr Christian's (BREAD; GROCERS & DELIS)
The Organic Grocer (HEALTH & ORGANIC FOODS)
Outpatients (GROCERS & DELIS)
P de la Fuente (GROCERS & DELIS)
Pierre Pechon (BREAD; PATISSERIE)
Planet Organic (HEALTH & ORGANIC FOODS)
Speck (GROCERS & DELIS)
The Spice Shop (HERBS & SPICES)
Summerill & Bishop (COOKWARE)
Tawana (ETHNIC)
Tea & Coffee Plant (COFFEE & TEA)
Tom's (GROCERS & DELIS)
Vom Fass (GROCERS & DELIS; WINE)
The Winery (WINE)

Hammersmith, Shepherd's Bush Olympia, Chiswick & Ealing (W4, W5, W6, W12, W14)

Adamou (ETHNIC)
L'Amandine Patisserie (BREAD)
As Nature Intended (HEALTH & ORGANIC FOODS)
GH Baxter (MEAT, GAME & POULTRY)
Bushwacker Wholefoods (HEALTH & ORGANIC FOODS)
TH Carr (FISH & SEAFOOD)
Covent Garden Fishmongers (FISH & SEAFOOD)
Damas Gate (ETHNIC)
Farm (HEALTH & ORGANIC FOODS)
Habitat (COOKWARE)
Kitchen Ideas (COOKWARE)
M&C Greengrocers (FRUIT & VEG)
Macken Bros (FRUIT & VEG; MEAT, GAME & POULTRY)
Maison Blanc (BREAD; CHOCOLATES & SWEETS; PATISSERIE)
Maquis (GROCERS & DELIS)
Maxwell & Kennedy (CHOCOLATES & SWEETS)
Mortimer & Bennett (GROCERS & DELIS)
Olympia Butchers (MEAT, GAME & POULTRY)

Portobello Road Market (FRUIT & VEG; HERBS & SPICES; MARKET)
Richardson's (MEAT, GAME & POULTRY)
Roberson (WINE)
Shepherd's Bush Market (MARKET)
Sri Thai (ETHNIC)
Stenton Family Butcher (MEAT, GAME & POULTRY)
Sutherlands (GROCERS & DELIS)
Theobroma Cacao (CHOCOLATES & SWEETS)
Thorogoods (MEAT, GAME & POULTRY)
HG Walter (MEAT, GAME & POULTRY)
West Ealing Farmers Market (MARKET)
Wine Cellar (WINE)

NORTH

Hampstead, W Hampstead, St John's Wood, Regent's Park, Kilburn & Camden Town (NW postcodes)

Ackermans (CHOCOLATES & SWEETS)
Ambala (CHOCOLATES & SWEETS; ETHNIC)
Amy's Cook & Dine (COOKWARE)
B&M Seafood (FISH & SEAFOOD)
Baker & Spice (BREAD; PATISSERIE)
FT Barrett (MEAT, GAME & POULTRY)
Belsize Village Delicatessen (GROCERS & DELIS)
Bifulco (MEAT, GAME & POULTRY)

The Bread Shop (BREAD)
Brian Lay-Jones (FRUIT & VEG)
Brown's (FISH & SEAFOOD)
Carmelli Bakeries (BREAD)
Church Street Market (MARKET)
Cockfosters Delicatessen (GROCERS & DELIS)
Cooksleys Butchers (MEAT, GAME & POULTRY)
Country Market (ETHNIC)
Daniel's Bagel Bakery (BREAD)
Fairfax Kitchen Shop (COOKWARE)
Fresh & Wild (BREAD; HEALTH & ORGANIC FOODS)
Giacobazzi's (GROCERS & DELIS)
Grodzinski (BREAD)
The Grogblossom (WINE)
Habitat (COOKWARE)
Hampstead Food Hall (GROCERS & DELIS)
Hampstead Seafoods (FISH & SEAFOOD)
MJ Hodges & Sons (FISH & SEAFOOD)
Hoo Hing (ETHNIC)
Ikea (COOKWARE)
The International Cheese Centre (CHEESE & DAIRY)
Inverness Street Market (MARKET)
Kent & Sons (MEAT, GAME & POULTRY)
Lea & Sandeman (WINE)
Louis Patisserie (PATISSERIE)
Maison Blanc (BREAD; CHOCOLATES & SWEETS; PATISSERIE)
Marine Ices (CHOCOLATES & SWEETS)

Oriental City (ETHNIC)
Panzer's (ETHNIC; FRUIT & VEG; GROCERS & DELIS)
Platters (GROCERS & DELIS)
La Reserve (WINE)
Richard Dare (COOKWARE)
Roni's Bagel Bakery (BREAD)
Rosslyn Delicatessen (GROCERS & DELIS)
Rumbolds (BREAD)
Salusbury Foodstore (GROCERS & DELIS)
Sam Stoller & Son (FISH & SEAFOOD)
JA Steele (MEAT, GAME & POULTRY)
Swiss Cottage Farmers Market (MARKET)
Willesden Fisheries (FISH & SEAFOOD)
Wing Yip (ETHNIC)

Hoxton, Islington Highgate, Crouch End, Stoke Newington, Finsbury Park, Muswell Hill & Finchley (N postcodes)

Amici (GROCERS & DELIS)
La Bottega (GROCERS & DELIS)
Bumblebee (HEALTH & ORGANIC FOODS; HERBS & SPICES)
Bunces (GROCERS & DELIS)
Café Mozart (PATISSERIE)
Casemir (CHOCOLATES & SWEETS)
Chapel Street Market (FRUIT & VEG; MARKET)

Area overviews

Cheeses
(CHEESE & DAIRY)

Clocktower Store
(FRUIT & VEG)

The Cooler
(GROCERS & DELIS)

Da Mario
(GROCERS & DELIS)

Dugans Chocolates
(CHOCOLATES & SWEETS)

Dunn's
(BREAD)

TJ Ellingham & Sons
(FRUIT & VEG)

Euphorium Bakery
(BREAD; PATISSERIE)

Fields
(GROCERS & DELIS)

The Food Centre
(HERBS & SPICES)

France Fresh Fish
(FISH & SEAFOOD)

Frank Godfrey
(MEAT, GAME & POULTRY)

Freeman's Butchers
(MEAT, GAME & POULTRY)

Fresh & Wild
(BREAD; HEALTH & ORGANIC FOODS)

La Fromagerie
(CHEESE & DAIRY)

Gallo Nero
(GROCERS & DELIS)

Gill Wing Cookshop
(COOKWARE)

Graham's Butchers
(ETHNIC; MEAT, GAME & POULTRY)

The Haelan Clinic
(HEALTH & ORGANIC FOODS)

Highgate Butchers
(MEAT, GAME & POULTRY)

Highgate Village Fruiterers
(FRUIT & VEG)

Islington Farmers Market
(MARKET)

James Elliott
(MEAT, GAME & POULTRY)

Johns
(FRUIT & VEG)

L & D Foods
(GROCERS & DELIS)

WM Martyn
(CHOCOLATES & SWEETS; COFFEE & TEA; HERBS & SPICES)

Monte's
(GROCERS & DELIS)

Olga Stores
(GROCERS & DELIS)

Palmers Green Farmers Market
(MARKET)

Sapponara
(GROCERS & DELIS)

A Scott & Sons
(FISH & SEAFOOD)

Stagnells Bakeries
(BREAD)

Steve Hatt
(FISH & SEAFOOD)

Walter Purkis & Sons
(FISH & SEAFOOD)

Yasir Halim Patisserie
(BREAD; ETHNIC)

Yildiz
(ETHNIC)

SOUTH

South Bank (SE1)

Absolutely Starving
(GROCERS & DELIS)

Borough Market
(BIG TEN; BREAD; CHEESE & DAIRY; FISH & SEAFOOD; FRUIT & VEG; HERBS & SPICES; MARKET; MEAT, GAME & POULTRY)

Coopers
(HEALTH & ORGANIC FOODS)

De Gustibus
(BREAD)

Fish! Shop
(FISH & SEAFOOD)

Konditor & Cook
(BREAD; PATISSERIE)

Lower Marsh Market
(MARKET)

Monmouth Coffee Company
(COFFEE & TEA)

Neal's Yard Dairy
(CHEESE & DAIRY)

Vinopolis
(WINE)

The Waterloo Wine Company
(WINE)

Battersea, Clapham, Wandsworth, Barnes, Putney, Brixton & Lewisham (All postcodes south of the river except SE1)

L'Amandine Patisserie
(BREAD)

As Nature Intended
(HEALTH & ORGANIC FOODS)

Balham Wholefood & Health Store
(HEALTH & ORGANIC FOODS)

Balthazar
(GROCERS & DELIS)

Bayley & Sage
(GROCERS & DELIS)

Belmont Bakery
(BREAD)

Blackheath Farmers Market
(MARKET)

Bon Vivant
(GROCERS & DELIS)

Botticelli
(PATISSERIE)

Brixton Market
(FISH & SEAFOOD; FRUIT & VEG; HERBS & SPICES; MARKET)

Brixton Whole Foods
(HEALTH & ORGANIC FOODS; HERBS & SPICES)

Brotherhood's
(GROCERS & DELIS)

Chadwicks
(MEAT, GAME & POULTRY)

Chanteroy
(GROCERS & DELIS)

The Cheese Block
(CHEESE & DAIRY)

The Cheese Board
(CHEESE & DAIRY)

Condon Fishmongers
(FISH & SEAFOOD)

Coppin Bros
(MEAT, GAME & POULTRY)

La Cuisiniere
(COOKWARE)

Dandelion Health Foods
(HEALTH & ORGANIC FOODS)

162

Area overviews

Davy's
(WINE)

De Lieto Bakery & Delicatessen
(GROCERS & DELIS)

Deepak Cash & Carry
(ETHNIC)

Dentons
(COOKWARE)

A Dove
(MEAT, GAME & POULTRY)

Estilo Kitchen Shop
(COOKWARE)

Fenners
(FRUIT & VEG)

Frankonia
(PATISSERIE)

Fresh & Wild
(BREAD; HEALTH & ORGANIC FOODS)

La Gastronomia
(GROCERS & DELIS)

Gennaro
(GROCERS & DELIS)

Get Fresh
(FRUIT & VEG)

The Grape Shop
(WINE)

The Ham Pantry
(GROCERS & DELIS)

Hamish Johnston
(CHEESE & DAIRY)

Hand Made Food
(GROCERS & DELIS)

Hesters
(MEAT, GAME & POULTRY)

The Hive Honey Shop
(HEALTH & ORGANIC FOODS)

The House of Chocolates
(CHOCOLATES & SWEETS)

I Sapori di Stefano Cavallini
(GROCERS & DELIS)

Indulgence
(CHOCOLATES & SWEETS)

Jeffreys & Son
(FISH & SEAFOOD)

Kelly's Organic Foods
(HEALTH & ORGANIC FOODS)

The Kew Cheese
(CHEESE & DAIRY)

Lea & Sandeman
(WINE)

Leena
(HERBS & SPICES)

Lighthouse Bakery
(BREAD)

AF Manuel
(BREAD)

Mise en Place
(GROCERS & DELIS)

M Moen & Son
(MEAT, GAME & POULTRY)

Northcote Fisheries
(FISH & SEAFOOD)

Northcote Road Market
(BREAD; FRUIT & VEG; MARKET)

Old Post Office Bakery
(BREAD)

Olivers Wholefood Store
(HEALTH & ORGANIC FOODS)

Organic World
(MEAT, GAME & POULTRY)

Pethers
(MEAT, GAME & POULTRY)

Philglas & Swiggot
(WINE)

Real Cheese Shop
(CHEESE & DAIRY)

Robert Edwards
(MEAT, GAME & POULTRY)

Salumeria Napoli
(GROCERS & DELIS)

Sandrine
(CHOCOLATES & SWEETS)

Sandy's Fishmongers
(FISH & SEAFOOD; MEAT, GAME & POULTRY)

J Seal
(MEAT, GAME & POULTRY)

Sonny's Food Shop & Cafe
(GROCERS & DELIS)

FC Soper
(FISH & SEAFOOD)

GG Sparkes
(MEAT, GAME & POULTRY)

Talad Thai
(ETHNIC; HERBS & SPICES)

Tawana
(ETHNIC)

The Teddington Cheese
(CHEESE & DAIRY)

Tony's Deli
(GROCERS & DELIS)

Tooting Market
(ETHNIC; HERBS & SPICES; MARKET)

Treohans
(GROCERS & DELIS)

Twickenham Farmers Market
(MARKET)

Two Peas in a Pod
(FRUIT & VEG)

Valentina
(GROCERS & DELIS)

The Village Delicatessen
(GROCERS & DELIS)

Vivian's
(GROCERS & DELIS)

Wimbledon Wine Cellar
(WINE)

Zoran's Deli
(GROCERS & DELIS)

EAST

Smithfield & Farringdon (EC1)

Brindisa
(GROCERS & DELIS)

Comptoir Gascon
(BREAD; GROCERS & DELIS)

Flâneur
(GROCERS & DELIS; PATISSERIE)

Fresh & Wild
(BREAD; HEALTH & ORGANIC FOODS)

G Gazzano & Son
(GROCERS & DELIS)

Meat City
(MEAT, GAME & POULTRY)

Patisserie Bliss
(PATISSERIE)

Simply Sausages
(MEAT, GAME & POULTRY)

Smithfield Market
(MARKET; MEAT, GAME & POULTRY)

St John
(BREAD)

L Terroni & Sons
(GROCERS & DELIS)

The City (EC2, EC3, EC4)

Butcher & Edmonds
(MEAT, GAME & POULTRY)

De Gustibus
(BREAD)

Godiva
(CHOCOLATES & SWEETS)

International Cheese Centre
(CHEESE & DAIRY)

Leadenhall Market
(MARKET)

Area overviews

Leonidas
(CHOCOLATES & SWEETS)

HS Linwood
(FISH & SEAFOOD)

Maxwell & Kennedy
(CHOCOLATES & SWEETS)

Porterford Meats
(MEAT, GAME & POULTRY)

Uncorked
(WINE)

The Wine Library
(WINE)

East End & Docklands (All E postcodes)

Billingsgate
(FISH & SEAFOOD; MARKET)

Brick Lane Beigel Bake
(BREAD)

Brick Lane Market
(MARKET)

Christophers
(GROCERS & DELIS)

Friends Organic
(HEALTH & ORGANIC FOODS)

A Gold
(GROCERS & DELIS)

Heroes of Nature
(HEALTH & ORGANIC FOODS)

Husseys
(MEAT, GAME & POULTRY)

Jones Dairy
(BREAD; CHEESE & DAIRY)

Maxwell & Kennedy
(CHOCOLATES & SWEETS)

Ridley Road Market
(MARKET)

Roman Road Market
(MARKET)

Spitalfields Organic Market
(HEALTH & ORGANIC FOODS; HERBS & SPICES; MARKET)

Taj Stores
(ETHNIC; HERBS & SPICES)

Turkish Food Centre
(ETHNIC)

Walthamstow Market
(MARKET)

Alphabetical index

Alphabetical index

A
A La Reine Astrid, 35
A&B Vintners, 134
Abel & Cole, 96
Absolutely Starving, 72
Ackermans, 35
Adamou, 51
Adnams, 134
Alara Wholefoods, 91
Algerian Coffee Stores, 41
Allen & Co, 107
Amandine Patisserie, 17
Amato, 119
Ambala, 35, 51
Amici, 72
Amy's Cook & Dine, 45
Angelucci, 41
Anything Left-Handed, 45
Arigato, 52
Artisan du Chocolat, 36
As Nature Intended, 91
Asda, 72
Athenian Grocery, 52
Australia & NZ Shop, 52

B
B&M Seafood, 58
Bagatelle Boutique, 18, 119
Baker & Spice, 18, 120
Balham Wholefood & Health Store, 91
Balthazar, 73
Barrett, 107
Baxter, 107
Bayley & Sage, 73
Beerbarons.co.uk, 134
Bella Sicilia, 73
Belmont Bakery, 18
Belsize Village Delicatessen, 73
Berry Bros. & Rudd, 41, 125
Berwick Street Market, 66, 98, 102
Betty's & Taylors of Harrogate, 44
Bibendum, 58
Bibendum Wines, 134
Bifulco, 108
Biggles, 108
Billingsgate, 58, 102
Blackheath Farmers Market, 102
Blagden's, 59
Bloomsbury Cheeses, 18, 29
Bluebird, 11, 19, 30, 59, 66, 73
Bon Appetit, 73
Bon Vivant, 74
Bonne Bouche, 19
Books for Cooks, 45
Borough Market, 12, 19, 29, 59, 67, 98, 102, 108
Bottega, 74
Botticelli, 120
Bottoms Up, 125
Bread Shop, 19
Breadstall, 20
Brian Lay-Jones, 67
Brick Lane Beigel Bake, 20
Brick Lane Market, 103
Brindisa, 74
Brixton Market, 59, 67, 98, 103
Brixton Whole Foods, 92, 98
Brotherhood's, 74
Brown's, 59
Bumblebee, 92, 99
Bunces, 74
Bushwacker Wholefoods, 92
Butcher & Edmonds, 108

C
Café Mozart, 120
Carluccios, 20, 74
Carmelli Bakeries, 20
Carr, 59
Casemir, 36
Caviar House, 60
Chadwicks, 108
Chalmers & Gray, 60
Chanteroy, 75
Chapel Street Market, 67, 103
Charbonnel et Walker, 36
Chateauonline, 134
Chatsworth Farm Shop, 75, 109
Cheese Block, 30
Cheese Board, 30
Cheeses, 30
Chelsea Fishery, 60
Choccywoccydoodah, 36
Chocolate Society, 36
Christophers, 75
Church Street Market, 103
City Meat, 109
&Clarke's 20, 30, 37, 120
Clearspring, 96
Clipper Teas, 44
Clocktower Store, 67
Cockfosters Deli, 75
Comptoir Gascon, 21, 75
Condon Fishmongers, 60
Conran Shop, 46
Cooksleys Butchers, 109
Cooler, 75

Alphabetical index

Coopers, 92
Copes Seafood Co, 60
Coppin Bros, 109
Corney & Barrow, 126
Country Market, 52
Covent Garden
  Fishmongers, 60
Cucina Direct, 50
Cuisiniere, 46
Cullens, 21
Culpeper, 99

D

Da Mario, 76
Damas Gate, 52
Dandelion Health
  Foods, 92
Daniel's Bagel Bakery, 21
David Mellor, 46
Davy's, 126
De Gustibus, 21
De Lieto Bakery &
  Delicatessen, 76
Deepak Cash & Carry, 52
Delizie d'Italia, 76
Dentons, 46
Divertimenti, 46
Domaine Direct, 135
Donald Russell, 117
Dove, 109
Drurys, 42
Du Pain Du Vin, 76
Dugans Chocolates, 37
Dunn's, 21

E

Elizabeth King, 76
Ellingham & Sons, 67
Esperya, 89
Estilo Kitchen Shop, 47
Euphorium Bakery, 22, 120
Europa Foods, 76
Exeter Street Bakery, 22

F

Fairfax Kitchen Shop, 47
Farm, 92
Farmaround, 96
Farr Vintners, 126
Felicitous, 77
Fenners, 68
Fields, 77
Fileric, 120
Finns of Chelsea Green, 77
Fish Shop, 61
Fish Society, 65
Fish! Shop, 61
Flâneur, 77, 121
Food Centre, 99
Food Ferry, 89
Forman & Son, 65
Fortnum & Mason, 12, 37,
  42, 77, 121, 126
Fox's Spices, 101
France Fresh Fish, 61
Frank Godfrey, 110
Frankonia, 121
Fratelli Camisa, 89
Freeman's Butchers, 110
Fresh & Wild, 22, 93
Friarwood, 126
Friends Organic, 93
Fromagerie, 30
Fry's of Chelsea, 68

G

Gallo Nero, 78
Garcia & Sons, 78
Gastronomia, 78
Gastronomia Italia, 78
Gazzano & Son, 78
Gennaro, 79
Gerry's, 127
Get Fresh, 68
Giacobazzi's, 79
Gill Wing Cookshop, 47
Godiva, 37
Golborne Fisheries, 61
Gold, 79
Golden Gate Grocers, 53
Goodness Direct, 97
Graham's
  Butchers, 53, 110
Grain Shop, 93
Grape Shop, 127
Green Valley, 53
Greenfields
  Supermarket, 53, 99
Grodzinski, 22
Grogblossom, 127

H

Habitat, 47
Haelan Clinic, 93
Ham Pantry, 79
Hamish Johnston, 31
Hampstead Food Hall, 79
Hampstead Seafoods, 61
Hand Made Food, 79
Handford, 127
Harrods, 13, 23, 31, 37,
  42, 47, 61, 68, 80, 110,
  121, 127
Hart's of Victoria, 110
Hart's the Grocer, 80
Harvey Nichols, 13, 23, 62,
  80, 111, 128
Haynes Hanson
  & Clark, 128
Heal Farm, 117

Alphabetical index

Heal's, 48
Here, 94
Heroes of Nature, 94
Hesters, 111
Higgins (Coffee-Man), 42
Highgate Butchers, 111
Highgate Village
 Fruiterers, 68
Hive Honey Shop, 94
Hodges & Sons, 62
Holland & Barrett, 94
Hoo Hing, 53
House of Chocolates, 38
Huge Cheese Direct, 34
Husseys, 111

I

I Camisa & Son, 81
I Sapori di Stefano
 Cavallini, 81
Ikea, 48
Indulgence, 38
International Cheese
 Centre, 31
Internet Cookshop, 50
Inverawe Smokehouses, 89
Inverness Street
 Market, 103
Islington Farmers
 Market, 103
Italian Fruit Company, 68

J

Jacobs, 81
Jago Butchers, 111
James Baxter & Son, 65
James Elliott, 111
Jane Asher
 Party Cakes, 121
Japan Centre, 54
Jeffreys & Son, 62
Jeroboams, 32, 81
Jeroboams (wine), 128
Jerry's Home Store, 48
John Armit Wines, 135
John Lewis/Peter Jones, 48
Johns, 69
Jones Dairy, 23, 32
Justerini & Brooks, 128

K

Kastner & Ovens, 122
Kelly's Organic Foods, 94
Kemptons
 of Kensington, 81
Kent & Sons, 112
King, 112
Kingsland, 112
Kitchen Ideas, 49
Kitchenware.co.uk, 50

Konditor & Cook, 23, 122

L

L & D Foods, 81
Laithwaites, 135
Lakeland, 50
Lay & Wheeler, 135
Lea & Sandeman, 129
Leadenhall Market, 103
Leapingsalmon.co.uk, 89
Leena, 99
Leon Jaeggi, 49
Leonidas, 38
Lidgate, 32, 112
Lighthouse Bakery, 23
Lina Stores, 82
Linwood, 62
Lisboa Patisserie, 122
Loon Fung
 Supermarket, 54
Louis Patisserie, 122
Lower Marsh Market, 104
Luigi's Delicatessen, 82
Luscious Organic, 95

M

M&C Greengrocers, 69
Macken Bros, 112
Maison Bertaux, 122
Maison Blanc, 24, 38, 123
Majestic Wine
 Warehouses, 129
Manuel, 24
Maquis, 82
Marée, 62
Marine Ices, 39
Marks & Spencer, 14, 24,
 32, 69, 113
Markus Coffee Co, 42
Maroc, 54
Martyn, 39, 43, 99
Maxwell & Kennedy, 39
Meat City, 113
Mediterranea, 82
Michanicou Bros, 69
Mise en Place, 82
Moen & Son, 113
Monmouth Coffee Co, 43
Monte's, 82
Montignac Boutique, 95
Moore Park Deli, 83
Morris & Verdin, 135
Mortimer & Bennett, 83
Mr Christian's, 24, 83

N

Neal's Yard Bakery, 25
Neal's Yard Dairy, 32
New Loon Moon, 54
Newport Supermarket, 54

Alphabetical index

Nicolas, 129
North End Rd
  Market, 33, 69, 104
Northcote Fisheries, 63
Northcote Rd
  Market, 25, 69, 104
Northfield Farm, 117
Notting Hill
  Farmers Market, 104

O
Oddbins, 129
Old Post Office Bakery, 25
Olga Stores, 83
Olivers Wholefood
  Store, 95
Olives et al, 90
Oliviers & Co, 83
Olympia Butchers, 113
Organic Grocer, 95
Organic World, 113
Organics Direct, 97
Oriental City, 54
Outpatients, 84

P, Q
P de la Fuente, 84
Pages Catering
  Equipment, 49
Palmers Green
  Farmers Market, 104
Panzer's, 55, 70, 84
Partridges, 84
Patisserie Bliss, 123
Pâtisserie Valerie, 123
Paul, 25, 124
Paxton & Whitfield, 33
Pethers, 113
Philglas & Swiggot, 130
Picena, 84
Pie Man, 85
Pierre Pechon, 25, 124
Planet Organic, 95
Platters, 85
Poilâne, 26
Porterford Meats, 114
Portobello Food
  Company, 90
Portobello Road
  Market, 70, 100, 104
Portwine & Son, 114
Prestat, 39
Pure Meat Company, 117

R
Randall's Butchers, 114
Real Cheese Shop, 33
Reserve, 130
Reza, 55
Richard Dare, 49
Richard Woodall, 118
Richardson's, 114
Ridley Road Market, 105
Rippon Cheese Stores, 33
Roberson, 130
Robert Edwards, 114
Rococo Chocolates, 39
Roman Road Market, 105
Roni's Bagel Bakery, 26
Rosslyn Delicatessen, 85
Rumbolds, 26

S
Safeway, 85
Sainsbury's, 14, 26, 33, 63,
  70, 96, 100, 115, 130
Salumeria Estense, 85
Salumeria Napoli, 86
Salusbury Foodstore, 86
Sam Stoller & Son, 63
Sandrine, 40
Sandy's
  Fishmongers, 63, 115
Sapponara, 86
Sara Jayne, 40
Scott & Sons, 63
Sea Harvest, 63
Seal, 115
See Woo Hong, 55
Seldom Seen Farm, 118
Selfridges, 15, 26, 33, 40,
  49, 55, 64, 70, 86, 100,
  115, 130
Shepherd's Bush
  Market, 105
Simply Organic, 97
Simply Salmon, 90
Simply Sausages, 115
Smithfield
  Market, 105, 116
Soho Wine Company, 131
Sonny's Food Shop
  & Cafe, 86
Soper, 64
Sparkes, 116
Speck, 86
Spice Shop, 100
Spitalfields Organic
  Market, 96, 100, 105
Sri Thai, 55
St John, 27
Stagnells Bakeries, 27
Starbucks, 43
Steele, 116
Stenton Family
  Butcher, 116
Steve Hatt, 64
Summerill
  & Bishop, 50
Sunday Times

Alphabetical index

Wine Club, 135
Super Bahar, 55
Sutherlands, 87
Swaddles Green Farm, 118
Swig, 136
Swiss Cottage
  Farmers Market, 105

T

Tachbrook Street
  Market, 27, 70, 106
Taj Stores, 56, 100
Talad Thai, 56, 101
Tawana, 56
Tea & Coffee Plant, 43
Tea House, 43
Terroni & Sons, 87
Tesco, 15, 27, 70, 131
Theobroma Cacao, 40
Thorntons, 40
Thorogoods, 116
Thresher, 131
Tom's, 87
Tony's Deli, 87
Tooting
  Market, 56, 101, 106
Tray Gourmet, 87
Treohans, 87
Truc Vert, 88
Turkish Food Centre, 56
Twickenham
  Farmers Market, 106
Twining & Co, 44
Two Peas in a Pod, 71

U, V

Uncorked, 131
Unwins, 131
Valentina, 88
Vigneronne, 132
Village Delicatessen, 88
Villandry, 27, 88
Vinopolis, 132
Vintage Cellars, 132
Virginwines, 136
Vivian's, 88
Vom Fass, 88, 132

W

Waitrose, 16, 27, 34, 64,
  71, 89, 101, 117, 132
Waitrose
  Wine Direct, 136
Walter, 117
Walter Purkis & Sons, 64
Walthamstow
  Market, 106
Waterloo Wine
  Comapny, 133
Weald Smokery, 90

West Ealing
  Farmers Market, 106
Whittard of Chelsea, 44
Willesden Fisheries, 65
Wimbledon Wine
  Cellar, 133
Wine Cellar, 133
Wine Library, 133
Wine Society, 136
Wine Wine Wine, 136
Winery, 134
Wing Yip, 56

X, Y, Z

Yapp Brothers, 136
Yasir Halim Patisserie, 28, 57
Yildiz, 57
Zoran's Deli, 89

Notes

Notes

Notes

Notes